T0375238

THE NEW FIBONACCI TRADER

WILEY TRADING

THE NEW FIBONACCI TRADER

TOOLS AND STRATEGIES FOR TRADING SUCCESS

ROBERT FISCHER
JENS FISCHER

JOHN WILEY & SONS
New York • Chichester • Weinheim • Brisbane • Singapore • Toronto

Published by John Wiley & Sons, Inc.
Published simultaneously in Canada.

Library of Congress Cataloging-in-Publication Data:

Fischer, Robert, 1942 June 17-
    The new Fibonacci trader : tools & strategies for trading success / Robert Fischer.
        p.   cm. — (Wiley trading)
    Continues with computer extrapolations: Fibonacci applications and strategies for traders / Robert Fischer. New York : J. Wiley, c1993.
    Includes index.
    ISBN 0-471-41910-9 (cloth : alk. paper)
    1. Speculation. 2. Stocks. 3. Commodity exchanges. 4. Fibonacci numbers.
I. Fischer, Robert, 1942 June 17-. Fibonacci applications and strategies for traders.
II. Title. III. Series.
HG6041.F575   2001
332.64—dc21
                                                      2001045527

10 9 8

ACKNOWLEDGMENTS

In April 2000, Claudio Campuzano at John Wiley & Sons, New York, asked whether we would be interested in writing a book to accompany *Fibonacci Applications and Strategies for Traders* (Wiley, 1993).

Thank you, Claudio, for convincing us that a second book would be meaningful to readers.

We wrestled with the challenge of improving a very well received book. We knew that we needed to integrate all the analytic features and ideas that had already been included with a Microsoft DOS-based graphics software package. However, we did not know whether additional enhancements would justify a new book.

Thanks to Kwansoo Kim, a friend from Chicago, not only was the existing Microsoft DOS version of the WINPHI software converted into a Microsoft Windows format, but all program features were brilliantly made so user-friendly that we were able to test and apply PHI-ellipses, PHI-spirals, PHI-channels, corrections, extensions, and Fibonacci time-goal days to various markets and products. Without the WINPHI software, this book could not have been written.

We are grateful that Anne Cavanagh, of Green Valley, Arizona, once again shared her in-depth knowledge of the markets, and her writing skills, with us.

We are thankful to all those who helped us with their expertise in making this book possible.

R. F.
J. F.

The following figures in this book are related to this disclaimer: 2.6, 2.7, 2.8, 2.9, 3.11, 3.12, 3.13, 3.14, 3.22, 3.23, 3.26, 3.28, 3.29, 5.25, 5.26, 5.28, 5.29, 5.34, 5.35, 5.36, 5.37, 5.38, 5.39, 5.40, 5.41, 5.43, 5.44.

PREFACE

In 1993, Robert Fischer published a book with Wiley and Sons under the working title *Fibonacci Applications and Strategies for Traders*. The book described basic findings and inventions of Fibonacci applied to sophisticated strategies for successful trading. The book became, and still is, an overwhelming success.

Almost eight years have passed, and the more popular the book becomes, the more evident it is that an integral part is missing from the first approach in order to make the all-fascinating Fibonacci principles tradable. The calculation power, graphics, and drawing power of state-of-the-art computer technology over the past half-decade have opened up horizons that are waiting to be explored. These opportunities must not be wasted. Computer technology has progressed markedly, and so has the power to successfully trade the markets using Fibonacci tools.

Making Fibonacci strategies profitable for traders is the authors' objective. The first book had the ideas, the rules, the principles, and all the Fibonacci tools on paper, but was not able to convert promising trading ideas into valid trading systems to be applied real-time to market data.

This new book focuses on the new Fibonacci trader. He or she still has the ideas and the skill, but, for the very first time, computer technology can be used to put ideas and skill together in powerful trading strategies.

We do not offer fully automated trading systems; rather, we write about the missing link that would graphically set up trading strategies and test them in a computerized environment.

In addition to academically describing our findings, we share our knowledge by delivering to readers the WINPHI software package that we use to graphically apply the Fibonacci tools to charts.

Some of the core principles of Elliott and Fibonacci have to be discussed again, even though they were explained in the original *Fibonacci Applications and Strategies for Traders*. The same holds true for some of the fundamental explanations of price and time targets in corrections, extensions, and Fibonacci time analysis. These subjects will be described again to adequately present the overall framework, but not in the same detail as in the first book. For newcomers as well as apprentices to Fibonacci and Elliott, we highly recommend rereading the 1993 predecessor.

Our purpose in this book is to introduce new tools not yet offered and never analyzed for the markets. The PHI-channel, the PHI-ellipse, the PHI-spiral, and the PHI-ellipse and the PHI-spiral combined with Fibonacci price and time goals, cover new territory and offer almost unlimited trading potential, if handled correctly.

The biggest difficulty when working with sophisticated Fibonacci concepts is that every trading tool has to be calculated with utmost precision. This problem can be addressed by hand when calculating price targets in extensions or corrections, but it is almost impossible to solve without the accuracy of a computer when it comes to PHI-spirals, PHI-ellipses, and similar concepts.

Our main challenge was to make the graphical use of PHI-spirals, PHI-ellipses, PHI-channels, corrections, and extensions just as simple as drawing a trend line on a chart—and, even more importantly, to have the ability to overlay and to combine different tools. As a reminder: The most powerful signals can be generated if different tools identify the same turning points in price and time.

Chapter 8 is dedicated to combinations of six geometrical Fibonacci devices that are allied in an integrated trading concept that proves reliable within the limits of the time spans traded on cash currencies and futures weekly, daily, and intraday. Our concept is also valid for volatile and marketable individual stocks worldwide. The latter factor is especially important because Fibonacci's and Elliott's principles and proposals claim global relevance and are not limited to the trading environment in the United States.

The first computerization of many Fibonacci tools was done in 1985 on a Microsoft DOS platform, but the true breakthrough came when the advantages of the Microsoft Windows operating system and its graphical surface and user interface became available to the mass market. Together with the vast power of today's personal computers and the huge storing capacity of hard files and removable media, the Fibonacci trading tools have almost unlimited potential.

And here lies our obligation vis-à-vis the investor. No matter how powerful the trading tools described in this book are, if interested investors cannot work with the tools, they are of very little use. Most of the tools described in *The New Fibonacci Trader* are not available elsewhere, not even with the most comprehensive and expensive trading software packages. Because we think that every investor should have the chance to work with the trading tools presented in this book, we decided to include the entire software package on a CD-ROM. The software is designed to work with ASCII O-H-L-C data on a daily basis, so that investors do not need to bother with multiple datafeeds, as long as they subscribe to a data vendor that includes a conversion utility for ASCII data with its data package.

Investors who do not feel comfortable with the need to convert data from their data vendors into an ASCII D-O-H-L-C format in order to be able to chart their data on the WINPHI program can rely on an online version of the WINPHI software package that is set up on a registered membership basis at www.fibotrader.com.

The Internet platform has the great advantage of supplying a much larger universe of trading vehicles to chart from various liquid international markets, and of allowing intraday trading on 60-minute and 15-minute bases. The Internet platform also closes the data gap from the time this book was written to any time in the future.

Again: The application of the Fibonacci trading tools takes knowledge and skill. Given the overwhelming response to the first attempt in *Fibonacci Applications and Strategies for Traders,* we know that serious believers in this kind of analysis can use the knowledge provided in this book to their benefit, as long as they have the ability to test and the discipline to follow these principles and then to execute their trading strategies.

All examples and strategies described in the book have been developed to the best of our knowledge. We do not offer fully automated trading approaches, but we introduce readers to some little known possibilities of beating the markets.

The fascination and beauty of graphic trading tools can be seen from day one. On the other hand, it is very difficult to have the discipline to wait until Fibonacci price or time goals are reached. The temptation of taking profits a little earlier, or placing protective stops a little wider, might dilute the overall performance profile.

The software has been carefully tested. The user manual for the program on the CD-ROM (see the Appendix) makes it easy for users to get started and to apply all tools to charts.

This book is intended to be educational. Concepts are thoroughly presented with detailed examples.

We hope that readers find our ideas inspiring and enlightening, useful and exciting.

New York, New York, 2001   ROBERT FISCHER

                                                                 JENS FISCHER

CONTENTS

1

Basic Fibonacci Principles

"Let your imagination soar." This phrase, this invitation, started the earlier book, *Fibonacci Applications and Strategies for Traders*. And once again, we do not hesitate to introduce readers to the fascination of the findings of Leonardo Di Pisa, commonly known as Fibonacci, by publishing this renewed appeal to creativity and imagination.

Eight years have passed since *Fibonacci Applications and Strategies for Traders* was published. The market environment has changed a great deal. What has remained unchanged, however, is the beauty of nature. Think of all the wonders of nature in our world: oceans, trees, flowers, plant life, animals, and microorganisms.

Also think of the achievements of humans in natural sciences, nuclear theory, medicine, computer technology, radio, and television. And finally, think of the trend moves in world markets. It may surprise you to learn that all of these have one underlying pattern in common: the Fibonacci summation series.

The Fibonacci summation series, the baseline of our pattern-oriented market analysis, is presented in this first chapter. After the meaning of this sequence of numbers has become clear, we take a quick look at the types of phenomena and achievements in human behavior that can be analyzed using the Fibonacci summation series. We then point out the conclusions drawn by engineer and trader Ralph Nelson Elliott. We look at the generalizations he made to provide analysts today with a nonstringent framework that can be used for the sake of profitable trading in global markets.

Chapter 1 is designed as a recap of *Fibonacci Applications and Strategies for Traders*. Readers who are familiar with the details of Fibonacci and Elliott in this first chapter may want to proceed to the overview of what is new in this book, on page 22.

THE FIBONACCI SUMMATION SERIES

Fibonacci (1170–1240) lived and worked as a merchant and mathematician in Pisa, Italy. He was one of the most illustrious European scientists of his time. Among his greatest achievements was the introduction of Arabic numerals to supersede the Roman figures.

He developed the Fibonacci summation series, which runs as

$$1 - 1 - 2 - 3 - 5 - 8 - 13 - 21 - 34 - 55 - 89 - 144 - \ldots$$

or, in mathematical terms,

$$a_{n+1} = a_{n-1} + a_n \text{ with } a_1 = a_2 = 1$$

The mathematical series tends asymptotically (that is, approaching slower and slower) toward a constant ratio.

However, this ratio is irrational; it has a never-ending, unpredictable sequence of decimal values stringing after it. It can never be expressed exactly. If each number, as part of the series, is divided by its preceding value (e.g., $13 \div 8$ or $21 \div 13$), the operation results in a ratio that oscillates around the irrational figure $1.61803398875 \ldots$, being higher than the ratio one time, and lower the next. The precise ratio will never, into eternity (not even with the most powerful computers developed in our age), be known to the last digit. For the sake of brevity, we will refer to the Fibonacci ratio as 1.618 and ask readers to keep the margin of error in mind.

This ratio had begun to gather special names even before another medieval mathematician, Luca Pacioli (1445–1514), named it "the divine proportion." Among its contemporary names are "golden section" and "golden mean." Johannes Kepler (1571–1630), a German astronomer, called the Fibonacci ratio one of the jewels in geometry. Algebraically, it is generally designated by the Greek letter PHI (φ), with

$$\varphi \approx 1.618$$

or, in a different mathematical form

$$\varphi = \frac{1}{2}\left(\sqrt{5}+1\right) \approx 1.618$$

And it is not only PHI that is interesting to scientists (and traders, as we shall see). If we divide any number of the Fibonacci summation series by the number that follows it in the series (e.g., 8 ÷ 13 or 13 ÷ 21), we find that the series asymptotically gets closer to the ratio PHI' with

$$\varphi' \approx 0.618$$

being simply the reciprocal value to PHI with

$$\varphi' = 1 \div \varphi = 1 \div 1.618 \approx 0.618$$

or, in another form,

$$\varphi' = \frac{1}{2}\left(\sqrt{5}-1\right) \approx 0.618$$

This is a very unusual and remarkable phenomenon—and a useful one when it comes to designing trading tools, as we will learn in the course of the analysis. Because the original ratio PHI is irrational, the reciprocal value PHI' to the ratio PHI necessarily turns out to be an irrational figure as well, which means that we again have to consider a slight margin of error when calculating 0.618 in an approximated, shortened way.

From here on, we analytically exploit PHI and PHI' and move ahead by slightly reformulating the Fibonacci summation series so that the following PHI series is the result:

$$0.618 - 1.000 - 1.618 - 2.618 - 4.236 - 6.854 - 11.090 - 17.944 - \ldots$$

In mathematical terms, it is written as

$$a_{n+1} = a_{n-1} + a_n \text{ with } a_1 = 0.618, \ a_2 = 1$$

In this case, we do not find an asymptotical process with a ratio because, in dividing each number of the PHI series by its preceding value (e.g., 4.236 ÷ 2.618 or 6.854 ÷ 4.236), the operation results in the approximated ratio PHI = 1.618. Running the division in the opposite direction—that is, dividing each number of the PHI series by the value that follows (e.g., 2.618 ÷ 4.236 or 4.236 ÷ 6.854)—results in the reciprocal value to the constant PHI, introduced earlier as PHI' = 0.618. Before progressing further through the text, it is important that readers fully understand how the PHI series has been derived from the underlying Fibonacci summation series.

We have discovered a series of plain figures, applied to science by Fibonacci. We must take another quick detour before we can utilize the Fibonacci summation series as the basis for the development of trading tools. We must first consider what relevance the Fibonacci summation series has for nature around us. It will then be only a small step to conclusions that lead us directly to the relevance of the Fibonacci summation series for the movement of international markets, whether in currencies or commodities, stocks or derivatives.

We recognize the dampened swings of the quotients around the value of 1.618 (or 0.618, respectively) in Fibonacci's series by either higher or lower numbers in the Elliott wave principle, which was popularized by Ralph Nelson Elliott as the rule of alternation. And we present the trading tools that we developed for exploration of the magic of PHI to the largest extent possible. Humans subconsciously seek the divine proportion, which is nothing but a constant and timeless striving to create a comfortable standard of living.

THE FIBONACCI RATIO

For us—and, hopefully, for our readers as well—it remains remarkable how many constant values can be calculated using Fibonacci's sequence, and how the individual figures that form the sequence recur in so many variations. However, it cannot be stressed strongly enough that this is not just a numbers game; it is the most important mathematical representation of natural phenomena ever discovered. The following illustrations depict some interesting applications of this mathematical sequence.

We have subdivided our observations into two sections. First, we deal briefly with the Fibonacci ratio and its presence in natural phenomena and in architecture. Then we briefly describe how mathematics, physics, and astronomy make use of the Fibonacci ratio.

The Fibonacci Ratio in Nature

To appreciate the great relevance of the Fibonacci ratio as a natural constant, one need only look at the beauty of nature that surrounds us. The development of plants in nature is a perfect example of the general relevance of the Fibonacci ratio and the underlying Fibonacci summation series. Fibonacci numbers can be found in the number of axils on the stem of every growing plant, as well as in the number of petals.

We can easily figure out member numbers of the Fibonacci summation series in plant life (so-called *golden numbers*) if we count the petals of certain common flowers—for example, the iris with 3 petals, the primrose with 5 petals, the ragwort with 13 petals, the daisy with 34 petals, and the Michaelmas daisy with 55 (and 89) petals. We must question: Is this pattern accidental or have we identified a particular natural law?

An ideal example is found in the stems and flowers of the sneezewort (Figure 1.1). Every new branch of sneezewort springs from the axil, and more branches grow from a new branch. Adding the old and the new branches together, a Fibonacci number is found in each horizontal plane.

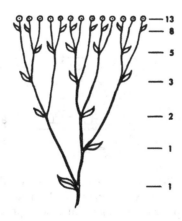

Figure 1.1   Fibonacci numbers found in the flowers of the sneezewort.

When analyzing world markets and developing trading strategies, we look for structures or chart patterns that have been profitable in the past (according to historical data) and therefore shall have a probability of continued success in the future. In the Fibonacci ratio PHI, we propose to have found such a structure or general pattern.

The Fibonacci ratio PHI is an irrational figure. We will never know its exact value to the last digit. Because the error margin approximating the Fibonacci ratio PHI gets smaller as the numbers of the Fibonacci summation series become higher, we consider 8 the smallest of all the numbers of the Fibonacci summation series that can be meaningfully applied to market analysis (calculating the sample quotients of 13 ÷ 8 = 1.625 and 21 ÷ 13 = 1.615, compared with PHI = 1.618).

At different times and on different continents, people have attempted to successfully incorporate the ratio PHI into their work as a law of perfect proportion. Not only were the Egyptian pyramids built according to the Fibonacci ratio PHI (as described in detail in *Fibonacci Applications and Strategies for Traders*), but the same phenomenon can be found in the Mexican pyramids.

It is conceivable that the Egyptian and the Mexican pyramids were built in approximately the same historical era by people of common origins. Figure 1.2a and Figure 1.2b illustrate the importance of the incorporated Fibonacci proportion PHI.

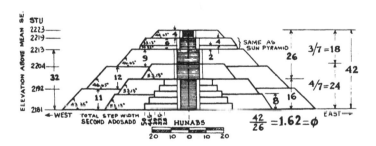

Figure 1.2a   Number PHI = 1.618 incorporated in the Mexican pyramid. *Source: Mysteries of the Mexican Pyramid,* by Peter Thomkins (New York: Harper & Row, 1976), pp. 246, 247. Reprinted with permission.

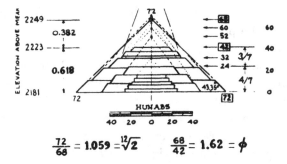

$$\frac{72}{68} = 1.059 = \sqrt[12]{2} \qquad \frac{68}{42} = 1.62 = \phi$$

Figure 1.2b   Number PHI = 1.618 incorporated in the Mexican pyramid. *Source: Mysteries of the Mexican Pyramid,* by Peter Thomkins (New York: Harper & Row, 1976), pp. 246, 247. Reprinted with permission.

A cross-section of the pyramid shows a structure shaped as a staircase. There are 16 steps in the first set, 42 steps in the second, and another 68 steps in the third. These numbers are based on the Fibonacci ratio 1.618 in the following way:

$$16 \times 1.618 = 26$$
$$16 + 26 = 42$$
$$26 \times 1.618 = 42$$
$$26 + 42 = 68$$
$$42 \times 1.618 = 68$$

Here we find (although not at first glance) Fibonacci's ratio PHI in a macrostructure familiar to all of us. Our task is to transfer this approach from nature and the human environment to the sphere of chart and market analysis. In our market environment, we must ask whether and where we can detect PHI as purely and exploitably as in natural plant life and manmade pyramids.

The Fibonacci Ratio in Geometry

The existence of the Fibonacci ratio PHI in geometry is also very well known. However, a workable way for investors to apply this ratio, as a geometric tool, to commodity price moves using PHI-spirals and

PHI-ellipses has not yet been published. It takes a programmer's knowledge and the power of computers to apply the PHI-spiral and the PHI-ellipse as analytic tools.

Because computer power is easily accessible today, the obstacle is not the hardware, but rather some missing knowledge and the lack of appropriate software.

The fully operational software package that accompanies this book allows every interested reader/investor to trace the examples shown and to generate similar signals in real-time trading.

PHI-spiral and PHI-ellipse consist of unusual properties that are in accordance with Fibonacci's ratio PHI in two dimensions: price and time. It is very likely that the integration of PHI-spirals and PHI-ellipses will elevate the interpretation and the use of the Fibonacci ratio to a much higher level. Up to now, Fibonacci's PHI has been generally accepted as a tool for the measurement of corrections and extensions of price swings. Forecasts of time have seldom been integrated because they did not seem to be as reliable as the price analysis, but, by including PHI-spirals and PHI-ellipses into a geometric analysis, both parts—price and time analyses—can be combined accurately.

To gain a better understanding of how Fibonacci's PHI is geometrically incorporated into PHI-spirals and PHI-ellipses, we begin by describing the golden section of a line and of a rectangle, and their respective relations to PHI.

A Greek mathematician, Euclid of Megara (450–370 B.C.), was the first scientist to write about the golden section and thereby focused on the analysis of a straight line (Figure 1.3).

The line AB of length L is divided into two segments by point C. Let the length of AC and CB be a and b, respectively. If C is a point

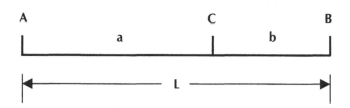

Figure 1.3   Golden section of a line. *Source: FAM Research,* 2000.

such that the quotient L ÷ a equals a ÷ b, then C is the golden section of AB. The ratio L ÷ a or a ÷ b is called the golden ratio.

In other words, point C divides the line AB into two parts in such a way that the ratios of those parts are 1.618 and 0.618; two figures we easily recognize from our analysis of the Fibonacci summation series as Fibonacci's PHI and its reciprocal value PHI′.

Moving from one cradle of science to another—from ancient Europe to ancient Africa, or from ancient Greece to ancient Egypt—we learn that in the Great Pyramid of Gizeh, the rectangular floor of the king's chamber also illustrates the golden section.

The golden section of a rectangle can best be demonstrated by starting with a square, a geometrical formation that served as the foundation for the Pyramid of Gizeh. This square can then be transformed into a golden rectangle as has been done schematically in Figure 1.4.

Side AB of the square ABCD in Figure 1.4 is bisected. With the center E and the radius EC, an arc of a circle is drawn, cutting the extension of AB at F. Line FG is drawn perpendicular to AF, meeting the extension of DC at G. AFGD is the golden rectangle. According to the formal definition, the geometrical representation of the golden section in a rectangle means that a rectangle of this form is 1.618 times longer than it is wide. Again, Fibonacci's ratio PHI appears, this time in the proportions of the golden rectangle.

Keeping in mind the representation of the Fibonacci ratio PHI in one-dimensional (line) and two-dimensional (rectangle) geometry, we can proceed to more complex geometrical objects that bring us closer

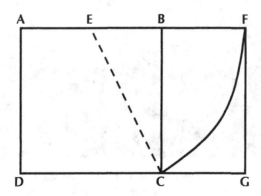

Figure 1.4   Golden section of a rectangle. *Source: FAM Research,* 2000.

to the tools we want to apply to analyze stock and commodity markets with regard to time and price.

The only mathematical curve that follows the pattern of natural growth is the spiral, expressed in natural phenomena such as *Spira mirabilis*, or the nautilus shell. The PHI-spiral has been called the most beautiful of mathematical curves. This type of spiral occurs frequently in the natural world. The Fibonacci summation series and the golden section, introduced above as its geometrical equivalent, are very well associated with this remarkable curve.

Figure 1.5 shows a radiograph of the shell of the chambered nautilus. The successive chambers of the nautilus are built on the framework of a PHI-spiral. As the shell grows, the size of the chambers increases, but their shape remains unaltered.

To demonstrate the geometry of the PHI-spiral, it is best to use a golden rectangle as the basis for geometrical analysis. This is done schematically in Figure 1.6.

Figure 1.5   The PHI-spiral represented in the nautilus shell. *Source: The Divine Proportion,* by H. E. Huntley (New York: Dover, 1970), p. iv. Reprinted with permission.

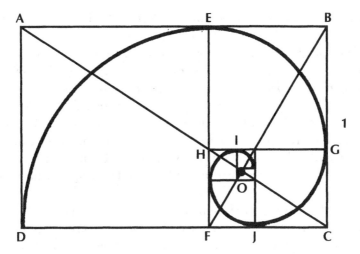

Figure 1.6   Geometry of the PHI-spiral. *Source: FAM Research,* 2000.

The quotient of the length and height of rectangle ABCD in Figure 1.6 can be calculated, as we learned previously, by AB ÷ BC = PHI ÷ 1 = 1.618. Through point E, also called the golden cut of AB, line EF is drawn perpendicular to AB, cutting the square AEFD from the rectangle. The remaining rectangle EBCF is a golden rectangle. If the square EBGH is isolated, the then remaining figure, HGCF, is also a golden rectangle. This process can be repeated indefinitely until the limiting rectangle O is so small that it is indistinguishable from a point.

The limiting point O is called the pole of the equal angle spiral, which passes through the golden cuts D, E, G, J, and so on. The sides of the rectangle are nearly, but not completely, tangential to the curve.

The relation of the PHI-spiral to the Fibonacci series is evident from Figure 1.6 because the PHI-spiral passes diagonally through opposite corners of successive squares, such as DE, EG, GJ, and so on. The lengths of the sides of these squares form a Fibonacci series. If the smallest square has a side of length d, the adjacent square must also have a side of length d. The next square has a side of length 2d (twice as long as d), the next of 3d (three times the length of d), forming the series 1d, 2d, 3d, 5d, 8d, 13d, . . . which is exactly the well-known Fibonacci sequence: 1–1–2–3–5–8–13– and so on, indefinitely.

The spiral is without a terminal point. While growing outward (or inward) indefinitely, its shape remains unchanged. Two segments of the spiral are identical in shape, but they differ in size by exactly the factor PHI. All those spirals whose rate of growth is an element of the PHI series 0.618–1.000–1.618–2.618–4.236–6.854–11.090– and so on, shall be referred to as PHI-spirals in the context of this book.

The PHI-spiral is the link between the Fibonacci summation series, the resulting Fibonacci ratio PHI, and the magic of nature that we enjoy all around us.

In addition to the PHI-spiral, other important geometric curves can be found in nature. Those most significant to civilization include the horizon of the ocean, the meteor track, the parabola of a waterfall, the arc the sun travels, the crescent moon, and, finally, the flight of a bird. Many of these natural curves can be geometrically modeled using ellipses.

An ellipse is the mathematical expression of an oval. Each ellipse can be precisely designated by only a few characteristics (Figure 1.7).

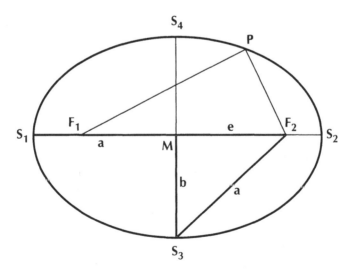

Figure 1.7   Geometry of the PHI-ellipse. *Source: FAM Research, 2000.*

S_1S_2 in Figure 1.7 represents the length of the major axis of the ellipse. S_3S_4 is the length of the minor axis of the ellipse. The ellipse is now determined by the equation

$$F_1P + F_2P = S_1S_2 = 2a$$

Of interest to us, in the context of Fibonacci analysis, is the ratio of the major axis and minor axis of the ellipse, in mathematical terms

$$S_1S_2 \div S_3S_4 = 2a \div 2b = a \div b$$

An ellipse is turned into a PHI-ellipse in all those cases where the ratio of the major axis to the minor axis of the ellipse is a member number of the PHI series 0.618–1.000–1.618–2.618–4.236–6.854– and so on. A circle is a special type of PHI-ellipse, with a = b and a ratio of a ÷ b = 1.

What makes PHI-ellipses preferable to all other possible ellipses (those with ratios of major axes divided by minor axes other than numbers of the PHI series) is the fact that empirical research has shown that people find approximations of PHI-ellipses significantly more visually satisfying.

When participants in a research project were confronted with different shapes of ellipses and were asked for their levels of comfort, a sample empirical study returned the results shown in Table 1.1.

Table 1.1   Preferences for PHI-Ellipses

Ratio Major Axis ÷ Minor Axis a ÷ b	Percentage of Preference
1.000	1.2
1.205	0.6
1.250	8.3
1.333	14.7
1.493	42.4
1.618	16.7
1.754	13.1
2.000	1.6

Source: *The Divine Proportion*, by H. E. Huntley (New York: Dover, 1970) p. 65. Reprinted with permission.

Three observers out of four favored ellipses shaped with axes whose ratios were either the PHI-ellipse (1.618) or so close an approximation to the PHI-ellipse as to be almost indistinguishable from it.

With this optimistic outlook, we can proceed to the second main part of our theoretical introduction of basic Fibonacci tools.

What conclusions can be drawn from our discussions so far? And what sort of conclusions did Elliott draw to integrate the Fibonacci summation series and Fibonacci's PHI with the forces that move international markets?

THE ELLIOTT WAVE PRINCIPLE

Ralph Nelson Elliott (1871–1948) began his career as an engineer, not a professional market analyst. Having recovered from a serious illness in the 1930s, he turned his interest to the analysis of stock prices, focusing on the Dow Jones Index.

After a number of remarkably successful forecasts, in 1939 Elliott published a series of major articles in *Financial World* magazine. In these articles, he first presented the contention that the Dow Jones Index moved in rhythms.

Elliott's market theory was based on the fact that every phenomenon on our planet moves in the same patterns as the tides: low tide follows high tide, reaction follows action. Time does not affect this scheme because the structure of the market in its entirety remains constant.

In this section, we briefly review and analyze Elliott's concepts. However, it is important that we address his ideas, because they explain the fundamental concepts that we have used in our analysis of the Fibonacci tools. We will not go into great detail here; most of the facts have been discussed extensively in *Fibonacci Applications and Strategies for Traders*.

Our attention will focus on the main sectors of Elliott's work, which have long-lasting value. Even if we do not agree with some of Elliott's findings, he must be admired for his ideas. We know how difficult it was to create new concepts for market analysis without the technical support that is available today. When we began to study Elliott's work, back in 1977, it was a tremendous struggle to get the data needed for an in-depth analysis. How much more difficult it must have been for Elliott in those years when he started his work! The computer technology available today gives us the ability to test and analyze quickly, but it is still necessary to have Elliott's ideas handy in order to begin.

Elliott wrote: "Nature's law embraces the most important of all elements, timing. Nature's law is not a system, or a method of playing the market, but it is a phenomenon which appears to mark the progress of all human activities. Its application to forecasting is revolutionary."*

Elliott based his discoveries on nature's law. He noted: "This law behind the market can only be discovered when the market is viewed in its proper light and then is analyzed from this approach. Simply put, the stock market is a creation of man and therefore reflects human idiosyncrasy" (p. 40).

The chance to forecast price moves using Elliott's principles motivated legions of analysts to work day and night. We will focus on the ability to forecast, and try to answer whether it is possible.

Elliott was very specific when he introduced his concept of waves. He said: "All human activities have three distinctive features, pattern, time and ratio, all of which observe the Fibonacci summation series" (p. 48).

Once the waves are interpreted, that knowledge may be applied to any movement because the same rules apply to the prices of stocks, bonds, grains, and other commodities.

The most important of the three factors mentioned is pattern. A pattern is always in progress, forming over and over again. Usually, but not invariably, one can visualize in advance the appropriate type of pattern. Elliott describes this market cycle as ". . . divided primarily into 'bull market' and 'bear market' " (p. 48).

A bull market can be divided into five "major waves," and a bear market, into three major waves. The major waves 1, 3, and 5 of the bull market are subdivided into five "intermediate waves" each. Then

---

* *The Complete Writings of R. N. Elliott with Practical Application from J. R. Hill,* by J. R. Hill, Commodity Research Institute, NC, 1979 (subsequent references will cite Elliott), p. 84.

waves 1, 3, and 5 of each intermediate wave are subdivided into five "minor waves" (Figure 1.8).

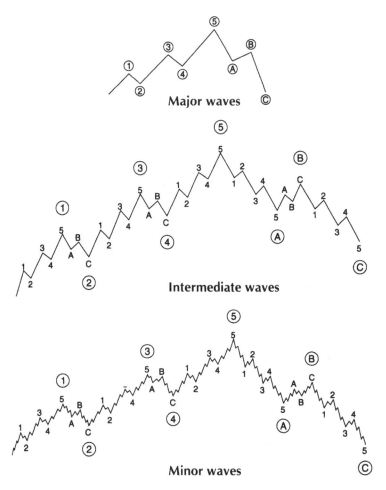

Figure 1.8 Elliott's "perfect" stock market cycle. *Source: Fibonacci Applications and Strategies for Traders,* by Robert Fischer (New York: Wiley, 1993), p. 13. Reprinted with permission.

The problem with this general market concept is that, most of the time, there are no regular 5-wave swings. The regular 5-wave swing is only the exception to a rule that Elliott tried to fine-tune via a sophisticated variation to the concept.

Elliott introduced a series of market patterns that apply to almost every situation in market development. If the market rhythm is regular, wave 2 will not retrace to the beginning of wave 1, and wave 4 will not correct lower than the top of wave 1 (Figure 1.9). In cases where it still does, the wave count must be adjusted.

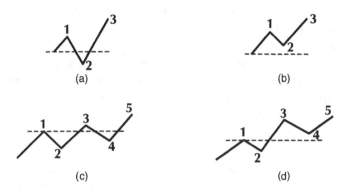

(a) (b)

(c) (d)

Figure 1.9 Counting is (a) erroneous in a 3-wave upmove; (b) correct in a 3-wave upmove; (c) erroneous in a 5-wave upmove; (d) correct in a 5-wave upmove. *Source: Fibonacci Applications and Strategies for Traders,* by Robert Fischer (New York: Wiley, 1993), p. 14. Reprinted with permission.

Each of the two corrective waves 2 and 4 can be subdivided into three waves of a smaller degree. Corrective waves 2 and 4 alternate in pattern. Elliott called this the *rule of alternation.* If wave 2 is simple, wave 4 will be complex, and vice versa (Figure 1.10). Complex in this respect is another term to describe the fact that wave 2 (or wave 4) consists of subwaves and does not go straight as the simple waves do.

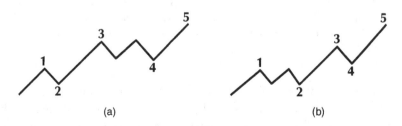

(a) (b)

Figure 1.10 Simple waves and complex waves (a) in wave 4; (b) in wave 2. *Source: Fibonacci Applications and Strategies for Traders,* by Robert Fischer (New York: Wiley, 1993), p. 14. Reprinted with permission.

Given his remarkable observation that simple and complex waves alternate, and his formulation of this as a rule for market development, Elliott linked nature's law to human behavior and thus to investors' behavior.

In natural phenomena such as sunflowers, pinecones, and pineapples, there are spirals that alternate by first turning clockwise and then counterclockwise. This alternation is seen as an equivalent of the alternation of simple and complex constellations in the corrective waves 2 and 4.

In addition to corrections as integral parts of any market move, Elliott analyzed extensions as reinforcements of trends to either side of the market, be they uptrends or downtrends. "Extensions may appear in any one of the three impulse waves, wave 1, 3, or 5, but never in more than one" (p. 55).

Combinations of impulse waves and extensions in the first, third, and fifth wave of a market uptrend are demonstrated in Figure 1.11. The three wave extensions shown can be reversed for impulse waves and extensions in downtrends.

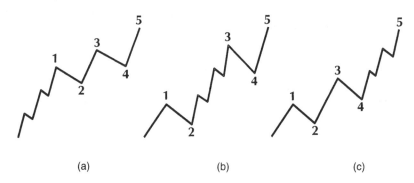

(a)   (b)   (c)

Figure 1.11   (a) First wave extension in an uptrend; (b) third wave extension in an uptrend; (c) fifth wave extension in an uptrend. *Source: Fibonacci Applications and Strategies for Traders,* by Robert Fischer (New York: Wiley, 1993), p. 17. Reprinted with permission.

At this point, we refrain from giving readers advice on all possible options given in Elliott's publications so that we can model the basic structure of market moves based on impulse waves, corrections, and extensions.

The purpose of this quick review is to show the essence of Elliott's ideas and follow them as they became more intricate. In their most complex stages, it is almost impossible, even for very experienced Elliott followers, to apply all of Elliott's wave pattern rules to real-time trading.

Elliott himself admitted: "Corrections in bull and bear swings are more difficult to learn" (p. 48). The problem is that the complex nature of the wave structure does not leave room for forecasts of future price moves in advance. The schemes and structures look perfect in retrospect. The multitude of rules and situations described by Elliott can be used to fit any price pattern after the fact. But that is not good enough for real-time trading.

To conclude our remarks on Elliott, we give a summary of those segments of Elliott's findings that can be exploited in order to devise trading concepts and trading tools that are easy to apply, and that relate to what we have stated about Fibonacci's PHI as the constant for natural growth.

Elliott's principles of markets steadily moving in a wave rhythm are brilliantly conceived. The principles work perfectly in regular markets and give stunning results when looking back at the charts.

The most significant problem is that market swings are irregular. This makes it difficult to give definitive answers to questions such as:

- Is the point at which we start our wave count part of an impulse wave or part of a corrective wave?

- Will there be a fifth wave?

- Is the correction flat or is it zigzag?

- Will there be an extension in wave 1, 3, or 5?

Elliott specifically wrote, regarding this point: "The Principle has been carefully tested and used successfully by subscribers in forecasting market movements" (p. 107). And: "Hereafter letters will be issued on completion of a wave and not await the entire cycle. In this matter, students may learn how to do their own forecasting and at no expense. The phenomenon and its practical application become increasingly interesting because the market continually unfolds new examples to which may be applied unchanging rules" (p. 137).

Our own work with Elliott's concepts, done from many different angles over 20 years, does not support the contention that the wave structure has forecasting ability. The wave structure is too complex, especially in the corrective waves. The rule of alternation is extremely helpful, but this abstract scheme does not tell us, for example, whether to expect:

- A correction of three waves,

- A double sideways correction, or

- A triple sideways movement.

It is even more unlikely that any 5-wave pattern can be forecast. The integration of extensions in wave 1, wave 3, or wave 5 complicates the problem further. The beauty of working with the Elliott concept is not the wave count. We can only agree when J. R. Hill reveals in his practical application: "The concept presented is extremely useful but has literally driven men 'up the wall' as they try to fit chart patterns to exactness in conformity with the Elliott wave" (p. 33).

Elliott focuses on pattern recognition. His whole work is streamlined to forecast future price moves based on existing patterns, but he does not appear to have succeeded in this area.

Elliott expressed uncertainty about the wave count himself, when he wrote in different newsletters: "The five weeks' sideways movement was devoid of pattern, a feature never before noted" (p. 167).

Elsewhere he wrote: "The pattern of the movement across the bottom is so exceedingly rare that no mention thereof appears in the Treatises. The details baffle any count" (p. 165).

Yet again: "The time element [meaning the Fibonacci summation series] as an independent device, however, continues to be baffling when attempts are made to apply any known rule of sequence to trend duration" (p. 180).

And last: "The time element is based on the Fibonacci summation series but has its limitations and can be used only as an adjunct of the wave principle" (p. 186).

Elliott did not realize that it is not the wave count that is important, but Fibonacci's PHI. The Fibonacci ratio represents nature's law and human behavior. It is no more and no less than Fibonacci's PHI that we try to measure in the observation of market swings. While the Fibonacci summation series and the Fibonacci ratio PHI are constant, the wave count is confusing.

Elliott tried to forecast a price move from point B to point C based on market patterns (Figure 1.12). We consider this impossible, and Elliott himself has never given a rule that showed he was able to do it mechanically.

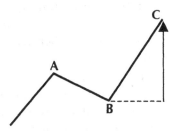

Figure 1.12   Forecasting a price move from point B to point C is not possible. *Source: Fibonacci Applications and Strategies for Traders,* by Robert Fischer (New York: Wiley, 1993), p. 23. Reprinted with permission.

By studying Elliott's publications more carefully, a rule with forecasting value can still be identified. "A cyclical pattern or measurement of mass psychology is five waves upward and three waves downward, a total of eight waves. These patterns have forecasting value: when five waves upward have been completed, three waves down will follow, and vice versa" (p. 112). We could not agree more with this statement. Figure 1.13 visualizes Elliott's latter findings.

Most likely, Elliott did not realize that his strategy had taken a complete shift. Elliott's latest statement takes an opposite strategy, compared to the approach shown in Figure 1.12. Instead of trying to

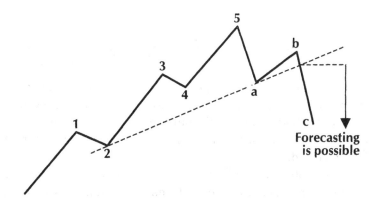

Figure 1.13   Forecasting a price move after the end of a 5-wave cycle is possible. *Source: Fibonacci Applications and Strategies for Traders,* by Robert Fischer (New York: Wiley, 1993), p. 23. Reprinted with permission.

forecast a price move from point B to point C, he waits, according to Figure 1.13, until the very end of the 5-wave move, because three waves in the opposite direction are to be expected.

We totally accept Elliott's approach here and will reinforce the idea with additional rules in later sections. Numbers 5 and 3 are valid in the Fibonacci summation series and therefore cannot mislead us in our analysis.

We will also introduce other investment strategies closely related to the Fibonacci ratio. We will cover corrections and extensions as Elliott did, but will do so differently, always with our focus on Fibonacci's ratio PHI and its representation in the instruments we analyze.

Elliott never worked with a geometric approach. We, however, have developed computerized PHI-spirals and PHI-ellipses ready for application to analysis. We strongly believe that this is the solution to the problem of combining price and time in an integral analysis approach. This goes far beyond what we initiated with our first book some eight years ago.

Using our Fibonacci trading tools, as well as our WINPHI computer program, our analyses in the forthcoming chapters will concentrate mainly on daily price bar charts.

All tools presented have been tested thoroughly and are ready to be used on the commodity and stock markets. Research shows that intraday data can also be used, but under different parameters. More historical tests are needed on a tick or intraday bar basis before definite rules can be set for real-time application of Fibonacci-related geometrical tools.

SUMMARY: GEOMETRICAL FIBONACCI TOOLS

Investigation into the Fibonacci summation series and Elliott's analysis of markets moving in regular waves has led us to six general tools that can be applied, almost without limit, to market data series, whether cash currencies, futures, index products, stocks, or mutual funds are involved.

The six tools are: (1) The Fibonacci summation series itself, (2) Fibonacci time goals, (3) corrections and extensions in relation to the Fibonacci ratio, (4) PHI-channels, (5) PHI-spirals, and (6) PHI-ellipses.

All six of these trading tools are described in this section, to give readers an overview of the functioning and the functionality of the geometrical instruments in any detailed analysis and application of the tools to market data.

The Fibonacci Summation Series

It might seem astonishing at first, but the Fibonacci summation series can easily be turned into a tool for market analysis that works in a stable and reliable manner.

We recapitulate the Fibonacci summation series as:

$$1-1-2-3-5-8-13-21-34-55-89-144-\ldots$$

The quotients of each number in the Fibonacci series, divided by the preceding number, asymptotically gets closer to the value PHI = 1.618 (which we call the Fibonacci ratio).

If we combine the findings of Fibonacci with those of Elliott, we can count out Elliott's theoretical waves—five plus three plus five plus three plus five, for a total of 21 major waves, a number of the Fibonacci summation series.

If each 5-wave move in an uptrend is broken down into five plus three plus five plus three plus five smaller or intermediate waves (a total of 21 waves), and if each of the resulting waves is broken down into five plus three plus five (or a total of 13) small waves, we end up with a total of 89 waves, a number that we again recognize as part of the Fibonacci summation series.

If we go through the same process for the three corrective waves, we come up with a total of 55 waves for the corrective 3-wave move and a grand total of 144 waves for the completion of one of Elliott's market cycles.

The general application of this principle shows that a move in a particular direction continues up to a point where a time frame—part of, and consistent with, the figures of the Fibonacci summation series—is completed.

A move that extends itself beyond three days should not reverse until five days are reached. A move that exceeds five days should last a minimum of eight days. A trend of nine days should not finish before 13 days have passed, and so on.

Our findings regarding the relation between Fibonacci's summation series and Elliott's wave principle can be summarized as shown in Figure 1.14.

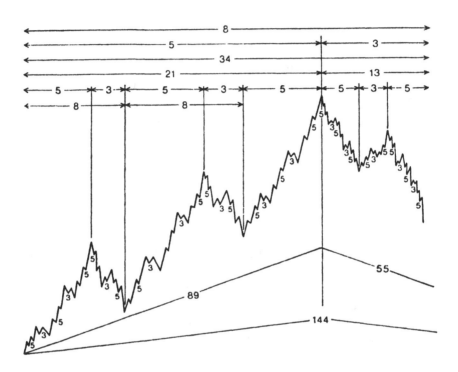

Figure 1.14   The Fibonacci summation series schematically integrated into the complete market cycle according to the Elliott wave count. *Source: Fibonacci Applications and Strategies for Traders,* by Robert Fischer (New York: Wiley, 1993), p. 20. Reprinted with permission.

This basic structure of calculating trend changes may be applied just as successfully on hourly, daily, weekly, or monthly data. But this is only an ideal type of pattern, and traders must never expect commodities, futures, stock index futures, or stocks to behave in such precise and predictable manners.

Deviations can and will occur both in time and amplitude, because individual waves and price patterns are not always likely to develop in a regular way. We also have to keep in mind that the simple application of the Fibonacci summation series is designed to forecast the length of trend moves, but the number of bars in sideways markets remains unpredictable.

However, as we will see later on, the figures 8, 13, 21, 34, and 55 can be of very practical value when applied to work in combination with other Fibonacci tools. One simple example: While looking for the length of a standard PHI-ellipse in a product we want to trade, the easiest way to identify a major trend change is to first check for moves of the length of the Fibonacci figures 8, 13, 21, 34, or 55. This does not mean that trend changes will always occur at the precalculated points after 8, 13, 21, 34, or 55 bars, but it happens too often to be ignored.

Elliott and his followers tried to calculate major trend changes in the stock market by applying the figures from the Fibonacci summation series to weekly, monthly, and yearly data. This made sense even though the underlying time frames became very long, and turning points in historical perspective on a weekly, monthly, or yearly basis often did not materialize at all. On intraday data, we consider the figures of very little value because (1) the markets are extended sideways, and (2) the much more erratic market moves during the day, compared to those from day to day, make the use of Fibonacci figures intraday almost impossible for serious analysis. In our analysis, therefore, we concentrate on daily data and the figures 8, 13, 21, 34, and 55.

Fibonacci Time-Goal Days

The use of time-goal days as the second of our geometrical Fibonacci tools is derived from the same rationale as the Fibonacci summation series.

Time-goal days are those days in the future when a price event will occur. If we were able to anticipate a day in the future when prices would reach a prescribed target or reverse direction, it would be a step forward in market analysis. If we could find a way to forecast the market, we would be able to enter trades or exit positions at the time of the price change rather than after the fact. In addition, a concept of time-goal days would be dynamic, allowing adjustments to longer or shorter swings of the market.

Our time analysis is based on the findings of Euclid of Megara and his invention of the golden section. This was previously discussed in the representation of the Fibonacci ratio in geometry and the golden section of a line.

We link nature's law, expressed in mathematical terms through the Fibonacci ratio PHI, to market swings, as is illustrated in Figure 1.15.

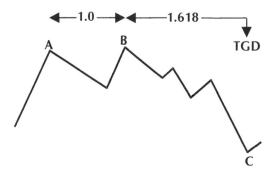

Figure 1.15 Calculation of time-goal days. *Source: FAM Research,* **2000.**

When we know the distance from peak A to peak B in days (or whatever the time unit is), we can multiply this distance by the Fibonacci ratio PHI = 1.618 to forecast the point C that will occur on that day:

$$C = B + 1.618 \times (B - A)$$

C is called a Fibonacci time-goal day. This is the day on which the market is expected to change direction. The forecast of Fibonacci time-goal days will not indicate whether the price will be high or low on particular days. The price can be either. In Figure 1.15, we have a high–high–low formation with a low at point C, but the formation could also be a high–high–high formation indicating a reversal to the downside on the precalculated time-goal day. The time-goal day only forecasts a trend change (a simple event) at the time the goal is reached; it does not indicate the direction of the event. By applying the Fibonacci ratio, the timing of objectives can be measured on intraday, daily, weekly, or monthly charts.

The Fibonacci summation series, Fibonacci's PHI, and the notion of time-goal days as the essence of both, are tools that we use to get closer to resolving the problem of forecasting markets. It cannot be stressed enough, however, that it is difficult to wait for a time goal or to wait for a precalculated period of time (according to the Fibonacci summation series) before finally being entitled to show trading action. Identifying a Fibonacci goal and patiently sticking to it, even when the odds are unfavorable (that is, if the market starts moving before the Fibonacci goal has been reached and one is not yet participating in the trend), are two sides of the same (golden) trading model.

Corrections and Extensions

Corrections and extensions are the third category of our geometrical Fibonacci trading tools. The most common approach to working with corrections is to relate the size of a correction to a percentage of a prior impulsive market move (Figure 1.16).

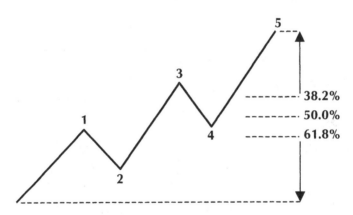

Figure 1.16   Corrections of 38.2%, 50.0%, and 61.8% after a 5-wave move. *Source: Fibonacci Applications and Strategies for Traders,* by Robert Fischer (New York: Wiley, 1993), p. 52. Reprinted with permission.

In our analysis, we are interested in the three most prominent percentage values of possible market corrections that can be directly derived from the quotients of the PHI series and the Fibonacci sequence:

- 38.2% is the result of 0.618 ÷ 1.618;

- 50.0% is the transformed ratio 1.000; and

- 61.8% is the result of the immediate ratio 1.000 ÷ 1.618.

Forecasting the exact size of a correction is an empirical problem; investing after a correction of just 38.2% might be too early, whereas waiting for a correction of 61.8% might result in missing strong trends completely. However, no matter what sizes of corrections are taken into consideration, the PHI-related sizes are the ones to focus on in the first place.

Extensions, in contrast to corrections, are exuberant price movements. They express themselves in runaway markets, opening gaps, limit up and limit down moves, and high volatility. These situations may offer extraordinary trading potential as long as the analysis is carried out in accordance with sensible and definite rules.

Considering extensions as graphical tools for market analysis, we again make use of the Fibonacci ratio as we derived it from the Fibonacci summation series (Figure 1.17).

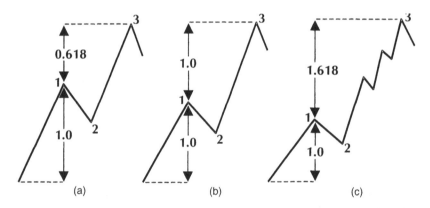

Figure 1.17 Extensions in the third wave of a trend, and the Fibonacci ratio PHI. (a) Ratio 0.618; (b) ratio 1.000; (c) ratio 1.618. *Source: Fibonacci Applications and Strategies for Traders,* by Robert Fischer (New York: Wiley, 1993), p. 52. Reprinted with permission.

The three ratios we work with in most of our analyses of extension sizes are 0.618, 1.000, and 1.618. But other elements of the PHI series, such as 2.618, 4.236, or 6.854, referred to in earlier sections, are also valid estimates for the strength of a market move once the size of the initial wave has been set to 1.000.

Strong trends can overshoot the initial wave by more than just PHI or 1.618 times the size of the initiating impulse wave. It can be tested empirically on various sets of data (using the ratio that best serves the need of the analyst) to get the most profit out of market rallies.

Remember: If 1.618 does not seem good enough, wait until the move has extended to 2.618, and do not stop somewhere in the middle.

There is no rationale behind the Fibonacci ratio, but by applying this ratio as a scheme for analysis, we get a hold on strong major market moves that are triggered by news of political or economic events, crop or storage reports, or any situation in which emotions take control of actions. Fear or greed, fast markets or stop-loss orders make the markets move. We measure the extent of these moves in Fibonacci's ratio PHI, the Fibonacci summation series, and the member numbers of the respective PHI series.

PHI-Channels

PHI-channels, so-called Fibonacci trend channels, constitute the fourth element in our set of geometrical tools. They are generated by drawing parallel lines through tops and bottoms of price moves.

The general idea behind PHI-channels as Fibonacci-related trading tools becomes clear when we look at the abstract schematic presentation in Figure 1.18.

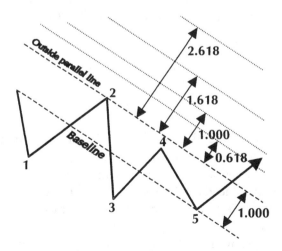

Figure 1.18   PHI-channel. *Source: FAM Research, 2000.*

The width of the PHI-channel is calculated as the distance between the baseline and the parallel outside line. This distance is set to 1.000. Parallel lines are then drawn in PHI series distance starting at 0.618 times the size of the channel, continuing at 1.000 times, 1.618 times, 2.618 times, 4.236 times the distance, and so on. We follow the wave pattern move through the PHI-channel. As soon as wave 5 has been completed, we expect a correction opposite to the trend direction to occur.

In contrast to our findings regarding corrections aiming at the prediction of price targets, PHI-channels provide us with an extra opportunity to make assumptions about the duration of the expected correction timewise. The correction will last until either one of the lines running parallel to the trend channel is touched. Which line we should wait for is another empirical question, but regardless of which line we consider reliable (0.618, 1.000, 1.618, 2.618, or beyond), we must make sure that we wait to the very end and do not act before the Fibonacci target line has been reached.

At the point our target parallel is realized, we might not have arrived at our Fibonacci goal pricewise on the basis of our calculation of corrections. This example shows how important it is to work with multiple Fibonacci targets and to try to identify points where different Fibonacci tools result in the same forecast pricewise and/or timewise.

In our example, an optimal Fibonacci target would be triggered when a correction out of a Fibonacci trend channel hit a parallel at 0.618, 1.000, 1.618, or 2.618 times the size of the channel, and pricewise at a level where a correction of 38.2%, 50.0%, or 61.8% is just or nearly completed.

In discussions of similar examples in later sections,we prove how this kind of multiple Fibonacci analysis is possible.

PHI-Spirals

PHI-spirals, fifth on our list of Fibonacci tools, provide the optimal link between price and time analysis.

In an earlier section on the representation of Fibonacci's PHI in geometry, we introduced the PHI-spirals as perfect geometric approximations of nature's law and phenomena of natural growth in the world around us.

In simple geometrical terms, the size of a PHI-spiral is determined by the distance between the center (X) of the spiral and the starting point (A). The starting point is usually given by wave 1 or wave 2: either a peak in uptrends or a valley in downtrends. The corresponding center of the spiral is usually set to the beginning of the respective wave. The PHI-spiral then turns either clockwise or counterclockwise around the initial line that goes from the center to the starting point.

As the PHI-spiral grows, it extends by a constant ratio with every full cycle. Returning to what we explained earlier in this chapter, all the spirals that have rates of growth corresponding to an element of the PHI series—0.618, 1.000, 1.618, 2.618, and so on—shall, in the context of this book, be referred to as PHI-spirals (Figure 1.19).

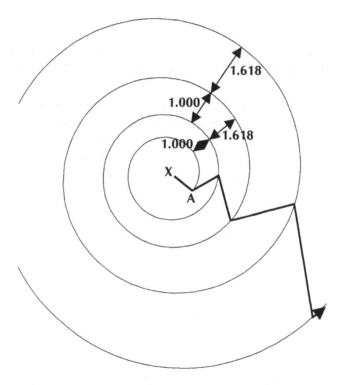

Figure 1.19   PHI-spiral. *Source: FAM Research,* 2000.

A growth rate of 1.618 is the one we will work with most, but all other ratios that can be generated using the PHI series are valid as well and can be tested individually with the WINPHI software package.

We can now conclude that each point on a PHI-spiral manifests an optimal combination of price and time. Corrections and trend changes occur at all those prominent points where the PHI-spiral is touched on its growth path through price and time.

With PHI-spirals as Fibonacci tools, we can make the best out of the stunning symmetry in the price patterns of charts, whether on a daily, weekly, monthly, or yearly basis, and whether they represent stocks, cash currencies, commodities, or derivatives. The stronger the behavioral patterns become in extreme market conditions, the better PHI-spirals work to inform investors in advance about tops and bottoms of market moves.

PHI-Ellipses

The sixth tool brings us back to the PHI-ellipse. In its geometry, it is like the PHI-spiral. This tool has been discussed in one of the earlier sections.

An ellipse is the mathematical expression of an oval. What we mainly are interested in when dealing with a Fibonacci tool is the ratio $e_x = a \div b$ of major axis a and minor axis b of the ellipse (Figure 1.20).

An ellipse is turned into a PHI-ellipse in all those cases where the ratio of the major axis, divided by the minor axis of the ellipse, is

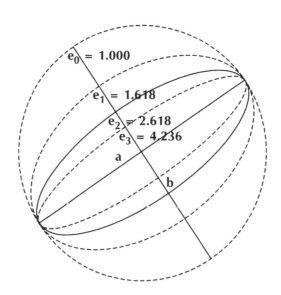

Figure 1.20   PHI-ellipses; $e_x = a \div b$. *Source: FAM Research,* 2000.

a member number of the PHI series—0.618–1.000–1.618–2.618, and so on. A circle, in this respect, is a special type of PHI-ellipse with a = b (ratio a ÷ b = 1).

What makes PHI-ellipses preferable to all other possible ellipses with ratios of major axis divided by minor axis other than numbers of the PHI series is that empirical research has shown that the majority of people find approximations of PHI-ellipses significantly more visually satisfying. But when it comes to using PHI-ellipses as tools for market analysis, satisfaction is not what we first consider. We are primarily looking for ellipses that fit well to market moves and can be utilized for forecasting purposes.

From Figure 1.20, we can conclude that PHI-ellipses with increasing ratios e_x = a ÷ b of major axis to minor axis turn very quickly into "Havana cigars"—and, in this process, lose part of their beauty. PHI-ellipses at ratios of 6.854 and above become so narrow that they can hardly be applied to charts as analytical tools. In Figure 1.21, however, we present a convincing solution that helps us with the dilemma and gives us a chance to maintain the beauty of PHI-ellipses up to ratios of at least 17.944.

To make PHI-ellipses work as tools for chart analysis, we have applied a transformation to the underlying mathematical formula that

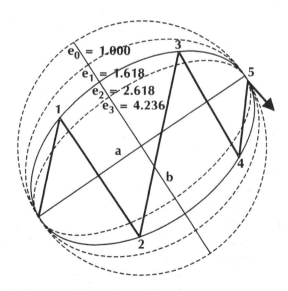

Figure 1.21   Fischer transformed PHI-ellipses; e_x = (a ÷ b)*. *Source: FAM Research,* 2000.

describes the shape of the ellipse. We still consider the ratio of major axis a to minor axis b of the ellipse, but in a different way—in mathematical terms $e_x = (a \div b)^*$.

It took us quite a while to come up with a solution to the problem of transforming PHI-ellipses for productive chart analysis and, at the same time, maintaining them as PHI-ellipses; that is, still incorporating the member numbers of the PHI series into our analysis of the ratio of the major axes and minor axes of the ellipse.

We protect our property in this case and hold the exact formula for transforming $a \div b$ into $(a \div b)^*$ proprietary, but readers will still benefit from our findings, because transformed PHI-ellipses are part of the WINPHI software on the CD-ROM and can easily be applied to charts, according to readers' preferences.

However, when we refer to the application of PHI-ellipses, keep in mind that we are referring to Fischer-transformed PHI-ellipses of the type demonstrated in Figure 1.21.

As long as we prefer a PHI-ellipse [meaning an ellipse with a ratio of major axis to minor axis $(a \div b)^*$, which is an element of the PHI series], we are free to test various ratios and ellipses on market data. The only thing we must make sure of is that once we have found an ellipse that fits well to a move (like the one at a ratio of $(a \div b)^* = 2.618$ in Figure 1.21), we do not alter it in the course of our analysis.

We will see in the upcoming chapters how this promising tool can be applied to charts and can be used to forecast market moves and targets in market developments.

Final Introductory Remarks on the WINPHI Software Package

The WINPHI software package that comes with this book allows interested investors to generate all the signals on historical data with the different Fibonacci tools (shown in examples).

All sample signals were tested, via our best efforts, by the time this book was completed early in 2001. Tests were done by hand and, of course, with the assistance of the WINPHI computer program.

Generating signals by hand can introduce the possibility of error. More important to mention, we did not test the products for demonstration purposes longer than 11 months backward on daily charts and three years backward on weekly charts. It would be too much for us to test each strategy presented in our entire historical database, which goes between 12 and 20 years backward, depending on the product. However, interested investors have the ability to do this on sample datasets for all major products and markets included with the CD-ROM, or on their own datasets.

We do not claim that, for each example shown, we have published the very best parameters, entry rules, stop-loss rules, or profit targets. There will certainly be other combinations that are somewhat superior to what we offer, but we want to distribute inspiration rather than optimization. We therefore provide a challenge for every investor who is especially interested in one of the tools or in a special strategy.

Test runs become more valid and reliable, the longer the time span selected to test a tool or a strategy. This holds true for all the examples and strategies we have described. Parameters, like swing sizes, never work equally well in sideways market conditions and in trending markets. This factor becomes especially important when we work with extensions or corrections where percentages are calculated relative to a minimum swing size. It is possible that the relevant parameters we use change over time with longer historical test runs.

In addition, the WINPHI software is basically restricted to plotting daily data on charts in ASCII D–O–H–L–C field order. We do not offer any conversion utility; the program does not change compression rates from daily to weekly, monthly, or yearly. However, weekly, monthly, yearly, and even intraday minute or hourly bar charts can be generated, if the data to plot are already in the respective ASCII D–O–H–L–C format. Monthly ASCII data files are plotted as monthly data, weekly data files as weekly data, and so on. And if data come as intraday minute or hourly ASCII D–O–H–L–C data, the correct data compression will also be plotted on the charts. Nevertheless, our default assumption remains that daily ASCII-coded D–O–H–L–C data files are intended to be analyzed by users.

All six Fibonacci tools are based on pattern recognition. These patterns can look very different if the price scale is varied. Generally speaking, online data vendors provide software packages that, by default, always scale full screen when information is updated. Depending on new highs or new lows, price scales are adjusted accordingly.

However, a constant scale is an absolutely necessary condition for any sort of convincing pattern recognition that is intended to run over longer periods of time (sometimes 20 years or more). One year of data, scaled full screen, is usually not good enough to cover an entire market cycle of trending and sideways periods. As soon as sophisticated tools, such as the PHI-ellipse, are employed to analyze market moves in price and in time, it is vital to have the angle of the PHI-ellipse remain free of influence from small variations in scaling.

Knowing that many data vendors do not have a feature for constant scaling included with their charting devices, we designed our software so that users can opt for either full-screen scaling of the most recent data loaded or constant scaling from highest high to lowest low of the entire data series for investors who do not feel comfortable with the need to convert data from their data series.

FINAL REMARKS

Elliott and his followers did not find a solution to the problem of whether to chart data on a linear scale or on a semi-log scale. Semi-log scales might be interesting to look at, especially when weekly or monthly charts analyze price and time, or when working with corrections or extensions. We consider the discussion on linear or semi-log scaling important to professional traders. Throughout the book, all sample applications of our tools have been conducted using linear scaling. Wherever we find it necessary—for example, when describing extensions and corrections on weekly data—we discuss the subject briefly. However, we do not consider the matter worth the effort of integrating an extra feature for semi-log scaling with our WINPHI software package.

So much for technical questions, parameters, scaling, and measurement. May the following chapters be inspiring and challenging. Readers should take our findings not as final solutions to the problem of making Fibonacci's PHI tradable, but as a promising starting point to verify, modify, improve, and apply our Fibonacci tools.

Trading according to Fibonacci principles is a journey. Come join us for an exciting trip.

2

APPLYING THE FIBONACCI SUMMATION SERIES

The Fibonacci summation series is the basis for all six tools that will be presented. Therefore, in Chapter 2, we focus on patterns of chart analysis that make use of no special tools other than the Fibonacci sequence. If by focusing only on the Fibonacci summation series, we can convincingly capture the rhythm of annual market swings already, just think of what we can do with the additional tools integrated as well.

The Fibonacci summation series will first be applied in principle. In the second and third steps, the Fibonacci summation series will be analyzed in depth, using samples of daily and weekly market data.

APPLYING FIBONACCI'S SUMMATION SERIES IN PRINCIPLE

As a quick recapitulation of the detailed description in Chapter 1, the Fibonacci summation series runs as

$$1 - 1 - 2 - 3 - 5 - 8 - 13 - 21 - 34 - 55 - 89 - 144 - \ldots$$

In mathematical terms, it can be written as

$$a_{n+1} = a_{n-1} + a_n \text{ with } a_1 = a_2 = 1$$

The key properties of the Fibonacci summation series can be condensed as follows:

- Each number that is part of the Fibonacci summation series, when divided by its preceding value (e.g., $13 \div 8$ or $21 \div 13$), results in a ratio that we approximate as PHI' = 1.618 (knowing that the oscillation of the numbers of the Fibonacci sequence toward the Fibonacci ratio PHI is an asymptotical process).

- The ratio PHI can be expressed algebraically according to the formula $\varphi = \frac{1}{2}\left(\sqrt{5} + 1\right) \approx 1.618$.

- Each number that is part of the Fibonacci summation series, when divided by its following value (e.g., $8 \div 13$ or $13 \div 21$), results in a ratio that we approximate as PHI' = 0.618 (that is, the reciprocal value to the ratio PHI).

- The ratio PHI' can be expressed algebraically according to the formula $\varphi = \frac{1}{2}\left(\sqrt{5} - 1\right) \approx 0.618$.

- Because the ratios PHI and PHI' are reciprocal values, multiplying the ratios PHI and PHI' results in (PHI $\times$ PHI' = 1.618 $\times$ 0.618 = 1).

- Each number that is part of the Fibonacci summation series (55–34–21–13), when divided by its value two below (e.g., $34 \div 13$ or $55 \div 21$), results in a ratio that we approximate as 1 + PHI = 2.618.

- Each number that is part of the Fibonacci summation series (13–21–34–55), when divided by its value two above (e.g., $13 \div 34$ or $21 \div 55$), results in a ratio that we approximate as 1 – PHI' = 0.382.

From the latter two properties of the Fibonacci summation series, we can generate a PHI series that runs as:

0.618 – 1.000 – 1.618 – 2.618 – 4.236 – 6.854 – 11.090 – 17.944 – . . .

In mathematical terms, it can be written as

$$a_{n+1} = a_{n-1} + a_n \text{ with } a_1 = 0.618, \ a_2 = 1$$

For means of analysis, the values of the Fibonacci summation series can be linked to the same method of counting market waves that Elliott used for the wave principle (Figure 2.1).

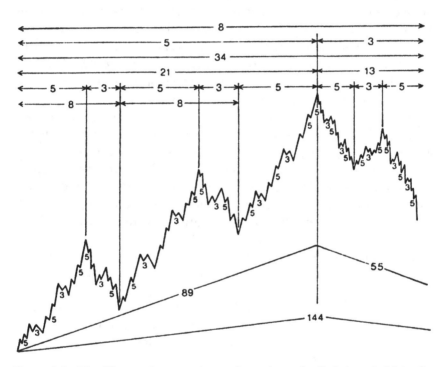

Figure 2.1   The Fibonacci summation series, schematically integrated into the complete market cycle according to the Elliott wave count. *Source: Fibonacci Applications and Strategies for Traders,* by Robert Fischer (New York: Wiley, 1993), p. 20. Reprinted with permission.

If we combine the findings of Fibonacci with those of Elliott, we can count out Elliott's theoretical waves—five plus three plus five plus three plus five major waves; or a total of 21 major waves—and we arrive at a number in the Fibonacci summation series.

If each 5-wave move in an uptrend is broken down into five plus three plus five plus three plus five smaller or intermediate waves (a total of 21 waves), and if each of the resulting waves is again broken down into five plus three plus five (a total of 13) small waves, we end up at a total of 89 waves—another number that is part of the Fibonacci summation series.

If we go through the same process for the three corrective waves, we come up with a total of 55 waves for the corrective 3-wave move and a grand total of 144 waves for one complete Elliott cycle.

The general application of this core principle is that a move in a particular direction should continue up to a point where a time frame that is part of, and is consistent with, the Fibonacci summation series is completed. A move that extends itself beyond three days should not reverse until five days is reached. A move that exceeds five days should last a minimum of eight days. A trend of nine days should not finish before 13 days have passed, and so on.

This basic structure of calculating trend changes can be applied equally well to sets of daily, weekly, or monthly data. However, this is only an ideal type of pattern, and investors must never expect commodities, futures, stock index futures, or stocks to behave in such a precise and predictable manner. Deviations, both in time and amplitude, can and will occur because individual waves and price patterns are not likely to always develop in a regular way. In addition, we have to keep in mind that the simple application of the Fibonacci summation series is designed to forecast the length of trend moves, and that the number of bars in sideways markets remains unpredictable.

However, as we will see later on, the numbers 8, 13, 21, 34, and 55 can be of very practical value to a trader when applied to work in combination with other Fibonacci tools. For example, while looking for the length of a standard PHI-ellipse in a product we want to trade, the easiest way to identify a major trend change is to first check for moves of the length of the Fibonacci figures 8, 13, 21, 34, or 55. This does not mean that trend changes will always occur at the precalculated points after 8, 13, 21, 34, or 55 bars, but it happens too many times to be ignored.

Elliott and his followers also tried to calculate major trend changes in the stock market by applying the figures from the Fibonacci summation series to monthly and yearly data. This made sense, even though the underlying time frames became very long and turning points in historical perspective on a weekly, monthly, or yearly basis often did not materialize at all. On intraday data, we consider the figures of very little value because extended sideways markets and much more erratic market moves during the day (compared to those from day-to-day) make using Fibonacci figures intraday almost impossible for serious analysis. In our analysis, therefore, we concentrate on daily and weekly data and on the numbers 8, 13, 21, 34, and 55.

To demonstrate how powerful individual values, like those in the Fibonacci summation series, can serve as analytic tools, we will analyze the nearest contract data of the S&P500 Index and the cash data of the Japanese Yen cash currency.

There is a reason for concentrating on widely used products. If the figures of the Fibonacci summation series represent nature's law, then human behavior is also expected to be expressed in these figures. Only on very rare occasions will market prices—on any given day, on any product, and on any exchange worldwide—represent the fair value of the underlying product. Most of the time, prices swing either above or below the fair value as an expression and a representation of nonfundamentals such as sensation, greed, excitement, fear, and frustration. The sum of these nonfundamentals or emotions is what we call human behavior.

The effects of human behavior are evident in market pricing at any given time. It is obvious that liquid and heavily traded instruments such as the S&P500 Index or the Japanese Yen cash currency are better indicators for the worldwide concentration of human behavior than niche products like futures contracts on pork bellies or lumber.

THE FIBONACCI SUMMATION
SERIES ON DAILY DATA

In this section, we present an analysis for six months (as of late November 2000) of daily bar charts of the S&P500 Index and the Japanese Yen cash currency.

The database for our analysis has been provided by Bridge/CRB, of Chicago, Illinois. The datasets for the different products we used are available on the WINPHI CD-ROM for readers who wish to trace our analysis and to proceed further.

We know that this time span (six months) is only an indication of what can be done with the Fibonacci summation series as an analytic tool, but this book does not offer a fully automated trading model. Our goals are to introduce some new trading tools and to give readers ideas for how these tools can be successfully applied to the markets.

Let us now get to the heart of the matter.

On the S&P500 Index market, we start counting Fibonacci numbers 8, 13, 21, 34, and 55 only from major highs (peaks) and major lows (valleys). A major high (vice versa for a valley) is confirmed when we have (a) at least two closing prices, on either side of the day with the highest high, that are lower than the low of the highest day, or (b) two closing prices that are lower than the close of the highest day (Figure 2.2).

(a)   (b)

Figure 2.2   Swing high formations based on (a) low of high day and (b) close of high day. *Source: FAM Research, 2000.*

The swing size has to be a minimum of 50 full S&P500 Index points (500 ticks). In other words, a price move in the S&P500 Index has to go from, for example, 1,400.00 to 1,450.00 and back to 1,400.00 before we can consider 1,450.00 to be the confirmed swing high.

In our Fibonacci count of days on the chart, we do not skip holidays; we include them as trading days.

Although we count, from every peak or valley every time, the distance of 8, 13, 21, 34, or 55 days, we use only those counts that equal or overlap and thereby multiply other counts (Figure 2.3).

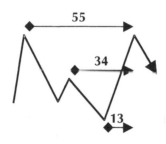

Figure 2.3   Confirmation of a peak by multiple Fibonacci numbers. *Source: FAM Research, 2000.*

If, for instance, we count 34 days from one peak, and this pre-calculated time is not confirmed with another count of 8, 13, 21, 55 days from any other confirmed peak or valley, we ignore this count.

The confirmation of a certain trend change by two or more values of the Fibonacci summation series indicates a price change in the future and eliminates many single counts that would create a lot of irritation while we are looking for relatively safe trend changes.

The counts from different peaks or valleys with different numbers do not often match exactly on the very same day when we are looking for a trend change.

What we find is a time band. We have established that a time band should not be longer than four days in order to still be acceptable and validly confirm a swing high or a swing low (Figure 2.4).

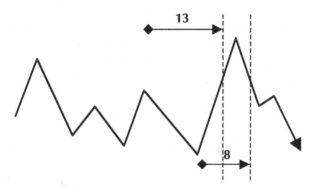

Figure 2.4 Confirmation of a peak by numbers of the Fibonacci summation series in a time band. *Source: FAM Research, 2000.*

In other words, a time goal calculated from a low with 13 days might arrive two days earlier or two days later than a time goal calculated from a high only 8 days beforehand.

The reason for the occurence of time bands when we apply alternative counts from the Fibonacci sequence is that different Fibonacci goals in time and price might be reached very closely together.

At a certain point, we do not know whether (a) Fibonacci price goals or (b) Fibonacci time goals are of bigger importance to stop price moves. But we do know that either goals, (a) or (b), can stop a price move.

The following charts illustrate this idea (Figure 2.5).

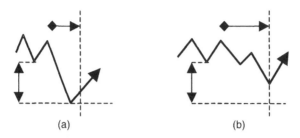

(a)   (b)

Figure 2.5   Dominance of (a) price goal and (b) time goal. *Source: FAM Research,* 2000.

The Fibonacci price-goal line in Figure 2.5 is calculated as an extension out of a 3-wave pattern. In Chapter 3, where various techniques for calculating corrections and extensions are described, readers will learn in detail how to find price goals in market patterns. In Chapter 7, we deal with the calculation and application of time-goal days. The Fibonacci time-goal line in Figure 2.5 is, for demonstration purposes, set in Fibonacci distance (meaning 8 or 13 or 21 or 34 or 55 days) from the last confirmed peak out of the underlying 3-wave pattern.

It is now easy to observe that, in Figure 2.5(a), the line for the Fibonacci price target is reached just a little bit before the Fibonacci time-goal line has been reached by the market move. The Fibonacci price goal in this respect is dominant and brings the market move to an end. In Figure 2.5(b), the case is exactly the opposite. The market movement arrives at the Fibonacci time-goal line, whereas the Fibonacci price-goal line has not yet been touched. Timewise, we are right on target; pricewise, we would have expected a stronger market move.

However, the existence of time bands when applying the Fibonacci summation series is one of the minor problems investors have to confront. We are satisfied if we can manage to calculate trend changes in advance, within a very small margin, by simply counting the duration of a market move in days, according to the rules of the Fibonacci summation series. In those cases where we reach our price target before our time has come, we are still satisfied. On the other hand, we might reach the time goal calculated on the basis of the

Fibonacci summation series, but might not have finished a move strong enough to get to the Fibonacci target pricewise. It is then up to the investor (and his or her risk preference) to decide whether to liquidate the position according to the established Fibonacci rule, or to wait longer, in case the price goal is reached. (For more details on price goals, see Chapter 3. Chapter 8 has details on combined applications of multiple Fibonacci tools.)

Let us return to our analysis of the developments in the S&P500 Index in the second half of 2000.

The parameters for the analysis are clear regarding definition of valleys and peaks, swing size, inclusion of trading holidays, and confirmation of major highs and major lows by multiple counts from the Fibonacci summation series.

In Figure 2.6, Fibonacci's summation series is applied to the S&P500 Index in order to demonstrate how big trend changes can be calculated by counting from swing highs and swing lows.

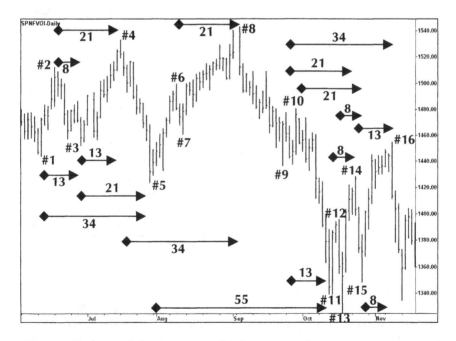

Figure 2.6 Chart of the S&P500 Index from 06–00 to 11–00. Base count of valid turning points in the market according to Fibonacci numbers. *Source: FAM Research,* 2000.

The total (16) turning points in the S&P500 Index market between June and November 2000 have been derived from Figure 2.6 and are based on the calculation in Table 2.1.

Counts for swing highs (peaks) or swing lows (valleys) are omitted in those cases where an insufficient number of days is available to complete one Fibonacci count. This factor is relevant for peak #2 and valley #1. Invalid counts occur when counts are not confirmed by overlapping Fibonacci numbers. Therefore, peaks #6, #10, and #12 and valleys #7, #9, and #13 are excluded from the table.

Table 2.1 Calculation of Valid Turning Points in the S&P500 Index from 06–00 to 11–00, Using the Fibonacci Summation Series

Turning Point	Type	Initiation (Days)	Reference	Type
#3	Valley	8	After #2	High
		13	After #1	Low
#4	Peak	13	After #3	Low
		21	After #2	High
#5	Valley	21	After #3	Low
		34	After #1	Low
#8	Peak	21	After #6	High
		34	After #4	High
#11	Valley	13	After #9	Low
		55	After #5	Low
#14	Peak	8	After #11	Low
		21	After #9	Low
#15	Valley	8	After #12	High
		21	After #10	High
#16	Peak	13	After #14	High
		34	After #9	Low

Source: FAM Research, 2000.

The same procedure can now be executed for a second set of sample data, using the daily chart of the Japanese Yen cash currency.

With the Japanese Yen cash currency, the general parameters we apply for our analysis do not differ widely from the parameters used with the S&P500 Index.

Again, we count the Fibonacci figures 8, 13, 21, 34, and 55 only from major highs (peaks) and major lows (valleys).

A major high (vice versa for a valley) is confirmed only when we have either: (a) at least two closing prices, on either side of the day with the highest high, that are lower than the low of the highest day, or (b) two closing prices that are lower than the close of the highest day (see Figure 2.2).

The swing size for valid peaks and valleys has to be a minimum of 150 Japanese Yen cash currency ticks (for example, a price move from 180.00 to 190.50 and back). Trading holidays are not skipped; they remain included as trading days in our Fibonacci count of days on the chart (Figure 2.7).

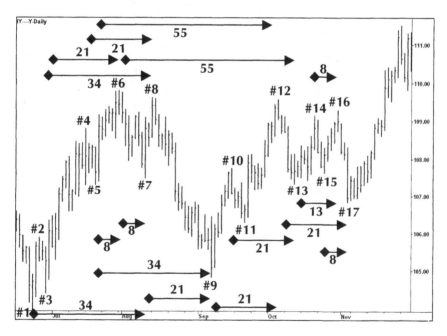

Figure 2.7 Chart of the Japanese Yen cash currency from 06–00 to 11–00. Base count of valid turning points in the market according to Fibonacci numbers. *Source: FAM Research, 2000.*

Although we count from every peak or valley every 8, 13, 21, 34, or 55 days, like the S&P500 Index, we use only those counts that equal or overlap each other and thereby multiply other counts.

The total (17) turning points in the Japanese Yen cash currency between June and November 2000 have been derived from the chart based on the calculation in Table 2.2.

Valleys #1, #3, #5, #11, and #15 and peaks #2, #4, #10, and #14 are omitted, either because there is less than the minimum Fibonacci number of eight days and no count is possible, or because they are invalid counts due to a lack of overlapping numbers.

Table 2.2 Calculation of Valid Turning Points in the
Japanese Yen Cash Currency from 06–00 to 11–00
Using the Fibonacci Summation Series

Turning Point	Type	Initiation (Days)	Reference	Type
#6	Peak	8	After #5	Low
		21	After #3	Low
#7	Valley	8	After #6	High
		34	After #1	Low
#8	Peak	21	After #4	High
		34	After #2	High
#9	Valley	21	After #7	Low
		34	After #5	Low
#12	Peak	21	After #9	Low
		55	After #5	Low
#13	Valley	21	After #10	High
		55	After #6	High
#16	Peak	8	After #14	High
		13	After #13	Low
#17	Valley	8	After #15	Low
		21	After #12	High

Source: FAM Research, 2000.

By now, it should have become clear to readers how easily the numbers of the Fibonacci summation series can be applied as a precise algebraic tool for the analysis of daily charts, and to detect major turning points in international markets.

In the same way we analyzed the daily charts of the S&P500 Index and the Japanese Yen cash currency, we will now deal with the weekly charts of the same two products.

In cases where we receive multiple confirmations of a price change on daily and weekly bases, the power of the Fibonacci summation series as a tool for market analysis and for the prognosis of trend changes is increased.

Regarding the accuracy of the tool, we must not forget the notion of time bands (explained earlier). Multiple Fibonacci goals might be reached at the same time in such a way that peaks and valleys are confirmed within a small margin. We accept this margin to a maximum of four days: two days before and after the exact Fibonacci count.

THE FIBONACCI SUMMATION SERIES ON WEEKLY DATA

Our analysis of the S&P500 Index on a weekly basis results in a series of prominent peaks and valleys similar to our findings for turning points in the S&P500 Index market daily (Figure 2.8).

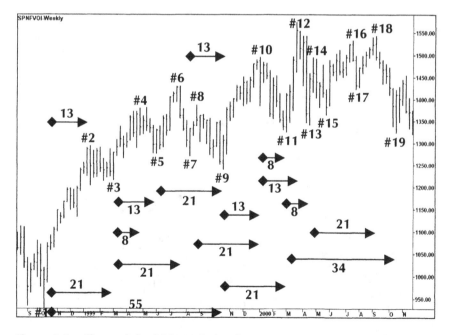

Figure 2.8 Chart of the S&P500 Index from 08–98 to 11–00. Base count of valid turning points in the market according to Fibonacci numbers. *Source: FAM Research,* 2000.

The minimum swing size we need weekly is 1,000 S&P500 ticks (for example, a move from 1,300.00 to 1,400.00). For the confirmation of a swing high on either side, we need two weeks with lower highs, and vice versa for a swing low. (This definition of swings is slightly different from our description for daily data; see Figure 2.2 in the previous section.)

Our Fibonacci count starts from swing highs or swing lows, and, again, we work with just five Fibonacci numbers (8, 13, 21, 34, 55). **The only major modification in parameters is that we no longer exclude those highs and lows that are designated by no more than one valid Fibonacci count.** The use of weekly data already works as a filter for noise in the market, which means that we do not need an additional filter for a multiple confirmation of peaks or valleys as valid turning points.

Changing the swing size to 2.00 JPY (200 ticks), we can analyze the Japanese Yen cash currency weekly in the same way that we have already analyzed the S&P500 Index weekly (Figure 2.9).

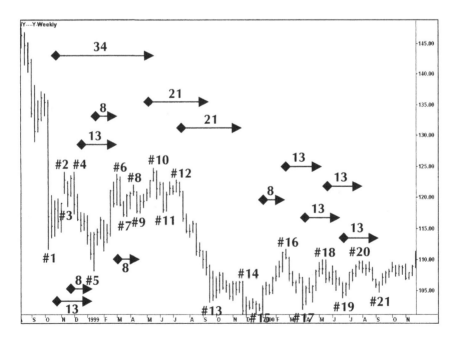

Figure 2.9 Chart of the Japanese Yen cash currency from 08–98 to 11–00. Base count of valid turning points in the market according to Fibonacci numbers. *Source: FAM Research, 2000.*

From Figures 2.8 and 2.9 we conclude that our Fibonacci count effectively catches the rhythm of the S&P500 Index market and the Japanese Yen cash currency market's movement over time.

It is important to notice that our weekly analysis covers a time span of 27 months, compared with just 6 months covered on a daily basis (as shown in the charts of the previous section).

It is not necessary to explain the Fibonacci count from weekly turning point to turning point, nor is it necessary for the S&P500 Index or the Japanese Yen cash currency. In this section and the preceding section, we have discovered how the Fibonacci count has to be handled if it is to serve as a highly promising instrument for chart analysis.

SUMMARY

The Fibonacci summation series is, by itself, a very powerful analytic tool for forecasting price changes.

Counting peaks and valleys with regard to a certain swing size, and observing only the Fibonacci summation series and its most important figures (8, 13, 21, 34, and 55), can be, in principle, successfully applied to any product and any market. The more investors participate in market action, and the higher the liquidity and volatility in a market, the greater the potential for correctly forecasting turning points in the respective market.

The Fibonacci summation series—and with it, the Fibonacci count—is expected to work best on data related to stocks or to stock market indexes, to index futures, or to cash currencies, because investors' behavior is most concentrated in those liquid trading vehicles.

In daily analysis, we look for multiple confirmations of swing highs and swing lows by a minimum two figures from the Fibonacci summation series. When dealing with weekly data, we work with single figures out of the Fibonacci summation series because weekly data work in our favor as filters. Having two figures on weekly charts is even better for our peak and/or valley confirmation. We then look for the trend reversal once the first number from the Fibonacci summation series is passed.

As we will see in later chapters, figures from the Fibonacci summation series can be easily combined with others in our set of Fibonacci tools. The effects of different Fibonacci tools must be considered when analyzing why time bands have emerged or why price or time goals were not reached. In the final chapter, we will give evidence that a solid combination of tools should be the goal of every skillful trader who considers Fibonacci tools to be relevant means of investment.

We do not want to introduce a trading model here. Trend changes can only be helpful as indications of the best side to trade a market, whether long, short, or flat. If used for trading, entry rules and stop-loss rules have to be integrated.

The Fibonacci count can also be used profitably for strategic decisions such as asset allocation or position management in a portfolio.

3

APPLYING THE FIBONACCI RATIO TO CORRECTIONS AND EXTENSIONS

Markets move in rhythms. This is the main conclusion drawn from our introductory analysis of Elliott's basic theoretical reflections.

As far as corrections in general are concerned, an impulse wave that defines a major market trend will have a corrective wave before the next impulse wave reaches new territory. This occurs in either bull market or bear market conditions.

Extensions, in contrast to corrections, are exuberant price movements. They express themselves in runaway markets, opening gaps, limit-up and limit-down moves, and high volatility. These situations may offer extraordinary trading potential as long as the analysis is carried out in accordance with sensible and definite rules.

Both corrections and extensions can serve as mighty trading tools if the correct link to the Fibonacci summation series and the corresponding Fibonacci ratio PHI is established.

In this chapter, we will look at how corrections and extensions are successfully utilized for chart analysis.

Sections A through C deal with corrections as trading tools. Corrections will first be linked to the Fibonacci ratio PHI in principle, and will then be applied as charting tools to sets of daily and weekly data of various products.

In Sections D and E, extensions and their relation to the Fibonacci ratio PHI are explained on the basis of 3-wave market patterns and 5-wave market patterns. In Section F, examples illustrate the analytic power of extensions in 5-wave patterns as trading tools in combination with numbers of the underlying Fibonacci summation series.

A. BASIC FEATURES OF CORRECTIONS

Analysis would be easy if we were able to detect one general pattern of corrections.

The problem is that when we work with corrections, we can have many more price patterns in the commodity, future, stock index future, stock, or currency markets than impulse waves. Markets move sideways for longer periods of time before a new impulse wave appears.

We can never predict which of the next waves will be an impulse wave instead of another false move in continuation of a sideways market. Therefore, every serious trading approach using corrections has to be designed to survive even the longest sideways market correction phase.

No market pattern can assure us of a profitable trade. At any time, we can be in a correction of an impulse wave or at the beginning of a new impulse wave.

It is a common belief that if market pricing reaches a new high, prices will go higher from there (and vice versa where market pricing falls to a new low).

Empirically, however, new highs (vice versa for new lows) are only trustworthy indications of higher (lower) prices in the future in strong bull markets (or strong bear markets, respectively), whereas the assumption of prices going higher on new highs and lower on new lows is, by no means, a valid rule for starting an investment if one gets stuck in a sideward market pattern.

One never knows in advance what kind of market situation prevails at a certain moment, so an assumption that markets will go higher on new highs can be very costly for an investor.

Markets are in sideward conditions about 70% of the time and in a trending state only about 30% of the time. Traders, thus, must always be aware of the appearance of some (a) irregular tops or (b) irregular bottoms (Figure 3.1).

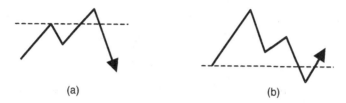

(a)   (b)

Figure 3.1 (a) False breakout to the upside; (b) false breakout to the downside. *Source: FAM Research,* **2000.**

So called "bull traps" on the upside, or "bear traps" on the downside, can frequently be seen especially when we are working with intraday data. Floor traders' common strategy is to buy at new lows and sell at new highs. We will come back to this market pattern in detail a little later when we deal with re-entry rules.

Working with corrections is a trend-following strategy. It is based on the assumption that after a correction of an impulse wave up or down, the next impulse wave will follow in the direction of the first wave. In many cases, the latter assumption is correct. Therefore, we consider working with corrections a valid investment strategy. However, it demands discipline because the investor must closely follow stop-loss rules, profit targets, or entry rules.

Corrections work equally well long and short, to the upside or the downside of the markets. The worst thing that can happen in trending markets is that the market runs away without correcting and leaves us without a valid signal. Of course, in markets moving sideways, we run the risk of getting stopped out in a streak of losing trades.

To explain our approach in making corrections tradable, we address the five basic parameters of corrections: (1) the size of the correction, (2) entry rules, (3) stop-loss rules, (4) profit targets, and (5) re-entry rules.

The Size of Corrections

The most common approach to working with corrections in research and in practical trading is to relate the size of a correction to a percentage of a prior impulse move.

In regard to Fibonacci's PHI, we are interested in three prominent percentages of possible market corrections that can directly be derived from the quotients 0.618, 1.000, and 1.618 of the PHI series (see also Figure 1.16 in Chapter 1):

- 38.2% is the result of the division 0.618 ÷ 1.618;

- 50.0% is the transformed ratio 1.000;

- 61.8% is the result of the immediate ratio 1.000 ÷ 1.618.

Forecasting the exact size of a correction is an empirical problem. Investing after a correction of just 38.2% might be too early, whereas waiting for a correction of 61.8% might result in missing strong trends completely. But no matter what sizes of corrections are taken into consideration, the PHI-related sizes are the ones to be focused on.

Any correction can (percentagewise) be a retracement in the market of 38.2%, 50.0%, 61.8%, or even 100.0% of the original price move at the beginning of the impulse wave.

However, if a price move goes below the value at the start of the previous impulse wave, we most likely will not have to consider a correction any longer. Instead, we must look for the beginning of a new impulse wave in the opposite market direction.

General rules for safe investments in corrections depend on a handful of conditions:

- The investment strategy (such as a buy-and-hold approach, or short-term trading);

- The volatility of a product (this varies very much among cash currencies, commodities, futures, single stocks, or mutual funds);

- The size of the initial swing on which a retracement is measured;

- The strength of a trend;

- The type of data used for the analysis and the calculation of retracements (monthly, weekly, daily, or intraday data compression).

The best way to establish a strong position in a correction is a sophisticated combination of the percentage of a correction with a second parameter, the swing size.

A price move is a continued move of the market in one direction. But as prices in market trends move up and down in bigger or in smaller swings, it is necessary to ignore some of the noise in the market by eliminating all those movements that do not continue in one direction for, at least, a minimum point value.

Abstractly speaking, we can model a market movement of a sample product in such a way that the product moves plus 70 ticks on day one, plus 100 ticks on day two, minus 20 ticks on day three, minus 20 ticks on day four, and another plus 70 ticks on day five. The market in this sample moves in the direction of an uptrend of net 200 ticks in five days. This move is not straight, however, because three days of very strong upmoves are interrupted by two minor moves to the downside.

Graphically, the market move of the abstract sample product can be done as shown in Figure 3.2. In the diagram, we suggest that the close of each of the five trading days shall equal the high on a "plus day" and the low on a "minus day." If we work with a filter that eliminates all movements smaller than 50 ticks, the whole move of the five trading days changes accordingly. The two days within the correction of 20 plus 20 ticks are eliminated because the correction of a total 40 ticks is smaller than the filter size of 50 ticks.

(a)   (b)

Figure 3.2   Sample market move of five days (a) without filter and (b) with filter. *Source: FAM Research, 2000.*

A minimum swing size is needed to make the best use of the Fibonacci ratio (or ratios to cover 0.618, 1.000, and 1.618) in a correction. That is why intraday charts and intraday samples in connection with swings are not used in this book. The shorter the time intervals become, the more the noise is contained in the respective periods. The magnitude of that noise is relatively large compared to a reasonable swing size that can be realized during a short interval.

The intent of this book is not to present empirical tests for every product available for trading the markets. Instead, we present concepts to interested traders, and we fill them with convincing trading strategies and examples.

As a guideline, for example, the swing size used in the Japanese Yen in the cash currency market is measured as 200 basis points. Each product has a typical swing size to work with. By exploring the utility program WINPHI, which is included with this book, interested investors have the chance to test corrections on historical data and to generate personal solutions.

If we stay with the concept of integrating a filter of 50 basis points to confirm swing highs or swing lows, we automatically end up with bigger swing sizes.

In the Japanese Yen cash currency, for example, we need the confirmation of a 200-basis-points swing size when working with Fibonacci ratios in corrections of 38.2%, 50.0%, or 61.8%. However, a correction of 38.2% in a swing of 200 basis points (meaning 76 ticks) might almost be too small to work with, because swings of 200 ticks and respective corrections of 76 ticks can occur in volatile markets once or twice a week.

On the other hand, 38.2% might be a very large correction when analyzed in combination with a minimum swing size of 1,000 basis points (in this case, it would mean a correction of 382 ticks, which is almost double the calculation of the initial swing size in the Japanese Yen cash currency with 200 basis points).

Entry Rules

Working with a percentage for a market correction of just 38.2% runs the risk that a market is entered too early and one gets stopped out when the market corrects beyond the 38.2% retracement level.

Nevertheless, if we wait for a larger 61.8% correction level, we might wait too long, the market price will not reach our retracement level, and we will miss the entire impulse wave for which we have been waiting.

To prevent both scenarios from happening, we look for a combination of percentage retracement and entry rule.

The reason for applying entry rules is: to be provided with an additional confirmation of a trend reversal. This approach is a compromise, because using entry rules means that we will always enter a market later than if we worked outright with the plain correction target as our entry indicator.

Our experience shows, however, that working with entry rules pays off in the long run.

Every time an investor chooses to enter a market according to a pattern of corrections to an initial impulse wave, he or she must make sure that the entry is realized by the time of the correction (or at least close enough to the time of the correction).

One reliable way to manage being on time (or at least close enough for the correction) is to combine swing size and correction with a convincing entry rule.

Table 3.1 gives an indication of how the percentage of the correction, the swing size, and the entry rule can vary and can also be combined.

Table 3.1   Swing Size, Correction, and Entry Rule

Swing Size in Ticks	Correction in %	Entry Rule: Previous High–Low in Days
100–200	61.8	3–4
200–400	38.2	3–4
200–400	50.0	2
200–400	61.8	1
400–800	38.2	3
400–800	50.0	1
400–800	61.8	1

Source: FAM Research, 2000.

Generally speaking, after a strong first-impulse wave and a strong correction, the second-impulse wave should be bigger than the first-impulse wave. Therefore, a more sensitive entry rule can be used.

Different entry rules in relation to different swing sizes are shown in Figure 3.3. (For abbreviations of trading signals, see the Appendix.)

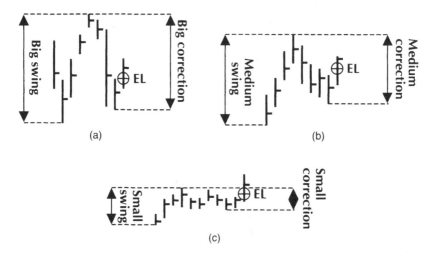

(a)   (b)

(c)

Figure 3.3   (a) Big swing, big correction, previous high entry; (b) medium swing, medium correction, previous two highs entry; (c) small swing, small correction, previous three highs entry. *Source: Fibonacci Applications and Strategies for Traders,* by Robert Fischer (New York: Wiley, 1993), p. 60. Reprinted with permission.

Many successful combinations of swing size, retracement, and entry rule are possible. The sample constellations in Table 3.1 and Figure 3.3 are intended to give readers an impression of the underlying general pattern and of how the three parameters go together in a productive way. It is then up to the reader to test even more productive combinations that are not included in our examples.

Stop-Loss Rules

Whenever a market position is entered, one must protect it with a stop-loss or a stop-reverse signal.

A strict stop-loss protection has an immediate effect on the performance profile. It reduces the size of losses and the frequency of profitable trades.

When analyzing and dealing with corrections, the best stop-loss protection should be below the starting point of the first impulse wave. The rationale is that if a correction goes below the starting point of the first impulse wave, there is a greater chance that the entire trend has changed, not just been corrected. Therefore, we can no longer expect the next impulse to be in favor of our current trading signal.

Let's assume that we set the stop-loss point to the low of the first impulse wave (which is below the entry price level). This means that the earlier we invest in the correction, the farther the stop-loss point is from the current market price. If we wait for a larger correction, we have a much closer stop-loss protection, but we run the risk, mentioned earlier, of never being invested.

The different risk profiles, when trading alternative percentages of corrections with stop-loss protection, are presented in Figure 3.4.

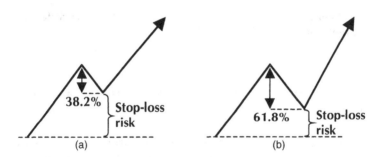

Figure 3.4   Different stop-loss risk profiles on investments into (a) a correction of 38.2% and (b) a correction of 61.8%. *Source: FAM Research,* 2000.

When we do not get stopped out and profits start accumulating, it will still be wise to protect our gains by taking profits as soon as a certain precalculated target is triggered.

Profit Targets

Profit targets, for use with corrections, can be created by directly applying the key ratios 0.618, 1.000, and 1.618 from the Fibonacci summation series.

For the calculation of profit targets, we take the total amplitude of the first impulse wave and multiply it by one of the aforementioned Fibonacci ratios (Figure 3.5).

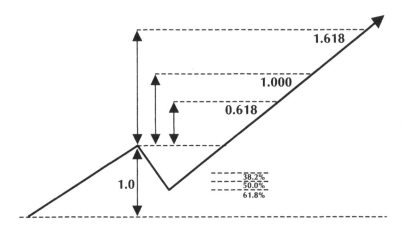

Figure 3.5 Alternative levels of corrections in combination with different ratios of profit targets. *Source: FAM Research, 2000.*

Working with profit targets in combination with corrections causes problems similar to those encountered when working with corrections alone.

In real-time trading, it seems that whatever profit target we choose, the market does not act in our favor. If the profit target is reached at 0.618 times the strength of the impulse wave, the market is moving higher. And if we place the profit target at 1.618 times the amplitude of the impulse wave, the market price does not reach this level.

What is important, at this point, is **consistency** in creating and in following trading signals. This is where computerized test runs become very important. If we compare the profitability of the respective profit targets with historical data that are available via computers, we will not always be correct. However, it will force us to act in a framework that provides us with the best average profit target available with our trading strategy.

To better protect profits in a market position, we recommend applying a trailing stop in addition to working with profit targets. The trailing stop is not always the best solution, but it protects at least some of the profits after the market price has moved in a profitable direction. On the other hand, one might get stopped out with a small profit before the market starts another strong rise, which then will be missed.

Depending on the product and its volatility, a three- to four-day trailing stop is always helpful. In the sample diagram (Figure 3.6) the trailing stop is four days.

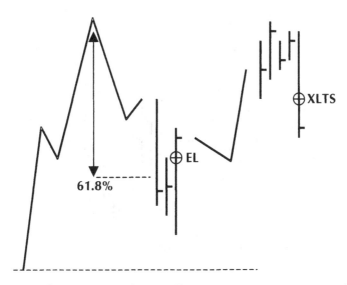

Figure 3.6   Profit protection using a trailing stop. *Source: FAM Research,* **2000.**

To complete our set of basic parameters for the analysis and application of corrections to the markets, re-entry rules—plus percentages of a correction, swing sizes, entry rules, stop-loss rules, and profit targets—will be described.

Re-Entry Rules

After a position is stopped out in a loss, one often questions whether it should be followed by a re-entry signal if the market price moves back to its original direction.

Working with corrections means one must always invest in the direction of the main trend.

When we work with a sensitive main entry rule, there is always the probability of getting stopped out when buying at a previous day's high after a 61.8% correction. If we suffer a stop-loss out of a long position (vice versa for a stop-loss out of a short position), we recommend a re-entry buy signal at the previous four days' high.

The slightly more conservative re-entry rule (compared with the main entry rule) is necessary in order to solidly confirm a trend reversal (Figure 3.7).

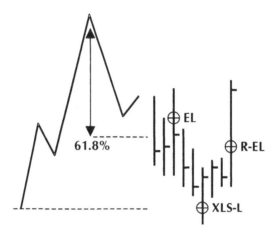

Figure 3.7 **Four days' high re-entry after stop-loss.** *Source: FAM Research, 2000.*

The re-entry rule makes sense if we begin by working with a very tight entry rule and a very close stop-loss protection. Using such a strategy, we limit the risk in our position. By applying a 61.8% correction level, we get very close to the bottom of the previous impulse wave and we reduce our risk to a reasonable size.

Even though we define the low of the initiating impulse wave as our stop-loss protection level, we know that the same level can serve as a support line for the original trend. Therefore, re-entry after a stop-loss can be a highly profitable trading approach. It allows us to take advantage of the (short-term) rallies that often occur when the low of the impulse wave is touched.

However, if we work with stop-loss protection levels that are a bit larger (as will be shown later, in examples of weekly charts), a re-entry rule cannot be recommended. Re-entries also are not useful for daily charts and conservative entry rules on daily charts, such as four days' previous high or low entries. The more conservative the entry rule, the farther we get away, on the entry, from the low of the first impulse wave as our stop-loss level definition.

Discussion of re-entry rules also becomes helpful when we are confronted with market patterns of bull traps and bear traps. (See Figure 3.1 for a recap.)

Bear traps and bull traps—in other words, irregular bottoms and tops—are two of the most difficult chart patterns to handle. Bull traps and bear traps are the reason why most trend-following systems fail in sideward markets.

Whenever new highs or lows are made, technical breakout systems—and trend followers—invest because they anticipate that prices will continue to rise in an uptrend or fall in a downtrend. Speculators, in particular, look for confirmations of the trend-following mentality and wait for prices to make new highs or new lows.

Statistically, however, commodity, future, or cash currency markets move sideways roughly 70% of the time (countertrend) and only about 30% in a trend direction.

In the formation of irregular tops or bottoms, we expect a very powerful move opposite the direction of the first impulse wave. The only difficulty comes when we must correctly identify whether the market is really building an irregular top or irregular bottom and reversing again, or whether it will continue to move strongly once new highs or new lows have been made.

One way to solve this problem is to work with a corridor above a swing high formation, or below a swing low formation. One must also make use of re-entries after being stopped out when the market reverses after a day or two out of the corridor and comes back in the direction of the original trend signal.

One may only practice this re-entry strategy out of a price corridor if large swings occur—for instance, 100 points (1,000 ticks) or more on the S&P500 Index, or at least 2.00 JPY (200 ticks) in the Japanese Yen cash currency.

Such trend reversals must happen fast—normally, within one to three days after new highs or lows have been made. Every time that chart pattern occurs, we recommend working with a four days' previous high or low re-entry rule.

Figure 3.8 shows the pattern of a bear trap, or an irregular bottom, in combination with a re-entry signal.

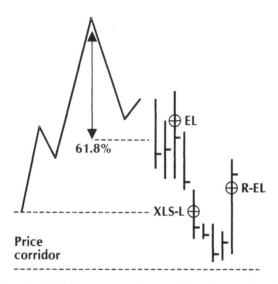

Figure 3.8 Four days' high re-entry rule out of a price corridor in a bear-trap chart formation. *Source: FAM Research,* 2000.

Chart formations such as bull traps or bear traps depend very much on the type of scaling selected for chart analysis. Before we apply our findings on retracement levels, entry rules, stop-loss protection, and profit targets on charts, we will discuss the pros and the cons of linear versus semi-log scaling.

Linear versus Semi-Logarithmic Scales

Elliott and his followers could never agree on whether analyses of chart patterns should be done using a linear or a semi-logarithmic scale, or both.

Assuming that many readers are not familiar with this problem, we present two sample charts from the weekly S&P500 Index, to demonstrate the difference between linear scaling and semi-logarithmic scaling (Figure 3.9).

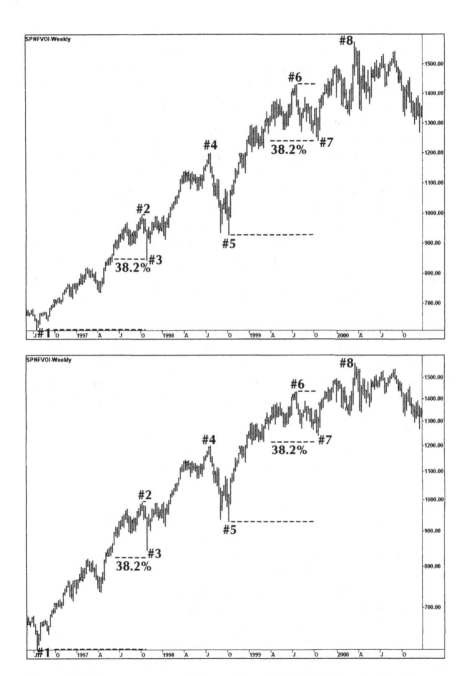

Figure 3.9 Linear versus semi-log scaling on S&P500 Index weekly. *Source: FAM Research,* 2000.

In Figure 3.9, the same set of weekly S&P500 Index bar data from June 1996 until December 2000 is charted twice: scaling is linear in the upper chart and semi-logarithmic in the lower chart.

Scales on sample linear charts show equal distances between all prices from 700.00 to 1,500.00; on the semi-log scale, the increments become smaller as the values on the price scale become higher. In other words, the scaling distance from 700.00 to 800.00 is much wider than the scaling distance from 1,400.00 to 1,500.00, meaning that when we are working with price and time and measuring distances, we end up with different results when choosing linear or semi-log scales.

At first glance, the differences between the two charts might not appear that great. But if we measure the distance from valley #1 to peak #2 and define this length as the strength of our impulse wave, we find that valley #3 touches the 38.2% retracement level on the linear chart but not on the semi-logartihmic chart. The same phenomenon can be found at valley #7: the market price does not touch the respective 38.2% retracement level.

To clarify: A correction in price of 38.2% on an impulse wave of 1,000 ticks remains 382 ticks, no matter what sort of chart scaling is applied. What we are presenting here is an approach in which corrections are not measured in points, but are graphically and geometrically calculated by measuring distances from swing highs to swing lows in centimeters (or equivalents).

The example shows that the size of the impulse wave from valley #5 to peak #6 is 3.9 centimeters for linear scaling and 3.4 centimeters for semi-log scaling. The respective corrections of 38.2% are 1.5 centimeters for linear scaling and 1.3 centimeters for semi-log scaling. The corrective move from peak #6 to valley #7 is 1.5 centimeters for linear scaling so that we have a valid correction according to our retracement level of 38.2%. For semi-log scaling, however, the corrective move is just 1.1 centimeters, which means that the retracement level is missed by a narrow but decisive margin of 0.2 centimeter.

Such deviations occur with semi-logarithmic scales because the starting point of a semi-log scale determines the final graphical appearance of a price move on a chart.

The starting point of a semi-log scale has to be chosen subjectively, regardless of whether we want to measure distances in price (vertically) or in time (horizontally).

On linear scales, our choice of the starting point of the time series does not affect the outcome of the graph because the distance from scale point to scale point remains constant. On the other hand, even considering the deviations, Elliott himself pointed out that working with semi-log scales can be helpful when applied in addition to linear scaling.

Now that all basic parameters of corrections as trading tools have been described in detail, we can put the pieces together and analyze datasets of different products from various segments in the international markets.

The analysis is split into two sections: corrections on a daily basis, and corrections on weekly data.

B. CORRECTIONS ON A DAILY BASIS

Working with corrections requires a lot of discipline and accuracy.

The profit chances are the biggest in very volatile products such as the S&P500 Index and DAX30 Index, or in cash currencies (the cash Japanese Yen against the US Dollar; or, recently, the cash Euro against the US Dollar).

Volatility alone is not enough. Both volatility and high volume are required for successful trading. If the volume is not high enough, slippage (getting in and out of positions in a product) becomes too big and trading is not recommended.

There is no perfect investment strategy that will work in any market at any time, because there is no easy way of knowing in advance whether a market move will be big or small, fast or slow. The biggest decision any investor has to make involves swing size and which corrections are being calculated. The size of a market swing determines whether a market move is considered big or small, slow or fast.

There is no simple and perfect rule. In our analyses, we work with a minimum sample swing size of 80 ticks (a move from 1,400.00 to 1,480.00) in the S&P500 Index, but we recommend a swing size of 180 ticks (a move from 110.00 to 111.80) for the Japanese Yen cash currency.

Another major problem that often faces investors is deciding when a market is in an uptrend, and when a trend has turned to the down side. The status of the market has to be addressed first; otherwise, investors will never be able to decide in what direction to invest.

As long as the market prices form new lows and the swing size from the previous peak is more than the minimum swing size, we will have a sell signal as soon as our precalculated correction level (61.8%, for instance) is reached. But we never know, in advance, whether we are selling into a correction of a previous impulse wave in a downtrend or into the impulse wave of a new uptrend.

This is why working with a higher correction level and a bigger swing size is recommended. We might calculate the direction of the impulse wave incorrectly, but the risk level remains low and we still have a chance of getting out of our position without too much damage (Figure 3.10).

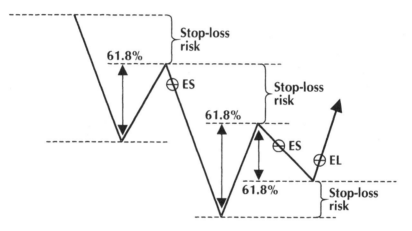

Figure 3.10   Risk levels if a correction is already the impulse wave of a new trend. *Source: FAM Research, 2000.*

Table 3.1 sums up a multitude of parameters with regard to percentage of retracement, swing size, and entry rules. We will now return to these rules.

Sample parameters for an investment in the S&P500 Index might look like this:

• The minimum initial swing size in the S&P500 Index is set to 80 basis points (a sample move from 1,400.00 to 1,480.00). If there is no correction as big as 61.8%, we do not get a signal.

- One must never try to catch up with a runaway market, no matter how strongly the S&P500 Index might start to move. This rule is strictly applied unless we get another entry chance that adheres to the rules of corrections.

- When a correction reaches the level of 61.8%, we have to enter long on the buy side at the previous day's high, or short on the sell side at the low of the previous day.

- After we are invested, we work with a profit target of 0.618 times the total swing size of the first impulse wave. We work with a trailing stop that is set at the lowest low of the past four days, as described in the previous section. Our stop-loss level is defined at the low of the starting day of the initiating impulse wave.

- We do not follow the general re-entry rule defined in the previous section. If we get stopped out, we wait for a full new swing high or swing low based on the minimum swing size, and only then do we start looking for new trading opportunities.

To better comprehend the buy and sell signals that will now be presented, it is very important to understand that all calculations have been made on a daily bar chart covering the last 11 months of the S&P500 Index (up to November 2000). As in the previous chapter, we have used nearest contract end-of-day O-H-L-C bar data supplied by Bridge/CRB Data Services.

We will not provide readers with years of computer test runs on various products. We have chosen two examples that will give readers ideas and will explain strategies on how money can be made, but we remain educational in this matter.

The book's CD-ROM enables every investor to generate the same results we show here, because the sample datasets we ourselves used are included with the software.

Based on the above set of parameters for swing size from highs to lows and lows to highs, retracement, entry rule, profit target, trailing stop, and stop-loss rule, nine sample trading signals can be generated for the S&P500 Index from January to November 2000.

Figure 3.11 and Table 3.2 show sample profits and losses in the S&P500 Index. (See the Appendix for abbreviations of trading signals.)

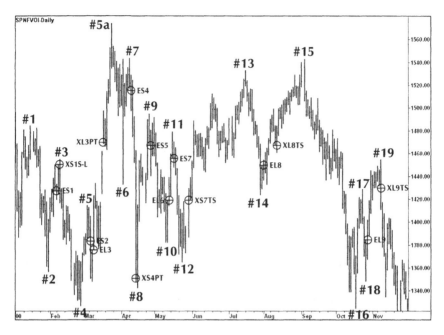

Figure 3.11   Chart of the S&P500 Index from 01–00 to 11–00. Simulation of trading signals based on corrections daily. *Source: FAM Research,* 2000.

Table 3.2   Calculation of Sample Signals in the
S&P500 Index from 01-00 to 11-00

High#/ Low# Reference	Entry Rule		At Exit Rule		At Profit/ Loss in Points
H#1/L#2	Entry sell	1,427.50	Stop-loss	1,449.80	(22.30)
H#3/L#4	Entry sell	1,386.20	Reverse buy	1,385.50	0.70
L#4/H#5	Reverse buy	1,385.50	Profit target	1,468.50	83.00
H#5a/L#6	Entry sell	1,517.50	Profit target	1,351.30	166.20
H#7/L#8	Entry sell	1,467.00	Reverse buy	1,419.00	48.00
L#8/H#9	Reverse buy	1,419.00	Reverse sell	1,456.00	37.00
H#9/L#10	Reverse sell	1,456.00	Trail. stop	1,418.00	38.00
L#12/H#13	Entry buy	1,449.00	Trail. stop	1,468.00	19.00
L#16/H#17	Entry buy	1,384.20	Trail. stop	1,430.00	45.80

Source: FAM Research, 2000.

To explain the use of corrections using a second data sample, we conducted a similar simulation of trading signals on the Japanese Yen cash currency (Figure 3.12).

Figure 3.12   Chart of the Japanese Yen cash currency from 01–00 to 11–00. Simulation of trading signals based on corrections daily. *Source: FAM Research, 2000.*

The basic underlying parameters for the analysis of the Japanese Yen cash currency were:

• Minimum swing size of 1.80 JPY (a sample move from 110.00 to 111.80); retracement of at least 61.8%;

• Entry rule at previous day's high or low; no re-entry;

• Profit target at 0.618 times the size of the impulse swing; trailing stop set to four-day low on buys and four-day high on sells;

• Stop-loss at previous swing's low on buys and high on sells.

The application of these parameters to the daily bar chart of the Japanese Yen cash currency results in a set of sample signals comparable to the ones in the S&P500 Index. By similarly analyzing the Japanese Yen cash currency, we can prove that the strong gains in the S&P500 Index were not accidental.

The nine sample trades in the Japanese Yen cash currency have been profitable overall. Six trades ended up in wins, and only three trades were losing trades. Profits totaled almost 9.00 points, which is a promising result for 11 months of sample calculation. The peak–valley references, as well as the profits and losses for the signals in the Japanese Yen cash currency against the US Dollar, are summarized trade-by-trade in Table 3.3.

To understand the table properly, readers must keep in mind that, when trading the Japanese Yen against the US Dollar, falling prices indicate a stronger Japanese Yen and rising prices indicate a stronger US Dollar. *Buy* signals in the table, therefore, refer to a speculation on rising prices, which means a stronger US Dollar and a weaker Japanese Yen. *Sell* signals refer to an opposite speculation on a stronger Japanese Yen and a weaker US Dollar. Therefore, we buy and sell US Dollars with reference to the Japanese Yen as the base value for our calculation of profits and losses.

Table 3.3 Calculation of Sample Signals in the Japanese Yen Cash Currency from 01-00 to 11-00

High#/ Low# Reference	Entry Rule		At Exit Rule		At Profit/ Loss in Points
L#2/H#3	Entry buy	105.90	Stop-loss	104.65	(1.25)
H#3/L#4	Entry sell	104.79	Stop-loss	105.76	(0.97)
L#4/H#5	Entry buy	104.94	Trail. stop	107.71	2.77
L#8/H#9	Entry buy	109.04	Reverse sell	109.05	0.01
H#9/L#10	Reverse sell	109.05	Trail. stop	107.91	1.14
H#11/L#12	Entry sell	107.67	Reverse buy	105.63	2.04
L#16/H#17	Reverse buy	105.63	Trail. stop	108.55	2.92
H#19/L#20	Entry sell	108.91	Profit target	106.15	2.76
H#23/L#24	Entry sell	108.25	Trail. stop	108.82	(0.57)

Source: FAM Research, 2000.

The results in the S&P500 Index and the Japanese Yen cash currency are very promising. However, the gains accumulated with our profitable strategy of combining corrections with parameters for swing size, entry rule, stop-loss rule, and profit target must not be overestimated. We have covered only a very limited time span of 11 months. During this sample time span, market conditions happened to favor our strategy of investing into corrective waves in the index future and cash currency markets.

The year 2000 was an ideal year for demonstrating the rationale behind corrections and the use of corrections. The main purpose of this book is educational; therefore, we refrain from testing more products and different daily time frames. We consider it more important to find out whether corrections work as trading tools on a weekly basis. This question is dealt with in the next section.

C. CORRECTIONS ON A WEEKLY BASIS

When we work with weekly data, we expect bigger trend changes and we want to exploit them by investing into corrections.

The S&P500 Index moved from about 1,250 points early in October 1999 to almost 1,600 points in 2000. The Japanese Yen cash currency rose from about 107.00 JPY per USD in August 1997 to almost 150.00 JPY per USD in 1998. In late 2000, it was trading at about 110.00 JPY per USD.

Long-term traders look for these swing sizes. However, even in long-term trending products, there are times when products like the S&P500 Index or the Japanese Yen cash currency are not trending at all. The year 2000 is a very good example of how these liquid products trade in a narrow price range.

Working with weekly data is problematic because one never knows beforehand whether markets are in trending or in sideward conditions. Compared with our analysis on daily data, we find exaggeration on a weekly basis where trading approaches can either be extremely good or very bad.

Big market movements can be caught when the size of a correction is calculated correctly. But if we choose the wrong retracement level, we either miss major moves completely or we suffer bigger losses than those we would incounter on a daily basis. This happens because we cannot stay as close to the markets' weekly data as we would otherwise. Swings from one week to another are larger than from day to day, so stop-loss levels, trailing stops, or profit targets might (pointwise) be far away from entry levels.

The following example illustrates, for the S&P500 Index, what can happen to an approach based on corrections in a weekly sideward market that lasts over a longer period of time (Figure 3.13).

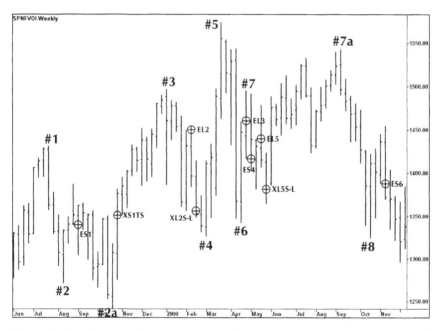

Figure 3.13 Chart of the S&P500 Index from 06–99 to 11–00. Simulation of trading signals based on corrections weekly. *Source: FAM Research,* 2000.

The underlying parameters for our analysis are:

• Minimum swing size of 140 points (a sample move from 1,400.00 to 1,540.00); retracement of at least 38.2%; entry rule at previous week's high or low;

• Profit target at 0.618 times the size of the impulse swing; trailing stop at two weeks' low on buys and two weeks' high on sells; stop-loss protection at previous week's high or low before entry.

Based on the weekly S&P500 Index chart in Figure 3.13, the set of sample signals shown in Table 3.4 can be found.

Table 3.4 Calculation of Sample Signals in the S&P500 Index from 06-99 to 11-00

High#/ Low# Reference	Entry Rule		At Exit Rule		At Profit/ Loss in Points
H#1/L#2	Entry sell	1,340.40	Trail. stop	1,348.00	(7.60)
L#2a/H#3	Entry buy	1,449.80	Stop-loss	1,357.00	(92.80)
L#4/H#5	Entry buy	1,459.50	Reverse sell	1,417.00	(42.50)
H#5/L#6	Reverse sell	1,417.00	Reverse buy	1,439.50	(22.50)
L#6/H#7	Reverse buy	1,439.50	Stop-loss	1,382.50	(57.50)
H#7a/L#8	Entry sell	1,388.50	Still running	1,337.70	40.80

Source: FAM Research, 2000.

This book is meant to be an educational tool. Therefore, it is important to present bad scenarios that can occur even within the best-planned trading strategies. Looking at failures and mistrades in the markets is just as helpful as showing how profitable a strategy may be. We might be successful at trading corrections on a daily basis, but at the same time, we may be getting completely hit by trading the S&P500 Index weekly, using an identical approach.

We will now look at the Japanese Yen cash currency as an alternative to the S&P500 Index. On a daily basis, this is one of the most reliable trending products available. To generate trading signals on weekly data, we work with the following parameters:

- Minimum swing size of 10.00 JPY (a sample move from 110.00 to 120.00); retracement of at least 38.2%;

- Entry rule at previous week's high or low; profit target at 0.618 times the size of the impulse swing; trailing stop at two weeks' high or low; stop-loss protection at one week's high or low before entry.

Signals on the chart of the Japanese Yen cash currency weekly are shown in Figure 3.14 and Table 3.5.

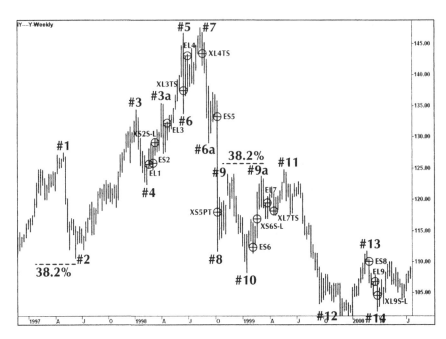

Figure 3.14 Chart of the Japanese Yen cash currency from 12–96 to 07–00. Simulation of trading signals based on corrections weekly. *Source: FAM Research,* 2000.

Table 3.5 Calculation of Sample Signals in the Japanese Yen Cash Currency from 06-96 to 11-00

High#/ Low# Reference	Entry Rule		At Exit Rule		At Profit/ Loss in Points
L#2/H#3	Entry buy	125.51	Reverse sell	125.88	0.37
H#3/L#4	Reverse sell	125.88	Stop-loss	128.98	(3.10)
L#4/H#3a	Entry buy	132.13	Trail. stop	137.48	5.35
L#4a/H#5	Entry buy	142.98	Trail. stop	143.43	0.45
H#7/L#6a	Entry sell	133.27	Profit target	117.00	16.27
H#9/L#10	Entry sell	113.35	Stop-loss	116.28	(2.93)
L#10/H#9a	Entry buy	119.39	Trail. stop	118.18	(1.21)
H#11/L#12	Entry sell	110.12	Reverse buy	106.69	3.43
L#12/H#13	Reverse buy	106.69	Stop-loss	104.65	(2.04)

Source: FAM Research, 2000.

Although the results in the Japanese Yen cash currency look much better than those in the S&P500 Index market, some major swings were missed. Valley #2 did not dip down enough to reach the 38.2% retracement level. The size of the correction in this particular case is calculated based on the swing low in the Japanese Yen cash currency at 79.78 on April 24, 1995, but this points too far back to be part of the chart. A proper retracement should have gone down to 109.25 in mid-1997, but the corrective move to form valley #2 stopped at 110.63. Therefore, the profit target move **long** on the way from valley #2 to peak #3 had not been caught. The same pattern occurred when peak #9, a year later, did not extend high enough to generate a new sell signal in the trend direction of valley #10.

Two key problems emerge when corrections weekly are concerned. As soon as we apply 38.2% retracement levels, market pricing moves to 50.0%, or even 61.8%, and we can suffer significant losses because we get stopped out easily. On the other hand, if we want to play safe and wait for 61.8% retracements, we might never get them.

Considering the advantages and the disadvantages of corrections on a weekly basis, we do not recommend the application of corrections as a means of analyzing weekly data.

Corrections have been analyzed in principle and also on daily and weekly data. We will now proceed to the description and analysis of extensions. Extensions are very useful trading tools and work just as effectively as corrections on a daily basis.

D. EXTENSIONS IN A 3-WAVE PATTERN

Extensions are exuberant price movements that result from runaway markets, opening gaps, or limit moves, up or down, at high volatility.

Most of the time, extensions occur when unexpected news, such as weather information, crop reports, or interest rates announcements by the Federal Reserve Board, reverse trend directions.

When news runs counter to investors' expectations, market situations with strong trading potential emerge. However, one can only take advantage of the situation if analysis is carried out in accordance with sensible and definitive rules. On the other hand, extensive market moves can also be very dangerous for investors who get caught by surprise with a wrong position in the marketplace.

However, this is only one way to look at extensions. They can also determine long-term trend changes in stocks, stock index futures, or cash currencies.

In our analysis of extensions in this section and in those that follow, we concentrate on two sets of sample data: (1) the DAX30 Index and (2) the Japanese Yen cash currency. Because we are looking for strong trend changes in the markets, as well as products with a high volatility *and* a high liquidity, we prefer those products to seasonal products such as futures contracts on soybeans or pork bellies.

Extensions take place primarily in the third wave of a 3-wave price pattern. In a regular 3-wave pattern in an uptrend, the correction does not go lower than the bottom of wave 1, whereas in extensions out of a bull trap or bear trap formation of irregular tops or bottoms, the correction can go higher than the high of the first impulse wave or lower than the low of the first impulse wave, respectively.

Two basic chart formations for extensions are illustrated in Figure 3.15.

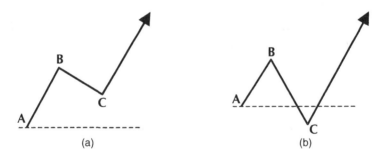

(a)   (b)

Figure 3.15   Extensions out of (a) a regular 3-wave pattern and (b) a bear-trap chart formation. *Source: FAM Research,* 2000.

Exploring extensions means investing against major trend directions. Working with extensions also suggests that an investor is looking for quick profits by taking advantage of imbalances in the marketplace. Therefore, it is important to know not only when to enter a position in advance, but also when to exit a position.

Three consecutive steps are needed when calculating price targets in extensions of the third wave out of a 3-wave chart formation:

1. A minimum swing size has to be defined and set to the size from peak to valley (or valley to peak) of the first impulse wave of the 3-wave pattern.

2. The swing size has to be multiplied by the Fibonacci ratio PHI, with PHI = 1.618.

3. The resulting value is added to the size of the initiating swing to define the price target.

Figure 3.16 is a visualization of the three-step approach to calculate Fibonacci target prices for extensions.

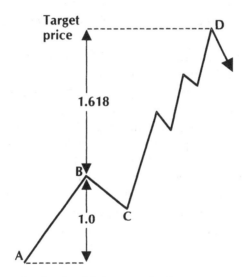

Figure 3.16 Extension in the third wave of a 3-wave pattern uptrend. Target price level measured by the Fibonacci ratio PHI = 1.618. *Source: FAM Research,* 2000.

When extensions as geometrical Fibonacci trading tools were introduced in Chapter 1, we described alternative ratios out of the PHI series as valid measurements for the size of extensions. This general statement still holds true. However, to explain the use of extensions, we limit our analysis to the ratio 1.618 that equals Fibonacci's PHI. Those who want to extend the analysis to alternative ratios can do so by choosing appropriate ratios from the menu bar of the WINPHI software.

Work with Fibonacci price targets in extensions leads to three different scenarios. Market prices can: (a) come close to the precalculated target price, but miss it by a small margin, (b) reach the exact target price, or (c) overshoot the target price.

The most important variable in the analysis of extensions is the swing size; therefore, the realization of one of the three scenarios will depend on the strength of the selected impulse wave.

If the swing size is too small, the thrust of the extension might be too big and the precalculated price target will be overshot by a wide margin. This makes the Fibonacci ratio PHI = 1.618, used for the calculation of the target price, unreliable. There also might be too much noise in the market, causing the underlying market swings to become unpredictable. Even more important: If the swing size is too small, profit targets might be reduced to such narrow margins that it will become difficult to execute them.

If the swing size is too big, it might take weeks, months, or even years, to reach a price target. The bigger the selected swing size, the more long-term-oriented the analysis has to be, especially if weekly charts are used. When long-term price targets are reached, they will determine major turning points in the products analyzed. Extensions calculated on large swings are of little use for average investors who invest with a short-term or mid-term time horizon.

In addition to the size of the impulse swing, a few other parameters determine a successful application of extensions. We will now explain entry rules, stop-loss rules, profit targets' rules, and re-entry rules, and will then conclude the section by demonstrating the trading potential of extensions.

Entry Rules, Stop-Loss Rules, Profit Targets, Re-Entry Rules

The general idea behind the use of extensions is to invest countertrend short once the target price of an extension upwards has been reached (and vice versa for buy signals at the target price of extensions to the downside).

By integrating an entry rule, this countertrend investment strategy can be fine-tuned. Because we have to deal with three scenarios, an entry rule is necessary to make the early stages of a market position more flexible and reliable.

The application of entry rules leads to a slightly reduced profit potential, because positions are entered with a time lag after the target price has been reached. Trades become safer, however, because positions are protected from excessive losses in cases where strongly rising or falling markets do not stop at precalculated price targets.

To properly handle the three aforementioned price target scenarios (being reached, missed by a small margin, or exceeded by some margin), the analysis must include small price bands above and below the line for the price target at the end of an extension. As long as the market price moves within the price band, the entry rule remains in effect. Should market pricing exceed the upper price band, no action will be taken because it has to be assumed that market prices will rise higher without a correcting countertrend.

Whenever a precalculated target price is triggered on a daily chart, we recommend working with an entry rule. This should be done with an uptrend set, either to the previous two days' low, or to a market on close rule if the close of the last trading day is lower than the close of the highest day within the price band (vice versa for entries on extensions to the downside).

Both patterns are shown in Figure 3.17.

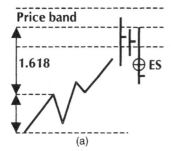 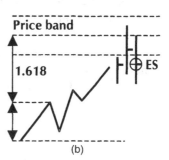

Figure 3.17   Entry rules out of a price band at the target price line of an extension: (a) entry on previous two days' low; (b) entry on close below highest day's close. *Source: FAM Research,* 2000.

The pattern that is realized in the end is decided by the market itself. The pattern that shows up first will be filled.

Whenever a market position (long or short) is established, it will be protected with a stop-loss. The rule for short positions is that the stop-loss protection is placed one tick above the highest high of the previous bars. For long positions, the stop-loss rule is reversed: the stop-loss level is set to one tick lower than the lowest low of the previous bars.

Figure 3.18 shows the stop-loss rule on a chart formation for a short position.

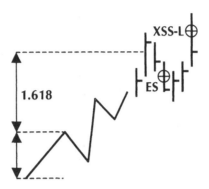

Figure 3.18 Stop-loss protection on a short position. *Source: FAM Research, 2000.*

In addition to stop-loss protection, profits that accumulate on a position are maintained by a profit target rule.

The profit target level for a short position is defined as 50.0% of the total distance from the swing low at the starting valley of the first impulse wave, up to the price target line of the extension (vice versa for a long position).

Figure 3.19 illustrates the 50.0% profit target definition for a short position.

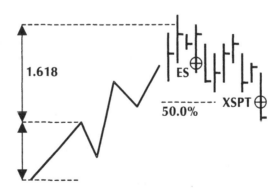

Figure 3.19 Profit target definition on a short position. *Source: FAM Research, 2000.*

The profit target has to be entered as a limit order once a position has been established. The smaller the chosen initial swing size, the closer entry level and profit target level are together. Traders have to be careful and attentive when placing and executing limit orders for profit targets on fast market action.

To further protect gains on market positions, trailing stops are useful supplements to profit targets.

Whenever the market moves toward a 50.0% profit target, we have the option of activating a trailing stop level that defines—for example—a previous four days' high or low as the exit rule. However, depending on the price pattern, the application of a trailing stop results in a set of various profit patterns compared to the simple 50.0% rule.

Different trailing stop configurations, combined with a 50.0% profit target level, are presented in Figure 3.20.

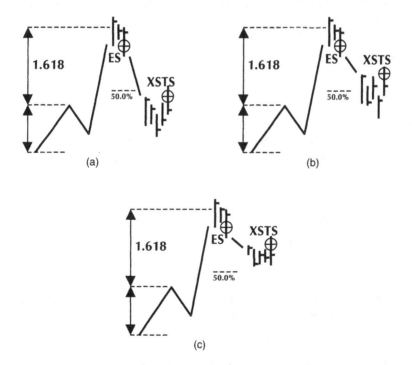

Figure 3.20 Trailing stop configurations. (a) Increased profit potential; (b) reduced profit potential; (c) profit potential even though profit target not reached. *Source: FAM Research, 2000.*

Working with trailing stops has advantages and disadvantages for an investment. If a short position is held and the market price falls far below the 50.0% profit target level, the profit potential on a position is increased. On the other hand, the profit potential is reduced if pricing goes up and the market reverses after the profit target level has been reached. As a third option, a small profit might be kept at the trailing stop level even if the profit target at the predefined 50.0% level has not been reached.

A re-entry rule will be effective in all cases where positions are stopped out in a loss, and then market pricing moves back in the direction of the previously held position. The rules for this type of re-entry are similar to the rules described above as a parameter for corrections.

In addition to this type of re-entry after a stop-loss, re-entries used with extensions can become important once market pricing exceeds the precalculated price target by a wider margin without getting filled on the entry point, and then, afterward, reverses in the direction of the originally defined entry point.

This pattern of a secondary entry rule to the market is represented in Figure 3.21.

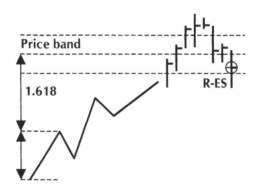

Figure 3.21 Re-entry rule (secondary entry rule) after a price move exceeds the price band around the price target line. *Source: FAM Research, 2000.*

The latter approach is a late entry rather than a re-entry, but, to be consistent in terminology, we will continue to use the term *re-entry* when defining a rule for a secondary entry to the market.

After a breakout from the price corridor, we wait for a correction signal. As soon as the market price returns to the price band, we re-enter (or late-enter) the market on a close below the precalculated price target level for a sell signal (vice versa for a buy signal). The same pattern of one close below (or above) the price target level is also used for re-entries in the true sense after a stop-loss. The stop-loss rule, profit target, and trailing stop apply to the re-entry signal in the same way as for the primary entry.

Our set of defined parameters—regarding entry, stop-loss, profit target, trailing stop, and re-entry—allows us to describe the trading potential of extensions based on two sets of sample data.

Sample Calculations for Extensions on Daily Data

The DAX30 Index and Japanese Yen cash currency are two liquid and volatile products that serve well to demonstrate how to basically trade extensions on daily data.

For the Japanese Yen cash currency, our first sample product, the following settings are being used for our parameters:

- Minimum swing size of 1.80 JPY (a sample move from 110.00 to 111.80); entry rule at previous two days' high on buy signals, and previous two days' low on sell signals.

- Price target in Fibonacci's PHI distance 1.618 times the swing size of the first impulse wave.

- Profit target at 50.0% of the distance from impulse wave to price target; trailing stop set to four days' low on buys and four days' high on sells.

- Stop-loss level at highest high before entry on sells, and lowest low before entry on buys.

Applying these parameters to a chart, we conducted the analysis twice. The result was four sample signals for the period from January to November 2000 daily.

In the first setup, we exit profitable positions as soon as the profit target level is reached. In the second setup, we use a trailing stop according to our definition and do not immediately close out positions at the profit target level.

The sample results for the two setups can be compared in Table 3.6a and Table 3.6b.

Table 3.6a   Calculation of Sample Signals in the Japanese Yen Cash Currency from 01-00 to 11-00 Exiting Positions with a Profit Target

High#/ Low# Reference	Entry Rule		At Exit Rule		At Profit/ Loss in Points
H#1/L#2	Entry buy	105.50	Profit target	107.60	2.10
H#3/L#4	Entry buy	105.65	Profit target	107.10	1.45
L#5/H#6	Entry sell	108.53	Stop-loss	109.38	(0.85)
H#7/L#8	Entry buy	106.45	Profit target	107.32	0.87

Source: FAM Research, 2000.

Table 3.6b   Calculation of Sample Signals in the Japanese Yen Cash Currency from 01-00 to 11-00 Exiting Positions with a Trailing Stop

High#/ Low# Reference	Entry Rule		At Exit Rule		At Profit/ Loss in Points
H#1/L#2	Entry buy	105.50	Trail. stop	107.71	2.21
H#3/L#4	Entry buy	105.65	Trail. stop	108.75	3.10
L#5/H#6	Entry sell	108.53	Stop-loss	109.38	(0.85)
H#7/L#8	Entry buy	106.45	Trail. stop	106.70	0.25

Source: FAM Research, 2000.

When the four sample trades are analyzed signal by signal, it becomes clear that trading extensions can be a profitable strategy. Signals are not very frequent, but on those four occasions (in the year 2000) where market patterns were in accordance with our parameter settings, convincing trading opportunities in the Japanese Yen cash currency were offered.

Nevertheless, it is difficult to decide on the appropriate exit rule. Both options—exiting immediately on the profit target level, and waiting a little longer for the trailing stop pattern to close the position—paid off equally well. We leave it to interested readers to test both patterns on different sets of data, and within different time frames, and develop their own personal preferences.

To better understand the conclusions we have drawn from the results of our simulation, the four relevant signals and the respective exit levels on profit target or trailing stop basis are shown in Figure 3.22. (See the Appendix for abbreviations of trading signals.)

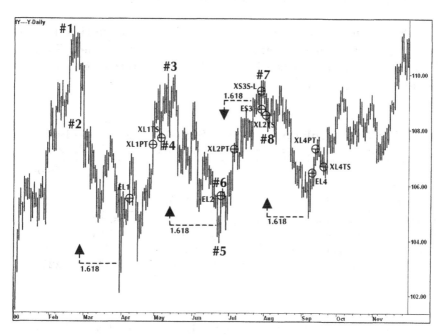

Figure 3.22   Chart of the Japanese Yen cash currency from 01–00 to 11–00. Simulation of trading signals based on extensions daily. *Source: FAM Research, 2000.*

Signals similar to the ones above can be generated for the DAX30 Index, using the following parameters:

- Minimum swing size of 400 points (a sample move from 6,500.0 to 6,900.0); entry rule at previous two days' high on buy signals and previous two days' low on sell signals;

- Price target in Fibonacci's PHI distance 1.618 times the swing size of the first impulse wave.

- Profit target at 50.0% of the distance from the impulse wave to the price target;

- Trailing stop set to four days' high or low, stop-loss level at the highest high or low before entry;

- Re-entry rule after a stop-loss, as well as after a correction back into the price corridor, on closes below the price target line for sells and above the price target line for buys.

Four sample signals for the DAX30 Index, for the time period from April 1998 to February 1999, are shown in Table 3.7a and Table 3.7b. Calculations have been conducted separately for profit target exits and for trailing stop exits.

Table 3.7a   Calculation of Sample Signals in the DAX30 Index from 04-98 to 02-99 Exiting Positions with a Profit Target

High#/ Low# Reference	Entry Rule		At Exit Rule		At Profit/ Loss in Points
L#1/H#2	Re-entry sell	6,005.0	Profit target	5,545.5	449.5
H#3/L#4	Entry buy	4,204.0	Stop-loss	3,861.0	(143.0)
H#3/L#4	Re-entry buy	4,299.0	Profit target	4,961.0	662.0
L#6/H#7	Entry sell	4,960.0	Stop-loss	5,189.5	(229.5)

Source: FAM Research, 2000.

Table 3.7b   Calculation of Sample Signals in the DAX30 Index from 04-98 to 02-99 Exiting Positions with a Trailing Stop

High#/ Low# Reference	Entry Rule		At Exit Rule		At Profit/ Loss in Points
L#1/H#2	Re-entry sell	6,005.0	Trail. stop	5,520.0	485.0
H#3/L#4	Entry buy	4,204.0	Stop-loss	3,861.0	(143.0)
H#3/L#4	Re-entry buy	4,299.0	Trail. stop	4,960.0	661.0
L#6/H#7	Entry sell	4,960.0	Trail. stop	4,720.0	240.0

Source: FAM Research, 2000.

The time period from April 1998 to February 1999 in the DAX30 Index sample has been chosen to demonstrate the practical use of re-entry rules with extensions out of a typical 3-wave pattern daily.

Signals on the basis of extensions generally occur only in volatile products, and even with those products, only four to five times a year. Re-entry constellations as a trading rule, therefore, have to be analyzed as exceptions to the majority of trading signals. Nevertheless, re-entries work exceptionally well.

In our DAX30 Index sample, however, we find a pair of re-entry situations within just four months. The first one is an example of re-entry after the market price left the price corridor without getting short on the entry rule and then corrected back toward the price target line. The second signal is an example of a true re-entry after getting stopped out at the stop-loss level.

Using the DAX30 Index chart in Figure 3.23, readers can trace the sample signals one-by-one.

Figure 3.23 Chart of the DAX30 Index from 04–98 to 02–99. Simulation of trading signals based on extensions daily. *Source: FAM Research, 2000.*

Extensions out of 3-wave moves are the easiest patterns to identify, which is why we dealt with the use of extensions with this simple pattern in our introductory section.

In practical trading, however, we must deal, most of the time, with multiple wave counts. Elliott based his principles on a 5-wave pattern, which is a static approach, but in strong bull or strong bear markets, we often find up to 10 or more waves in the same trend direction. Normally, the wave count will not exceed five waves; therefore, we add the 5-wave count to our analysis as well.

E. EXTENSIONS IN A 5-WAVE PATTERN

When analyzing extensions in a 5-wave pattern, we look for an additional parameter, based on the Fibonacci summation series, that will confirm our price target calculation for extensions out of a 3-wave pattern based on Fibonacci's PHI.

To analyze a 3-wave pattern, we multiplied the size of the first impulse wave by the Fibonacci ratio 1.618. The product was then added to the swing size of the initial move to calculate a Fibonacci price target line. It was at this line that we expected the third wave to reverse.

Because we usually have more than three waves in a trending market, our approach to calculating a Fibonacci target price needs to be modified slightly. The most common price pattern has at least five waves, three of which are impulse waves and two of which are corrective waves (Figure 3.24).

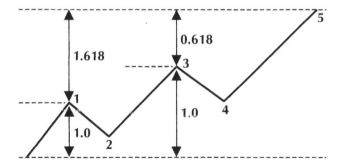

Figure 3.24 Calculation of Fibonacci price target in a regular 5-wave move. *Source: FAM Research, 2000.*

In a regular 5-wave move in an uptrend, the price target line for the end of wave 5 is calculated by multiplying the amplitude of wave 1 by the Fibonacci ratio PHI = 1.618, and then multiplying the amplitude from the bottom of the wave to the top of wave 3 by the reciprocal value to the Fibonacci ratio PHI (PHI' = 0.618). In a downtrend pattern, we also multiply the initial swing size by 1.618 and multiply the amplitude from the high of wave 1 to the low of wave 3 by the ratio 0.618.

By combining the two calculations—using ratios 0.618 and 1.618—we can precalculate the end of wave 5 exactly at the same price, given that the market moves in a regular price pattern as described.

In practical terms, however, most of the time this is not the case. Instead of finding one and the same price level calculated with both ratios, we get two different prices that are closer together or wider apart from each other, depending on the amplitude of wave 1 and wave 3. We find an upper and a lower price target, defined as a Fibonacci price target band.

Do we know whether our price forecast will ever be reached? Absolutely not. But we know in advance whether the price band calculated at 1.618 times the size of wave 1 and at 0.618 times the distance from the top or bottom of wave 1 to the bottom or top of wave 3 will be close together or far apart.

If the upper and the lower levels of the Fibonacci price target band are close together in relation to the underlying swing size of the initial move of the first impulse wave, the price target band is worth considering.

Price goals out of extensions in regular 3-wave patterns are normally related to soft commodities such as soybeans, orange juice, or pork bellies. They can move dramatically, depending on crop reports, storage reports, and weather forecasts. Extensions in these products can be reached within a couple of days. Working with extensions in these products is riskier, however, because price goals tend to be missed by a small margin, exceeded by a small margin, or even exceeded by a wider margin.

Fibonacci price targets in extensions in cash currencies, financial products, futures, stock index futures, or stocks are very rarely achieved in 3-wave moves. It generally takes five or more waves to reach a price target. As a consequence, weeks or months may pass before we get to our price target. The exact time will depend largely on the amplitude of the initial impulse wave.

When we analyzed corrections earlier in this chapter, we did not recommend conducting analysis via week-by-week charts. In contrast, with extensions as Fibonacci tools, we opt for a combination of daily and weekly analysis. Compared to a day-by-day approach, weekly analysis on extensions provides us with a more definite picture of potential turning points in the markets, even though the 5-wave count might not be as clear as on daily charts.

Because extensions need longer to develop and are tools for more of a midterm-oriented analysis, we are mainly interested in major trend changes and major moves in the markets. Often, we find five major waves on a weekly basis when a price target is triggered. Part of the major swings weekly, of course, are many smaller daily waves that might show the formation of extensions. These waves are not used, however, because the respective swing size is too small to execute profitable trades.

Elliott's analysis gave priority to the 5-wave count on a daily basis. When identifying 5-wave patterns to calculate extensions, we consider a daily chart first. If we do not find peak–valley configurations at an appropriate swing size, we check weekly data and carry out our count of waves from there.

The analysis of extensions out of 3-wave patterns made us question whether price targets could be multiply confirmed by additional Fibonacci ratios. If the integration of 5-wave moves into our analysis now allows us to calculate Fibonacci price target corridors, investors will get a very good indication of what price target to use. As long as the upper end and the lower end of a price band are close together, we can use them as valid price indicators.

A decision on whether price bands are close enough together depends on the type of underlying trading product. The DAX30 Index is presented as a first example of how to successfully apply extensions in 5-wave patterns. For the DAX30 Index, we consider a Fibonacci price target band to be close enough, as long as the distance from the lower end to the upper end is less than 200 points (for example, from 6,500.0 to 6,700.0).

The DAX30 Index is analyzed for the time period January 2000 to December 2000 in a combination of daily and weekly approaches. The Fibonacci price target corridor is calculated on a weekly basis. A daily chart is then analyzed to designate entry points and exit points for sample signals when price moves in the DAX30 Index have reached the price corridor.

If we set the Fibonacci price target corridor to 200 points, we can calculate a sample price band for the respective period in the DAX30 Index (Figure 3.25).

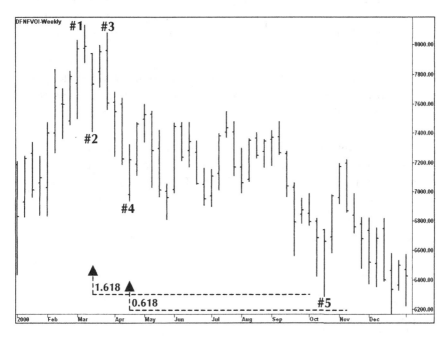

Figure 3.25   Chart of the DAX30 Index from 01–00 to 12–00. Price target corridor calculated using Fibonacci's PHI = 1.618 and PHI' = 0.618. *Source: FAM Research,* 2000.

The swing size of the impulse move, from the high in Figure 3.25 at 8,136.0 to the low at 7,412.0, multiplied by 1.618, leads us to the upper end of the price target corridor of 6,305.0. The lower end of the price band is calculated from the high of wave 1 at 8,136.0 to the low of wave 3 (peak #3 to valley #4, as in Figure 3.25) at 6,937.0, multiplied by 0.618, and resulting in 6,197.0. The distance from 6,305.0 to 6,197.0 is less than the setting of 200 points for the maximum size of the Fibonacci price target corridor.

Working with price bands is important because we do not apply additional entry rules to our strategy as we did in our analysis of corrections and extensions in a 3-wave pattern. Instead, we immediately enter the market on the close of the day when the price band is reached. Additional parameters for the generation of sample signals in the DAX30 Index, using extensions with price bands, and based on a 5-wave move, are:

- Minimum swing size of 300 points (a sample move from 6,500.0 to 6,800.0); profit target at 50% the total distance from high of wave 1 to low of wave 5 for buy signals (vice versa for sell signals);

- Trailing stop at four days' high or low; stop-loss level at the peak or valley before entry; re-entry rule after a stop-loss on the close which is higher or lower than the closing price on primary entry.

As previously explained, price targets calculated on weekly data are integrated and turned into signals on daily charts. Figure 3.26 is an illustration of a buy signal in the DAX30 Index out of the Fibonacci price target corridor.

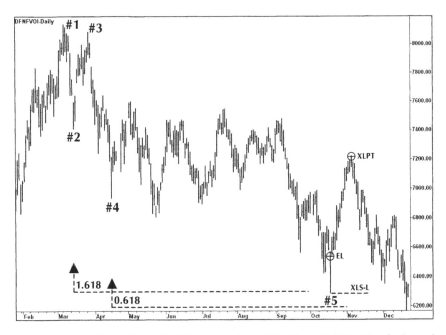

Figure 3.26   Chart of the DAX30 Index from 01–00 to 12–00. Simulation of trading signals based on extensions and Fibonacci price targets. *Source: FAM Research, 2000.*

In terms of a profit/loss calculation, the long trade in the DAX30 Index, starting at 6,534.5, turns out a profit of almost 700 points. As far as the exit rule is concerned, we consider only the profit target level that is triggered to sell flat at 7,222.0, just before the market reverses to the downside again. A trailing stop exit would sell flat the position four days later at a slightly reduced profit margin.

To prove that the sample profitable long trade in the DAX30 Index does not occur as a singular event, and also that it is possible to use 5-wave counts to calculate extensions on daily data (if large enough initial swings can be exploited), we calculate a similar price target corridor based on the Fibonacci ratios 1.618 and 0.618 for the Japanese Yen cash currency daily.

Beginning with the high of wave 1 (110.03) and the corresponding low (107.72), multiplied by 1.618, we reach a price target of 103.99. The confirmation from the high of wave 1 to the low of wave 3, multiplied by 0.618, leads us to a second price target at 104.08 (Figure 3.27).

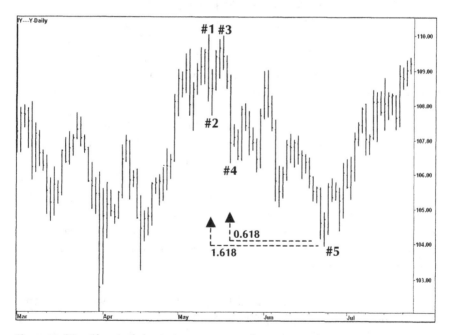

Figure 3.27   Chart of the Japanese Yen cash currency from 03–00 to 07–00. Price target corridor calculated using Fibonacci's PHI = 1.618 and PHI' = 0.618. *Source: FAM Research, 2000.*

The resulting Fibonacci price band is extremely narrow and is an ideal example of what we are looking for in the markets. The Japanese Yen cash currency dropped down to 103.94 and then immediately reversed its trend direction to the upside.

As soon as Fibonacci price target bands out of 5-wave moves are created, the multiple confirmation of price targets on extensions will open up horizons for forecasting major price changes in the marketplace. Price bands are the most important parameter in the analysis of extensions in 5-wave moves. We can never be sure whether market pricing will get to the price targets, but if the corridors are entered, they can be very powerful and reliable Fibonacci trading tools.

We have defined the Fibonacci ratio PHI and its derivatives as incarnations of nature's law and human behavior. To close this chapter, we will link our findings on extensions in 5-wave patterns to the Fibonacci summation series and analyze both tools in an integrated approach.

F. A 5-WAVE PATTERN AND
SUMMATION SERIES COMBINED

In the previous section, we pointed out how important it is for the quality of a price target to be confirmed by different waves and also to be precalculated by making use of more than one of the Fibonacci-related ratios.

In our example of extensions on the DAX30 Index, we learned that our weekly precalculated price target corridor was almost perfectly met before the market reversed its trend direction.

But the more confirmations of a potential turning point we can generate in advance, the better for our trading decisions. To get additional confirmation of the price target corridor, we integrate the figures of the Fibonacci summation series into the weekly chart on the DAX30 Index data. This will be described as it was in Chapter 2.

The results of our calculation are stunning:

- A total of 33 weeks spanned the gap between the week with the highest day (8,136.0 in March 2000) and the week with the lowest day (6,340.0 in October 2000). The number 34, a member number of the Fibonacci summation series, was reached one week after the lowest low was made.

- It is a Fibonacci 21 weeks from the major valley (6,811.0 in May 2000) to exactly one week before the lowest low in October 2000.

- It is a Fibonacci 13 weeks from the major peak (7,550.0 in July 2000) to exactly one week before the lowest low (6,340.0) in October 2000.

The successful combination of price target corridor calculation and Fibonacci summation series is illustrated in Figure 3.28.

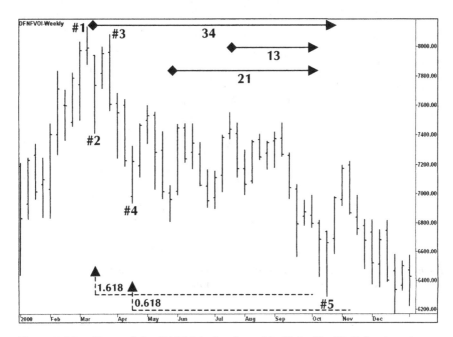

Figure 3.28 Chart of the DAX30 Index from 01–00 to 12–00. Price target corridor and Fibonacci summation series combined. *Source: FAM Research,* 2000.

The price target band was precalculated by multiplying the amplitudes of wave 1 and wave 3 with the respective Fibonacci ratios, 1.618 and 0.618. In addition, we are able to create a time band by simply counting the weeks from peaks and valleys, according to the Fibonacci summation series. The combination of price band and time band allows us to identify, months in advance, possible major turning points in the DAX30 Index market.

A similar calculation of a time band as a supplement to the price target corridor established in the previous section can be conducted for the daily Japanese Yen cash currency from March 2000 to July 2000 (Figure 3.29).

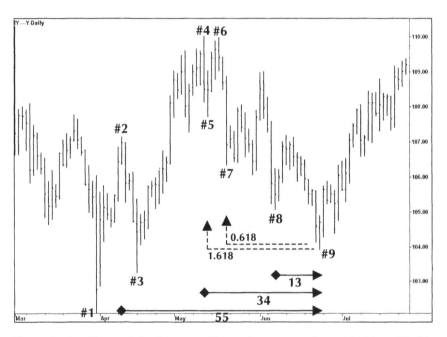

Figure 3.29 Chart of the Japanese Yen cash currency from 03–00 to 07–00. Price target corridor and Fibonacci summation series combined. *Source: FAM Research*, 2000.

The time band for the prediction of a change in trend direction in the Japanese Yen cash currency at valley #9 is based on the following Fibonacci count:

• We predict that a possible time event in market pricing will occur 55 days from peak #2. At the time of peak #2, we do not know whether there will be a high or a low 55 days later, but we do know that 55 is a powerful number when conducting analysis with the Fibonacci summation series.

- It is 34 days from peak #4 down to valley #9. This calculation suggests the same point as our count of 55 days from peak #2. At the time of the calculation from peak #4, the market price is high at 110.03, and nothing indicates that the Japanese Yen cash currency will fall below the 104.00 level.

- It is a Fibonacci 13 days from valley #8 to reach the turning point at valley #9.

The examples of the weekly DAX30 Index chart and the daily Japanese Yen cash currency chart were presented to demonstrate two important elements of our analysis:

1. When dealing with extensions, in contrast to corrections, signals on daily data and on weekly data will mutually strengthen each other. Short-term, midterm, and long-term analyses are possible with extensions as a Fibonacci trading tool.

2. Both price analysis and time analysis can lead us to identical turning points in different sorts of market environment.

We strongly believe that the combination and integration of price targets and time targets, on the basis of extensions in 5-wave patterns and the counts of the Fibonacci summation series, create cumulative support for market price action in the DAX30 Index at a level of 6,300.0 points, and also in the Japanese Yen cash currency at a level of 104.00 JPY per USD. As soon as investors' behavior is manifested pricewise, at a Fibonacci extension target level, and timewise, in overlapping Fibonacci counts, we consider trading signals generally safe.

Our overall findings on corrections and extensions as Fibonacci trading devices shall be summarized before Chapter 4's presentation of PHI-channels (also known as Fibonacci trend channels).

SUMMARY

In the first three sections of this chapter, corrections were discussed in principle, as daily occurrences, and as weekly data. The application of corrections out of a wave count is interesting because corrections mean investments against the short-term trend and, simultaneously, in the direction of the main trend established by the first impulse wave.

Three correction levels (38.2%, 50.0%, and 61.8%; all directly derived from the Fibonacci summation series and the Fibonacci ratio PHI) are prominent in our analysis. To decide which of the three ratios will be the best retracement level with which to work, one must consider the volatility of a product, the risk preference of an investor, the investment strategy, the underlying time horizon, and the managed account size available for investment. It also makes a big difference whether daily or weekly charts are created and studied.

In volatile products such as the Japanese Yen cash currency or the S&P500 Index, we suggest working with a correction level of 61.8%. However, the swing size of the initial first impulse wave from which we calculate the retracement is just as important as the correction level itself. The larger the swing size, the better the chances for a profitable investment as soon as the 61.8% retracement level is reached. Also, the larger the swing size, the more sensitive the entry rules that we can choose for an investment.

Corrections show up more often in sideward markets than in trending markets. Commodity, future, and cash currency markets tend to move about 70% of the time in sideward markets and only about 30% of the time in trending conditions, so waiting for a 61.8% correction might pay off. Another possibility is that the market does not retrace to the expected level and the investor misses the entire second impulse wave.

Corrections may be combined with entry rules, stop-loss rules, profit targets, trailing stops, and re-entry rules.

Calculated examples lead us to believe that corrections open up profitable trading opportunities on a daily basis. Entry rules, exit rules, and re-entry rules are calculated to the best of our knowledge. However, it will require many more tests of historical data to confirm these rules for various products and for alternative time frames. The tests required to fine-tune our general strategies can be conducted individually by interested investors with this book's WINPHI software package and the historical sample datasets that are included.

Compared with our analysis of daily data, we find an exaggeration on a weekly basis, where trading corrections can either be very good or extremely bad. Big market moves can be caught when the size of a correction is calculated accurately, but if we choose the wrong retracement level, we might either miss major moves completely or suffer losses bigger than those experienced on a daily basis. This may happen because, given only weekly data, we cannot stay as close to the market action as we could otherwise. Swings from one week to the next are larger than from day to day, so stop-loss levels, trailing stops, or profit targets might, pointwise, be far away from entry levels. Considering the advantages and disadvantages of corrections on a weekly basis, we do not recommend the application of corrections as a means of analyzing weekly data.

Extensions, as a Fibonacci trading tool, have been discussed in this chapter—first out of 3-wave patterns, then out of 5-wave patterns, and, finally, out of 5-wave patterns in combination with the counts of the Fibonacci summation series.

Investing based on extensions always means investments against the main trend, which is defined by the first impulse swing in a 3-wave move or a 5-wave pattern.

Extensions are important Fibonacci trading tools because they show up not only in fast moves over a couple of days or weeks in soft commodities, but also in financial instruments, derivatives, or currencies, as indicators of major trend changes.

Extensions occur at extreme points when media coverage sets investors on fire. Investing countertrend, under such circumstances, requires commitment and confidence in the underlying Fibonacci pattern. One must also be very patient and disciplined because extensions are patterns that can rarely be detected in the markets. As stated before, markets are in a trending state less than one-third of the time. Therefore, we receive many more signals on the basis of corrections rather than extensions.

Generally speaking, extensions are defined on the basis of a 3-wave pattern. A target price is calculated from the initial swing size of the first impulse wave, and then multiplied by the Fibonacci ratio 1.618. The resulting product is once again added to the swing size. As soon as the price target line is touched, a countertrend entry takes place.

Price targets are met only occasionally. Usually, they are either missed by a small margin, or exceeded by a smaller or a wider margin. Therefore, we integrate into our analysis a price band set a little below and a little above the precalculated target price. We must also integrate an entry rule, a stop-loss protection, a profit target, a trailing stop, and a re-entry rule, to make investments in extensions reliable.

The price band on a 3-wave pattern is somewhat artificial. This is because we have only a single point, and not the upper and the lower border, of the price band confirmed by a rule that comes from the Fibonacci summation series and the Fibonacci ratio.

The most important modification to the general calculation of extensions out of a 3-wave move is the additional use of 5-wave patterns to get to a multiple confirmation of a Fibonacci price target in a price band.

In a 5-wave pattern, price targets are calculated by multiplying the total swing from the top or bottom of wave 1 to the bottom or top of wave 3 by the ratio 0.618, and then adding the product to the total size of the underlying move. We receive a second independent price target as a supplement to the target price, determined by the plain swing size of wave 1 and the ratio 1.618. A countertrend entry on this modified (and, we think, improved) rule takes place as soon as the market price reaches the price target corridor.

A second and final improvement to the tradability of extensions is the combination of price target corridors generated from 5-wave moves with the Fibonacci summation series.

Using the Fibonacci summation series and the Fibonacci count as presented in Chapter 2, we are able to calculate a time band that perfectly complements the Fibonacci price target corridor. The combination of price and time is an important element of our analysis. Time and price targets do not come together on the same day or in the same week very often, but when they do, it is a powerful indication of major trend changes ahead. In contrast to technical analysis, where market moves are followed with a time lag, working with Fibonacci tools aims at calculating major highs or lows in advance. If applied properly, there are few investment tools that are able to forecast with the same accuracy as Fibonacci trading tools.

Examples in the DAX30 Index and the Japanese Yen cash currency already show how major changes in the trend direction of the markets can be caught. We never know in advance whether precalculated price targets will ever be reached, but if market prices get there, the target levels form a relatively safe entry-points countertrend.

The successful combination of two different Fibonacci-related tools is only the first step toward using other Fibonacci trading tools that are able to identify turning points in the markets.

4

PHI-CHANNELS

Human behavior is not only reflected in chart patterns as large swings, small swings, trend formations, or sideward markets. Human behavior is also expressed in peak–valley formations.

By introducing PHI-channels, or Fibonacci trend channels, as independent Fibonacci trading tools, we make use of peak and valley formations in the markets and come to conclusions on how to safely forecast major changes in trend directions.

To familiarize readers with trend channels, this chapter gives a brief description of the general structure of regular trend channels, discusses PHI-channels as specific types of trend channels, and presents examples of how to successfully work with PHI-channels as indicators for market trend changes.

STRUCTURE OF REGULAR TREND CHANNELS

Every peak or valley in the markets serves as a prominent indication of what the majority of investors are or were thinking at any particular moment in time.

The significance of peaks or valleys becomes evident only through the passing of time. Intraday peaks or intraday valleys are less meaningful indicators than peaks or valleys monitored on a daily basis, and they, in turn, are not as revealing as peaks or valleys on weekly charts. To demonstrate how regular trend channels can be powerful investment tools, we will concentrate on daily and weekly charts.

In contrast to the corrections and extensions described in the previous chapter, we do not use trend channels to generate trading signals. Instead, we strengthen our overall analysis by applying trend channels as indicators for trend changes. They then serve as additional instruments to confirm trading signals generated with alternative Fibonacci trading tools.

Peak and valley formations in general trading are often of much greater significance than traders' estimates suggest. It is important to analyze peaks and valleys not only as stand-alone patterns of trend reversals, but also as being related to each other in several ways (Figure 4.1).

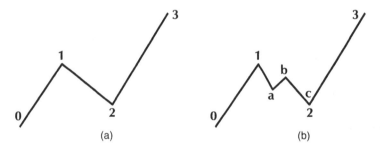

Figure 4.1   (a) Regular correction in an uptrend; (b) irregular correction in an uptrend. *Source: FAM Research,* 2000.

In Figure 4.1, we see that in an uptrend, the peak at point #3 will be higher than the preceding peak at point #1 (if the correction from point #1 to point #2 is regular). An irregular correction in an uptrend results in a peak that is lower than the preceding peak. We then have an a–b–c correction: the peak at point #b is lower than the corresponding peak at point #1.

This general constellation gets even more complicated if bull traps on the upside (or bear traps on the downside, respectively) are integrated into the basic picture. To keep things simple, however, we concentrate our analysis mainly on 3-swing patterns and 5-swing patterns in uptrends or downtrends, and on a 3-swing pattern in the respective corrective moves.

Regular trend channels are graphically generated by drawing parallel lines through tops (peaks) and bottoms (valleys) of market price moves. The basic graphical scheme for creating regular trend channels is illustrated in Figure 4.2.

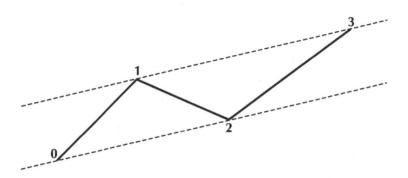

Figure 4.2   Regular trend channel in an uptrend. *Source: FAM Research,* 2000.

In a regular price move, we can connect the bottom of the first impulse wave at point #0 with the bottom of the correction at point #2 and then draw a parallel through the top of the first wave at point #1. The resulting line will be considered an indication of an upcoming peak of wave 3 as soon as wave 3 touches the line.

This general 3-wave model can be used to calculate trend channels on the basis of 5-wave moves.

In a regular price move, the bottom of wave 4 is expected to touch the extension line drawn from point #0 through point #2. The corresponding peak at the end of the wave lies on the parallel line that marks the upper border of the trend channel. Wave 5, in this respect, is the third impulse wave of a regular 5-wave move.

Following Elliott's observations, we recognize that regular 5-wave patterns are important because, often, the end of a regular 5-wave swing pattern is also the point of a trend reversal.

A perfect example is the S&P500 Index in late 1999 and early 2000. For three months, it has moved in a regular 5-wave swing exactly inside our trend channel. The valley at point #5 at a low,

1,327.00, was a major trend reversal to the upside from which the S&P500 Index market moved straight up 247 points to the highest high at 1,574.00 (Figure 4.3).

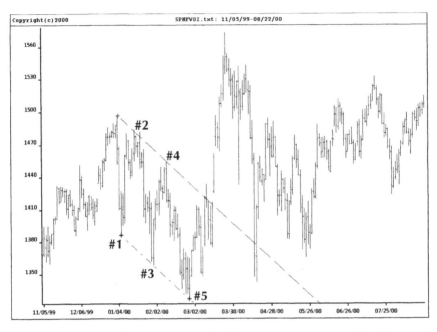

Figure 4.3 Chart of the S&P500 Index from 11–99 to 08–00. Regular trend channel in a 5-wave pattern. *Source: FAM Research,* 2000.

Regular 5-wave price patterns, as shown in the sample chart of the S&P500 Index, appear only on very rare occasions.

Most of the time, peaks #1, #3, and #5 will not be on the same line because, in general, market moves are irregular.

Irregular price patterns do not show up in the first three waves of a 5-wave price pattern because we always have an initial 3-swing pattern at the beginning of impulse waves or corrections in an up-trend or downtrend. Irregular price moves occur after the first 3-wave pattern is completed.

To properly capture irregular 5-wave price patterns with trend channel analysis, we must modify our trend channels.

The modification we choose can, once again, be demonstrated on a sample S&P500 Index chart. The relevant time period runs from spring to late summer 2000 (Figure 4.4).

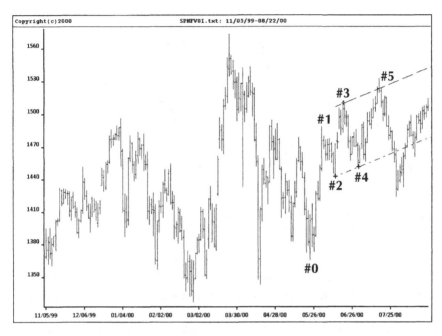

Figure 4.4   Chart of the S&P500 Index from 11–99 to 08–00. Trend channel in an irregular 5-wave pattern. *Source: FAM Research, 2000.*

In Figure 4.4, if peak #3 is not on the line drawn parallel to the line through point #0 and point #2, then peak #5 is on a different trend line. We can capture the peak at point #5 by drawing a line through the valley at point #2 and the valley at point #4 and then add a parallel to this line which runs through peak #3.

Regarding trend channels, Elliott noted, "Usually wave 5 will end approximately at the parallel line, when an arithmetic (linear) scale is used. However, if wave 5 exceeds the parallel line considerably and the composition of wave 5 indicates that it has not completed its pattern, then the entire move from the beginning of wave 1 should be graphed on a semi-log (arithmic) scale. The end of wave 5 may reach, but not exceed the parallel line" (Elliott, p. 60).

We can graph a sample price move on a linear scale and on a semi-logarithmic scale to receive two independent trend channels. See Figure 4.5.

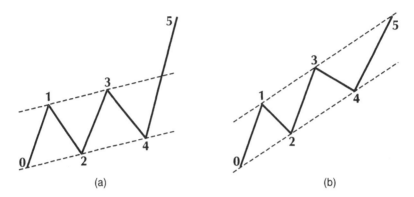

Figure 4.5 Trend channel in an uptrend. (a) Linear scale; (b) semi-log scale. *Source: FAM Research, 2000.*

The market move in Figure 4.5(b) comes out as a regular 5-wave pattern because the appropriate scaling technique has been chosen. The trend channel fits perfectly.

The problem when working with regular trend channels is that one can never be certain how a price pattern will develop in the future. Most of the time, linear scaling is more reliable than semi-log scaling to follow price patterns developing through trend channels. That is why we focus exclusively on linear scaling in the WINPHI software. Professional analysts are asked to consider charting on semi-logarithmic scales, too.

After a general discussion of trend channels as trend indicators, we will proceed to PHI-channels as a special kind of Fibonacci-related geometrical trading tool.

STRUCTURE OF PHI-CHANNELS

In the previous two chapters, we applied the numbers of the Fibonacci summation series as instruments to forecast possible major trend changes in time, and then analyzed corrections and extensions as Fibonacci tools to forecast significant trend changes in price.

PHI-channels as geometrical Fibonacci tools are different from the plain numbers of the Fibonacci summation series, corrections, and extensions, because they are designed to designate the support and resistance points in price and time simultaneously.

PHI-channels vary in distinct ways from regular trend channels. To begin, we will detect the same initial pattern structure as regular trend channels, and a 3-wave price move. But instead of isolating the outside points—connecting highs with highs and lows with lows to come up with trend lines—PHI-channels are based on peak-to-valley and valley-to-peak connections.

The baseline of a PHI-channel can be generated out of a 3-wave market move. See Figure 4.6.

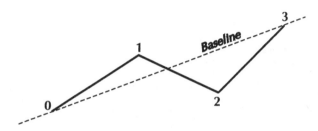

Figure 4.6   Baseline of a PHI-channel. *Source: FAM Research,* 2000.

The baseline of a PHI-channel is the connection of the price moves from the bottom, at point #0, to the top, at point #3. By connecting the high point #3 with the low point #0, we eliminate the biggest problem that occurs when working with regular outside trend channels: staying close enough to fast changes in price patterns.

Once the baseline of the PHI-channel is established, we draw a parallel line to the baseline, using the low at point #2 as our outside point to the right of the price pattern. The distance from the baseline to the parallel line is the width of the PHI-channel.

Trend channels are turned into PHI-channels (and thereby into geometrical Fibonacci trading tools) by using the width of the PHI-channel, from the baseline to the outside parallel line, for calculating the distance of further parallels. These can be drawn in PHI series distances at ratios of 0.618 times, 1.000 times, 1.618 times, 2.618 times, and so on, the width of the PHI-channel.

The resulting parallels are designed to work as trend indicators for market moves, once market pricing leaves the PHI-channel. The procedure of adding outside parallels in PHI series distances from the PHI-channel is visualized in Figure 4.7.

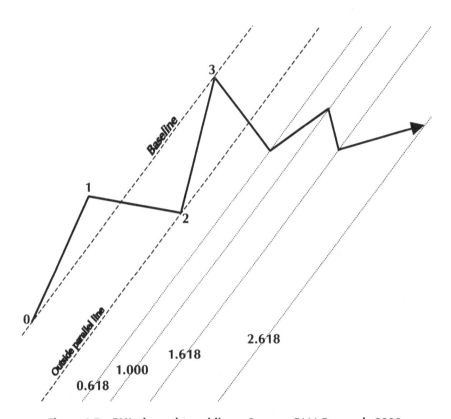

Figure 4.7   PHI-channel trend lines. *Source: FAM Research, 2000.*

PHI-channel trend parallels, derived from the connection of impulse waves, are indications of support and resistance levels for price action in the direction of the main trend.

It is also possible to draw PHI-channels on the basis of corrective waves in a price pattern. PHI-channels based on corrections provide us with resistance levels counter to the main trend. Baselines in this type of PHI-channel are determined by the high or low at point #3 and the low or high at point #6 in a 4–5–6 corrective move.

PHI-channel resistance lines drawn parallel to a corrective move in the price pattern are shown in Figure 4.8.

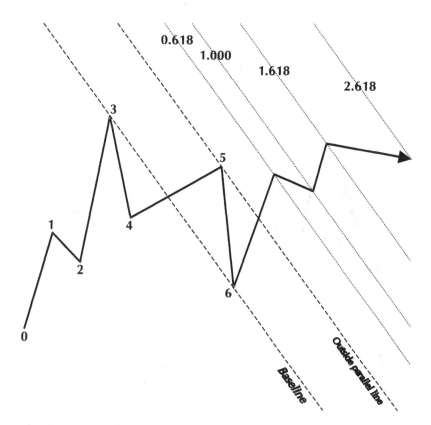

Figure 4.8   PHI-channel resistance lines. *Source: FAM Research,* **2000.**

PHI-channel trend lines drawn parallel to the main trend direction can easily be combined with PHI-channel resistance lines drawn parallel to corrections counter to the main trend. The result is a "cobweb" of trend lines and resistance lines based on different ratios of the PHI series. All crossovers of trend lines and resistance lines out of a PHI channel are the places to expect future market action.

Crossover points of trend lines and resistance lines are determined by the number of ratios used from the PHI series. Therefore, only major peaks and major valleys in the market can be regarded as valid when calculating a PHI-channel baseline and the corresponding parallel lines outside the PHI-channel.

Crossovers of the combination of trend lines and resistance lines out of a PHI-channel are presented in Figure 4.9.

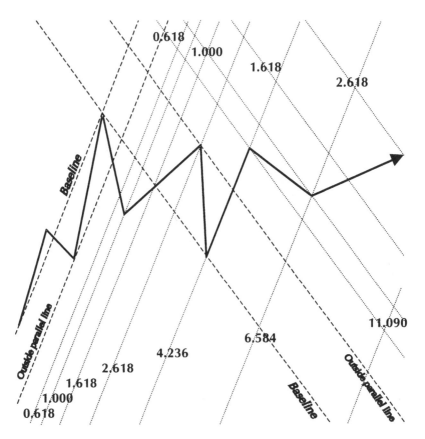

Figure 4.9 PHI-channel trend lines and resistance lines combined. *Source: FAM Research,* 2000.

Generating crossovers of PHI-channel trend lines parallel to a main trend and PHI-channel resistance lines' countertrend promises a projection of future investor behavior in price and in time.

Because we rely on high–low to low–high connections, angles of PHI-channels will vary quite a lot. But it does not matter whether a PHI-channel runs steep or flat. What is most important about

PHI-channels is that peak and valley formations have a major impact on price moves in the future. This is the only way to explain why, in many instances, PHI-channel lines serve as support and resistance lines with stunning accuracy. We may never know which line will be reached and when a crossover point will be triggered, but trend lines and resistance lines out of PHI-channels can be of major significance to confirm buy and sell signals, especially when used with other Fibonacci tools.

PHI-channel support and resistance lines are often expressions of perfect symmetry within price patterns. This factor is in contrast to the regular trend channels (discussed earlier in this chapter), which may not have enough built-in flexibility to adjust quickly to price patterns, and therefore are of less forecasting value.

The use of prominent peaks and valleys for the calculation of PHI-channels, in combination with the ratios from the PHI series, shows that price moves are not random. Price patterns, by themselves, can be predicted if they are analyzed correctly.

The secret of PHI-channels is to identify the correct valleys and peaks to work with. Support and resistance lines can be drawn weeks and months into the future, once the appropriate tops and bottoms in the market have been detected.

Identifying the appropriate PHI-channel is not difficult. Close market observation reveals how market pricing will either use or not use the cobweb formation (see Figure 4.9) as support and resistance. Once the first line is triggered, the quality of the lines drawn at higher ratios from the PHI series is confirmed.

Essentially, PHI-channel lines drawn at ratios higher than 2.618 lie too far in the future to be reliable, but sometimes even a ratio of 4.236 can be productive. Ratios that can be used meaningfully to calculate PHI-channel lines depend on the width of the PHI-channel from the baseline to the outside line.

PHI-channels that have been correctly identified and parallels that have been properly calculated often follow Elliott's rule of alternation, which is also a very important pattern in nature. Whenever an outer parallel is triggered, prices move back toward the line drawn at the preceding ratio from the PHI series. This happens before a move to the next outer line begins.

Still another factor points to the findings of Elliott. When a trend line is not just touched, but strongly broken, and is followed by a trend reversal, market pricing will penetrate the next PHI-channel line as well. This observation correlates with Elliott's claim that when a market price exceeds a number in the Fibonacci summation series in time, we can expect that the next following number of the Fibonacci summation series will also be reached.

There are cases where market prices stop at special points and reverse direction. This is often due to the overlapping of other Fibonacci tools. In the current chapter, and more so in Chapter 8, we will discuss useful combinations of Fibonacci trading tools in detail.

Now that the overall structure of PHI-channels has been explained, we will present examples of how to apply PHI-channels to sample market data.

WORKING WITH PHI-CHANNELS

PHI-channels can be seen as direct reflections of investor behavior and as indicators for major trend reversals in the marketplace.

To provide readers with a variety of examples, this section is divided into three parts. We first demonstrate the use of regular trend channels on a perfect 5-wave move in the S&P500 Index market. We then proceed to a step-by-step description of how to apply PHI-channels to market data using an S&P500 Index example. Finally, we present evidence of the incredible utility of PHI-channels on sample data of the DAX30 Index.

Regular Trend Channels in 5-Wave Moves

As explained earlier in this chapter, we can sometimes identify regular 5-wave price patterns in the markets.

In these cases, we can define the width of a trend channel by drawing parallel lines from peak to peak and valley to valley. The width of the trend channel—multiplied by the ratios 0.618, 1.000, 1.618, 2.618, and so on, of the PHI series—results in a set of parallel lines that indicate levels of trend support. On narrow trend channels, the resulting parallels might be very close together. If the parallel lines appear too close together, one should omit the first two lines and start at a ratio of 1.618, followed by 2.618, and so on.

A perfect 5-wave chart pattern from December 1999 to March 2000 is found in the S&P500 Index.

Assuming normal circumstances and a regular market environment, we can anticipate a strong move opposite to the main trend direction as soon as a 5-wave price move is completed and the market price breaks out of a trend channel. This pattern is easy to see in Figure 4.10, a chart of the S&P500 Index.

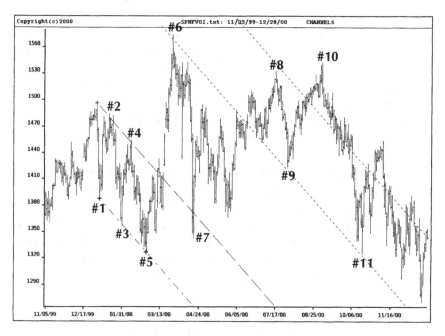

Figure 4.10   Chart of the S&P500 Index from 11–99 to 12–00. Regular trend channel and parallel lines in a 5-wave pattern. *Source: FAM Research,* 2000.

The S&P500 Index had an extremely strong price move after it broke out of the trend channel and reached its highest high at 1,574.00. Once the market price reached its highest high at peak #6, the market touched the trend channel parallel, which was calculated by multiplying the total width of the trend channel by the ratio 1.618.

The S&P500 Index hit the trend channel parallel in such exactness that we knew this trend channel parallel would be of importance for the market swings to come.

At this point, we could also predict that the next following trend channel line, calculated at a ratio of 2.618, would be of importance because historical test runs have shown that regular price patterns penetrate at least two trend channel lines.

These observations are based on the rule of alternation discovered by Elliott, who said that new highs are followed by retracements back to the previously broken trend channel line before a move toward a new trend channel line is initiated.

In our example, the market price penetrated the trend channel line at peak #6. The retracement went all the way back to the original trend channel at valley #7 before the trend channel parallel, calculated at a ratio of 2.618, was almost reached at peak #8. It was broken once the peak at point #10 was realized. Whenever a peak reaches a resistance line, as was the case at peak #8, the previous trend channel parallel becomes the support line. This can be seen very clearly at valley #9 and valley #11 in Figure 4.10.

Price patterns are not random. Market prices follow an underlying law based in the Fibonacci ratio and the ratios of the PHI series. The secret is to identify the correct trend channels.

As mentioned above, regular 5-wave patterns are seldom seen. To bring our trend channel analysis closer to the irregularities of market action, we transform regular trend channels into PHI-channels, which have a built-in flexibility to successfully capture irregular 5-wave moves.

PHI-Channels on S&P500 Index Sample Data

Trend channels are transformed into PHI-channels when parallel lines are no longer drawn from peak to peak and from valley to valley. Instead, a PHI-channel baseline is established—a peak-to-valley and valley-to-peak connection of the first and the second impulse waves in a 5-wave move. PHI-channel trend lines are calculated as parallels to this channel baseline using the ratios of the PHI series.

To demonstrate the best way to work with PHI-channel lines in irregular market patterns, we will look at the S&P500 Index for 1999 and 2000.

We will explain step-by-step how to generate a PHI-channel, PHI-channel trend lines, and PHI-channel resistance lines on the S&P500 Index. Each step will be described on a separate chart, so as not to add confusion by combining different steps in one chart and overlapping PHI-channel lines.

After all elements of the analysis have been explained, we will show the final result in one chart. It will demonstrate that PHI-channel trend lines and PHI-channel resistance lines, drawn weeks and months into the future, define very important support or resistance points once the actual market price reaches them.

The first step in our PHI-channel application is the generation of PHI-channel trend lines.

As mentioned earlier, the greater the peaks and valleys are, the more valuable the PHI-channel trend lines based on these peaks and valleys become.

We numbered the most prominent peaks and valleys in a daily bar chart O–H–L–C of our S&P500 Index sample data from point #0 to point #9 (Figure 4.11).

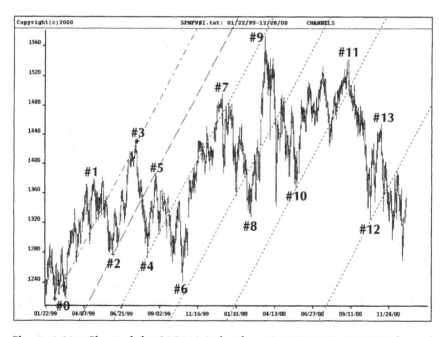

Figure 4.11   Chart of the S&P500 Index from 01–99 to 12–00. PHI-channel trend lines. *Source: FAM Research,* 2000.

We establish the baseline of the PHI-channel by connecting the low at point #0 and the high at point #3. Both points are part of the first significant 3-swing pattern. A parallel line to the right of the baseline is then drawn through the valley at point #2. Again, parallel to the PHI-channel, trend lines are drawn in PHI series distances that are 1.000 times, 1.618 times, 2.618 times, and 4.236 times the width of the PHI-channel.

Very interesting patterns can be detected in the movements of the S&P500 Index after the market price has left the PHI-channel to the downside (July 1999). The market price penetrated the first PHI-channel trend line at point #4. It went back to the original PHI-channel at point #5. It made the next attempt to reach the second PHI-channel trend line at point #6, and then went all the way back up to reach the first PHI-channel trend line at point #7.

Whenever a new PHI-channel trend line is broken, there is a tendency for market price patterns to go back to the previous PHI-channel trend line. This follows the flow of the market action and shows a general pattern of how investors behave.

It is amazing to discover how accurately PHI-channel trend lines, drawn weeks and months into the future of market pricing, work as support and resistance areas. We can only repeat that we will never know at what point in time PHI-channel trend lines might be reached, but when PHI-channel trend lines are triggered, they can be of significant importance.

PHI-channel trend lines are generated by connecting the highs and lows of impulse waves. In the general description of the structure of PHI-channels, we pointed out that PHI-channel resistance lines can also be created if we select a corrective move in the wave pattern to define the baseline of the PHI-channel.

Instead of connecting the valley at point #0 with the peak at point #3 to define a PHI-channel for trend lines, we can use the peak at point #1 and connect it with the significant valley at point #6. In this case, we get to a baseline of a PHI-channel that makes use of a 3-wave corrective move.

The baseline of the PHI-channel out of the correction is drawn in such a way that it intersects an imaginary line, running from the low at point #2 to the following high at point #3. The final point of the baseline at point #6 is at a significant low. A parallel line to the right of the baseline can be drawn through peak #3 to finish the definition of the PHI-channel.

As in the previous example, parallel lines to the PHI-channel run in PHI series distances 1.000 times, 1.618 times, 2.618 times, and 4.236 times the width of the PHI-channel to the right.

We draw the baseline of the PHI-channel from peak #1 to the valley at #6; therefore, the parallels to the PHI-channel run against the main market trend, and there are resistance lines. Although they indicate a negative trend direction, they may act as support and resistance lines for price action in the future. The width of the PHI-channels, multiplied by 1.618, creates a resistance line that indicates a trend change once the market price triggers the line at the peak at point #7.

All our findings on PHI-channel resistance lines are summed up in Figure 4.12. The reader should contrast these with PHI-channel trend lines.

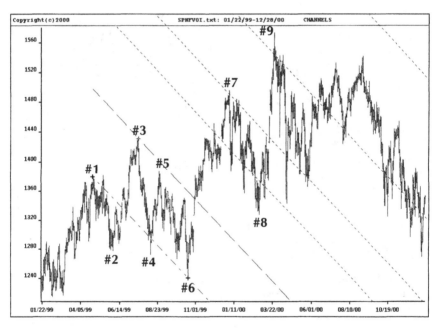

Figure 4.12   Chart of the S&P500 Index from 01–99 to 12–00. PHI-channel resistance lines. *Source: FAM Research,* **2000.**

As soon as the significant peak at point #7 has been established, we can draw a new PHI-channel baseline from valley #0 to peak #7, which leads us to a different set of PHI-channel trend lines.

The outside parallel of the PHI-channel is drawn through valley #4. We do not choose valley #6 because the PHI-channel baseline only intersects the movement from peak #3 to valley #4, and not the move from peak #5 to valley #6. In addition, using the valley at point #6 would increase the width of the PHI-channel too much, and it would no longer be symmetrical.

The PHI-channel trend line drawn at a ratio 1.000 times the width of the PHI-channel, from baseline to outside parallel, creates support for the market price at valley #6 and at valley #8 (Figure 4.13).

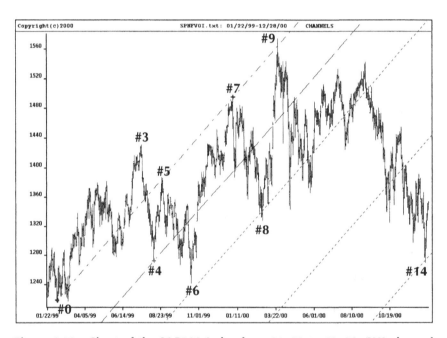

Figure 4.13   Chart of the S&P500 Index from 01–99 to 12–00. PHI-channel trend lines. *Source: FAM Research,* 2000.

Although the PHI-channel had already been established by January 2000, the width of the PHI-trend channel, multiplied by 4.236, was still the support level for the market action in December 2000 at valley #14. Whether this valley will be the lowest low in the S&P500 Index, or whether even lower price levels will be reached in the short-term or mid-term future, cannot be determined from the PHI-channel trend line analysis alone. However, we will learn more by combining Fibonacci tools in Chapter 8 and then analyzing this question again.

Staying consistent in our PHI-channel analysis, we connect peak #3 and valley #8 to get to a baseline of a PHI-channel for a second set of resistance lines. The outside parallel to this baseline is drawn through the peak at point #7 (Figure 4.14).

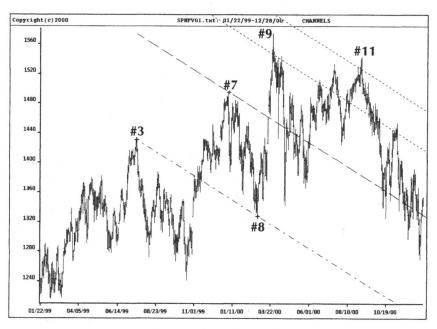

Figure 4.14 Chart of the S&P500 Index from 01–99 to 12–00. PHI-channel resistance lines. *Source: FAM Research, 2000.*

The resulting PHI-channel is very wide. That is why we start drawing PHI-channel resistance lines at a ratio 0.618 from the PHI series—a smaller ratio compared to the starting ratios used in the other examples. The PHI-channel line, drawn at a ratio 0.618 times the distance from the baseline to the parallel line of the PHI-channel, works as a resistance line for the peak at point #9. The next PHI-channel parallel generated at a ratio of 1.000 is the resistance line for peak #11. Again, we can observe that the high at point #11 has been reached only after the market reverted to the original outside parallel drawn through peak #7.

In the third and final example of how to generate PHI-channel trend lines, a baseline is drawn as a connecting line from valley #6 to peak #9. The parallel to this baseline is drawn through the outside valley at point #8. The width of the PHI-channel, multiplied by the two ratios 1.000 and 2.618 from the PHI series, leads us to a pair of PHI-channel trend lines that intersect the peak at point #11 and the valley at point #12 (Figure 4.15).

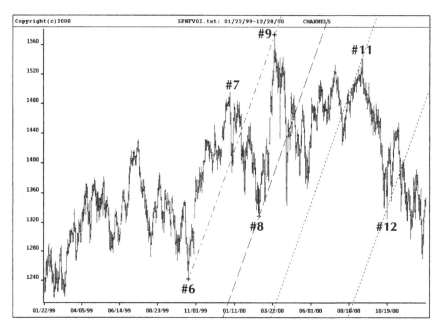

Figure 4.15   Chart of the S&P500 Index from 01–99 to 12–00. PHI-channel trend lines. *Source: FAM Research,* 2000.

Three detailed examples of PHI-channel trend lines plus two examples of PHI-channel resistance lines on the S&P500 Index daily bar chart should be sufficient for readers to grasp the general functioning of PHI-channels.

We now take the separate instruments of PHI-channel trend lines and PHI-channel resistance lines and integrate them into the cobweb design described earlier in this chapter.

When we observe the cobweb on the S&P500 Index market price moves, it is evident that PHI-channels can be very important for analysts who look for guidance through the ups and downs of market patterns.

Figure 4.16 covers the cobweb of PHI-channel trend lines drawn parallel to a baseline connecting the valley at point #0 with the peak at point #3, and PHI-channel resistance lines drawn from a baseline connecting peak #1 and valley #6. Turning points are marked the same way as in the previous five examples.

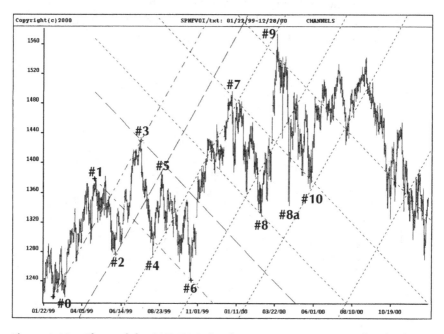

Figure 4.16 Chart of the S&P500 Index from 01–99 to 12–00. Cobweb of PHI-channel trend lines and PHI-channel resistance lines. *Source: FAM Research, 2000.*

Looking at the chart, one can easily see that the S&P500 Index market price reached its highest high at point #9. This was well captured by a crossover of PHI-channel trend line and PHI-channel resistance line.

The quality of our PHI-channel analysis depends on whether PHI-channels have the built-in flexibility to automatically adjust from bull market to bear market conditions, working only with significant peaks and valleys. Moreover, significant peaks and valley have to be analyzed in consecutive order; otherwise, we are left with too much room for interpretation.

Peak #9 and valley #10 are directly identified by working with the different PHI-channel baselines, and by using the consecutive peaks and valleys from #1 to #7. If only valley #10 had been considered significant, we would not have known how to properly handle the extraordinary market moves on April 14 and April 17, 2000, in the S&P500 Index, that led to the formation of valley #8a.

A second example of a cobweb design that can deal with this problem is one that reached the peaks marked #7 and #9 and the valleys marked #8, #8a, #10, and #10a in Figure 4.17.

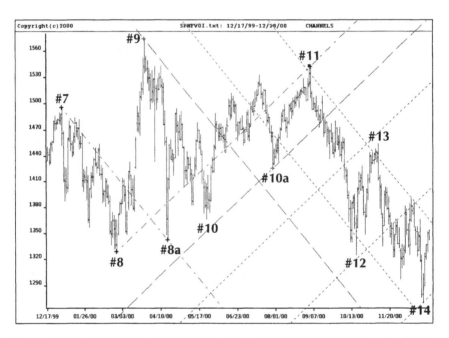

Figure 4.17   Chart of the S&P500 Index from 12–99 to 12–00. Cobweb of PHI-channel trend lines and PHI-channel resistance lines. *Source: FAM Research, 2000.*

We can establish a new baseline of a PHI-channel using the peak at point #7 and the valley at point #8a. The outside parallel line of the PHI-channel can be drawn through peak #9. By using the ratio 1.000 from the PHI series, we can draw a PHI-channel resistance line that marks peak #11 and peak #13. The PHI-channel resistance line drawn at a ratio of 0.618 is triggered by the valley at point #12 and is almost reached by the lowest low, which follows at valley #14.

The baseline of the PHI-channel intersects the distance from the side points at valley #8 and peak #9. This pattern of intersection benefits the overall symmetry of the PHI-channel.

To adjust to the S&P500 Index market action, we can also draw the baseline of a PHI-channel between the significant valley at point #8 and the significant peak at point #11, with the outside parallel line of the PHI-channel crossing through the valley at point #10a.

By multiplying the total width of the PHI-channel (from baseline to parallel line) by the ratios 1.000, 1.618, and 2.618 from the PHI series, we get to a set of PHI-channel trend lines that turn out to be support levels for valley #12 and valley #14, as well as a resistance level for peak #13. Once again, we find that the combination of trend lines and resistance lines derived from a PHI-channel is of indisputable value for the confirmation of trend changes.

Working with PHI-channels requires a long-term analysis of market price action. PHI-channel analysis finds its limitations in the Fibonacci ratios themselves. The higher the ratios chosen from the PHI series for drawing trend lines and resistance lines, the further into the future the PHI-channel lines reach. Therefore, it is recommended that analysts work with the latest major swing peaks and swing valleys.

The integration of weekly data might also be helpful when analysts attempt to capture trend changes in the marketplace far ahead of time.

PHI-channel analysis worked well in the S&P500 Index market. We will now present the DAX30 Index to prove to readers that the application of PHI-channels as Fibonacci tools is not limited to the United States of America.

PHI-Channels on DAX30 Index Sample Data

The DAX30 Index, like the S&P500 Index, is a very liquid and volatile trading device. Its market price moves in rhythms, and significant peaks and valleys are frequently identified.

We charted the DAX30 Index for 31 months in a cobweb design of PHI-channel trend lines and PHI-channel resistance lines that was very similar to our presentation of the S&P500 Index.

Figure 4.18 shows the DAX30 Index daily from June 1998 until
December 2000.

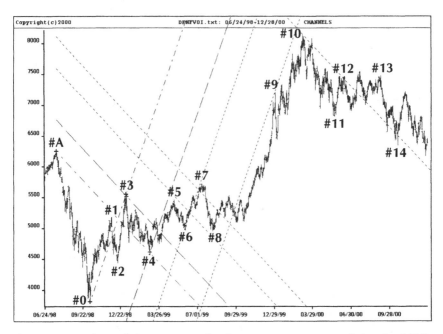

**Figure 4.18   Chart of the DAX30 Index from 06–98 to 12–00. Cobweb of PHI-
channel trend lines and PHI-channel resistance lines.** *Source: FAM Research,
2000.*

The DAX30 Index had a significant low at 3,810.0 on October 8,
1998. This valley is our starting point (#0) for the baseline of the first
PHI-channel. The underlying pattern marks an impulse wave in an
uptrend.

Peak #3 of the 3-wave uptrend price pattern, following the lowest low, is connected with the valley at point #0 to mark the ending
point of the baseline of the PHI-channel. The parallel to the baseline
is drawn through the outside valley at point #4.

The resulting width of the PHI-channel, multiplied by the ratio
0.618, leads us to a PHI-channel trend line that acts as a support and
resistance level for the valley at point #6 and the peak at point #7.
What is even more important, the PHI-channel trend line, generated
at a ratio 1.618, is the resistance line for the strong uptrend when
peak #9 touches the PHI-channel line. This all occurs just as the

DAX30 Index is on its way from a level of 5,000.0 up to a highest high: above 8,136.0 points.

This finding corresponds with what we have learned from our analysis of the S&P500 Index market movements: PHI-channels can serve as trend lines *and* resistance lines, depending on whether we work with peak-to-valley formations (countertrend lines) or valley-to-peak formations (trend lines) in an uptrend (vice versa in a downtrend).

The starting baseline for a second PHI-channel follows the pattern of an impulse wave in a downtrend. We connect the significant peak at point #A in Figure 4.18 with the valley at point #4. To this baseline we draw the parallel through the outside peak at point #3.

The width of the PHI-channel from baseline to parallel outside line, multiplied by the ratio 1.618, is the resistance point for peak #5. The PHI-channel line created by ratio 2.618 is the resistance line for peak #7. Even more amazing, the PHI-channel line, drawn at a ratio 11.090, turned out to be an adequate resistance line once the DAX30 Index reached its highest high at peak #10.

Researchers, analysts, and traders are surprised that a PHI-channel line drawn at a ratio 11.090 parallel to the baseline, connecting a peak in 1998 and a valley in 1999, creates a level of perfect resistance for the DAX30 Index almost one year later (2000) at its highest high. It is also quite amazing that the same PHI-channel resistance line defines the median line of the strong downtrend that follows the highest high in the DAX30 Index. The resistance line, which starts at the peak at point #10, intersects the imaginary connection from valley #12 to peak #13.

Once again, we find a perfect symmetry in market action—one that can only be captured by working with the Fibonacci summation series and the ratios from the PHI series.

To cover the price movements of the DAX30 Index after the highest high above 8,000.0 points in March 2000, we have the options of drawing PHI-channel trend lines using a baseline in the direction of the main trend, or PHI-channel resistance lines using a baseline out of a correction counter to the main trend.

We start with the baseline in the direction of the main trend and connect the lowest low in the DAX30 Index in October 1998 with the highest high in March 2000. We analyze the entire trend movement from 3,800.0 points to 8,000.0 points as a single long-term 3-wave pattern consisting of two impulse waves (from the valley in October 1998 to the significant peak on January 11, 1999, and from the valley on October 18, 1999, up to the highest high) and one corrective move from the peak in January 1999 to the valley in October 1999. The relevant peaks (#1, #3) and valleys (#0, #2) of the long-term 3-wave uptrend are marked accordingly in Figure 4.19.

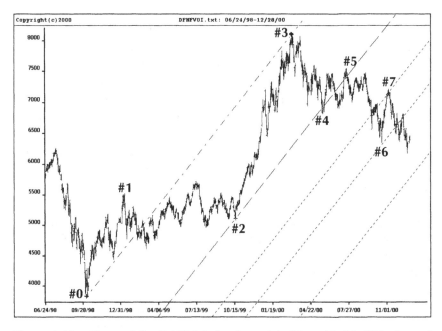

Figure 4.19   Chart of the DAX30 Index from 06–98 to 12–00. PHI-channel trend lines. *Source: FAM Research,* 2000.

The PHI-channel is established by drawing a parallel to the baseline through the outside valley at point #2. The parallel outside line of the PHI-channel, in this example, is also a support line for the market action at valley #4 and a resistance line for peak #5.

The PHI-channel in Figure 4.19 is very wide because of the long-term orientation of the analysis. Therefore, we start by drawing PHI-channel trend lines at small ratios of 0.618 and 1.000 from the PHI series. The price move in the DAX30 Index (down from the highest high) is strongly supported by the PHI-channel trend line at valley #6. The intermediate rally from valley #6 to peak #7 finds resistance at the PHI-channel line drawn at the ratio 0.618.

The DAX30 Index price action following the all-time high in March 2000 can also be captured by resistance lines generated on the basis of a PHI-channel analysis (Figure 4.20).

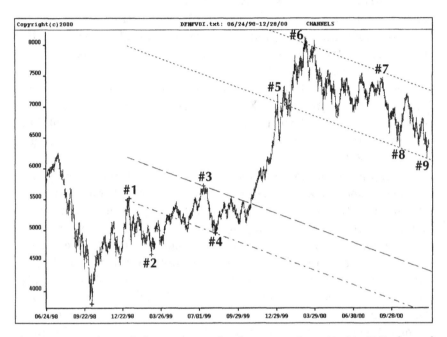

Figure 4.20 Chart of the DAX30 Index from 06–98 to 12–00. PHI-channel resistance lines. *Source: FAM Research,* 2000.

The initial baseline of the PHI-channel follows the correction from the major peak at point #1 to the major valley at point #4. The baseline intersects the imaginary line of the move from valley #2 to peak #3. Because the distances from the baseline to valley #2 and the baseline to peak #3 are almost identical, a very symmetrical pattern of market behavior can be identified, just as before. By detecting the correct peaks and valleys and working with high-to-low and low-to-high formations in accordance with Elliott's rule of alternation, the PHI-channel lines are of significant predictive value for future market action.

The parallel outside line to the baseline of the PHI-channel is drawn through the peak at point #3. The width of the PHI-channel, from baseline to parallel, and multiplied by the ratio 2.618, established a support line months in advance of the downtrend that began in March 2000. The respective resistance was given by the PHI-channel line drawn at a ratio 4.236 times the width of the PHI-channel, from baseline to outside parallel line.

PHI-channel analysis provides us with a multitude of options for setting baselines and parallel lines of different PHI-channels, and for drawing support and resistance lines from them. The overall quality of PHI-channel trend lines and PHI-channel resistance lines will, however, vary from case to case.

We now realize that when the resistance line drawn at a ratio 2.618 was broken by the DAX30 Index trend move to the upside at peak #5 in Figure 4.20, the market price jumped to the next level. This level was established at peak #6 and a PHI-channel line was created at a ratio 4.236.

It is impossible to predict which PHI-channel line is going to be the perfect one. We know, however, that if a market behaves in a regular manner, the peak at point #5 would be an extreme high for the market action. In historical perspective, we see that a move from one extreme point to an even higher extreme point, without a significant correction, has occurred very rarely (not only on the DAX30 Index). Even if investors had taken the extreme point at peak #5 as a strategically important point and had liquidated some of their positions, they could have felt comfortable with the investment decision again six months later, because ultimately the market price traded significantly lower than on the day of peak #5.

In Chapter 8, we will describe in detail how investment decisions can be made safer by combining various Fibonacci tools. An intelligent combination of Fibonacci tools would have answered all of our questions when the DAX30 Index market made the significant peak at point #5 in Figure 4.20.

On the previous charts, we were very much in line with the analysis, and the established long-term PHI-channel trend and resistance lines were of high value. We can now look at other options in order to stay even closer to the market action.

For example, we might start our PHI-channel analysis at the level of the highest high ever traded in the DAX 30 Index. We could reduce the time period analyzed and start in January 2000 instead of June 1998. Without going into too much detail, we will map the market situation in a cobweb design from a sample pointing into 2001. (By this time, readers will have gotten more information on the actual price

moves of the DAX30 Index than we had in December 2000. With the
help of the WINPHI software, they will see how valuable our analysis has been.)

Our choice of PHI-channels in the DAX30 Index is shown in Figure 4.21.

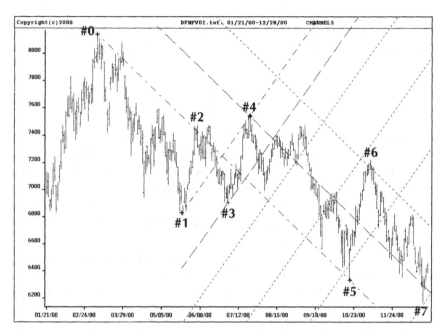

Figure 4.21   Chart of the DAX30 Index from 01–00 to 12–00. Cobweb of PHI-
channel trend lines and PHI-channel resistance lines. *Source: FAM Research,
2000.*

The impulse wave baseline is established from the peak at point
#0 to the valley at point #5; an outside parallel line is drawn through
the peak at point #4.

A PHI-channel resistance line is then defined by multiplying the
width of the PHI-channel (from baseline to parallel outside line) by
the ratio 1.000. This PHI-channel line is the resistance line for the
market price. The peak at point #6 on the DAX30 Index chart was
made when the PHI-channel resistance line was penetrated.

The second baseline following a corrective move is established by
connecting the valley at point #1 and the peak at point #4. The PHI-
channel is completed by choosing a parallel line through valley #3.

PHI-channel trend lines are then created based on the ratios 1.000, 1.618, 2.618, and 4.236, from the PHI series. The valley at point #7 touches the PHI-channel trend line drawn at a ratio 4.236.

Graphing the major peaks and valleys in market moves, and showing the cobweb designs of trend lines and resistance lines derived from PHI-channels, contributes to the valuable Fibonacci strategy of capturing trend reversals in the markets.

We will briefly summarize our findings before introducing PHI-ellipses (fourth on our list of geometrical Fibonacci trading tools).

SUMMARY

Investors' behavior expresses itself not only in chart patterns, trend formations, or sideward markets, but in peaks and valleys as well. Every peak or valley can be seen as an indication of what the majority of investors expect at any moment in time; however, intraday peaks or valleys are not as meaningful as those on daily or weekly charts. Our analysis, therefore, focuses on daily data but may easily be extended to sets of weekly data, too.

Significant peaks and valleys in the markets are much more relevant than is often assumed. Trend channels are generated by establishing major peak-to-peak and valley-to-valley connections out of regular 3-wave or 5-wave market moves. This is why trend channels should be the primary step when analyzing markets.

When PHI-channels are improvements of regular trend channels they are generated slightly differently. Our PHI-channel analysis works with baselines as connections of significant high-to-low and low-to-high formations.

PHI-channels can be drawn either from impulse waves or from corrective waves, by determining the outside parallel line of a PHI-channel on the basis of the next significant peak or valley to the right of the baseline. As soon as a PHI-channel has been established, the width of the PHI-channel, measured as the distance from baseline to parallel line, can be multiplied by the ratios 0.618, 1.000, 1.618, 2.618, 4.236, and so on. Depending on whether the baseline of the PHI-channel is trend-following or countertrend, PHI-channel trend lines (or PHI-channel resistance lines) can be drawn in PHI series distances from the outside parallel line of the PHI-channel. Combinations of

PHI-channel trend lines and PHI-channel resistance lines led us to a cobweb design that allows us to map market price action and predict future market moves.

The S&P500 Index and DAX30 Index are analyzed to explain the use and the functionality of PHI-channels. Because this book is purely educational, we refrain from conducting the analysis on more than two products and time frames beyond the years 1998 to 2000. The results presented are convincing and leave plenty of room for creative readers to fine-tune and to cross-examine our examples for alternative, and perhaps even more productive, PHI-channels.

Once they are triggered, PHI-channel trend lines and PHI-channel resistance lines are indicators of forthcoming market action. They do not have immediate forecasting value, but they can be very important as support or resistance levels for market trends. In the selected examples, we demonstrated that PHI-channel lines drawn weeks or months ahead do not lose any degree of quality. The biggest limitation of PHI-channels lies in the ratios of the PHI series, which quickly get too big to create meaningful PHI-channel lines for the future. To solve this problem and to stay close to the markets, we have to work with every significant peak or valley in sequence.

The mapping of historical daily bar charts of the S&P500 Index and the DAX30 Index proves that market price action is symmetrical, not random. Just as Elliott said, market price movements are like the tide; they swing forward and back again very smoothly.

Newcomers to Fibonacci tools and graphic means of market analysis often find it difficult to correctly detect PHI-channel baselines and the peaks and valleys through which to draw the outside parallel lines. The initial mistake that almost everyone makes, is to overlook the most significant peaks or valleys and to use, instead, smaller ones that bring PHI-channel lines closer to the markets. The final example in the section on DAX30 Index data shows clearly that investors who chose to conduct their analysis on prominent peaks and valleys back in 1998 and 1999 might have gotten far closer to the market action today if they had worked with better PHI-channel lines.

How can correct PHI-channels be distinguished from false ones? A correct PHI-channel is identified by looking at whether the first major turning point in the market, after the PHI-channel is drawn, finds its support or resistance in the first PHI-channel trend line or resistance line drawn at a ratio 0.618 or 1.000 (at the most). Once this condition is met, we can be sure that the following PHI-channel lines drawn at higher ratios from the PHI series will be important support or resistance lines as well.

Explicit buy-and-sell signals are not part of this chapter's analysis because we strongly believe that the greatest value for the serious investor is to combine the PHI-channel trend and resistance lines with other Fibonacci trading tools. The PHI-channel lines are only a part of the total picture of geometrical Fibonacci trading devices. Other combinations will be discussed in Chapter 8. But PHI-channels can be helpful as additional ways to make trading safer and more profitable.

PHI-channel lines can be drawn exclusively with the WINPHI software package. Readers should check the User Manual on how to quickly and easily get to PHI-channel trend lines and PHI-channel resistance lines. All examples presented in this chapter, and additional sets of sample market data, can be referenced using the WINPHI program.

PHI-channel lines are terrific tools for mapping out price action and making investors' behavior visible. Market swings can be followed up and down like a road map, as long as the correct PHI-channel lines are selected.

5

PHI-ELLIPSES

In the previous chapter, we described the risks of working with peak and valley formations in 3-wave patterns and 5-wave patterns.

Because swing formations are easy to identify and easy to integrate into computerized trading environments, peak and valley formations are often used, especially by traders or managers investing in smaller accounts. Many profitable trades can be made, as long as there are regular wave patterns and each impulse wave defines new highs or new lows by a wide margin. However, in multiple corrections with many false breakouts, swing systems are of little use because they are based only on price analysis.

The conditions change as soon as we add the time element to the market analysis. The time element filters noise out of the market moves and brings more stability into investment strategies. This is where PHI-ellipses come in.

Working with PHI-ellipses is not easy. The basic structure of PHI-ellipses is very simple, but because price patterns may change over time, the final shape of a PHI-ellipse that circumvents a price pattern may also vary.

At the beginning, the application of PHI-ellipses will be confusing because there are different forms and wave structures within a PHI-ellipse. In addition, different PHI-ellipses can sometimes be linked together. Therefore, it takes a lot of skill and imagination to properly work with PHI-ellipses as investment tools.

Because of their complexity, we will first describe the basic features and parameters of PHI-ellipses in great detail. Examples of how to apply PHI-ellipses as Fibonacci devices to real-time trading are presented in the second section.

By introducing PHI-ellipses, we touch only the tip of the iceberg, for there are no limits for creativity.

BASIC FEATURES AND PARAMETERS OF PHI-ELLIPSES

The PHI-ellipse is one of the unique Fibonacci trading tools that can only be drawn by a computer.

What makes PHI-ellipses so interesting? PHI-ellipses identify underlying structures of price moves. PHI-ellipses circumvent price patterns. When a price pattern changes, the shape of the PHI-ellipse circumventing the respective market price pattern changes, too. We find long and short PHI-ellipses, fat and thin PHI-ellipses, and even PHI-ellipses that are flat or have a steep angle. There are very few market price moves that do not follow the pattern of a PHI-ellipse.

PHI-ellipses are related to the Fibonacci ratio PHI in a way that is similar to the Fibonacci summation series and the corrections and extensions that were explained in Chapter 2 and Chapter 3.

Generally speaking, the shape of an ellipse is defined by the ratio of major axis a to minor axis b. Ellipses are turned into PHI-ellipses in all cases where the ratio of major axis to minor axis $e_x = a \div b$ is a member number of the PHI series.

To make PHI-ellipses work as tools for chart analysis, we have applied a (proprietary) transformation to the mathematical formula that describes the shape of the ellipse. We still consider the ratio of major axis a to minor axis b of the ellipse, but in a Fischer-transformed way. In mathematical terms, $e_x = (a \div b)^*$.

We introduce PHI-ellipses as instruments for investments that represent a countertrend to market action. In other words, we observe whether a price move stays within a PHI-ellipse, and we invest accordingly if a price move breaks out of a PHI-ellipse at the very end.

Looking backward on historical charts, one finds that very few price moves in commodities, futures, stock index futures, or stocks show up that cannot be circumvented with a PHI-ellipse. However, finding the correct PHI-ellipse is an art. It takes skill, experience, patience, and trust in the analysis to effectively utilize PHI-ellipses as Fibonacci investment tools.

It is impossible to forecast the final shape of a PHI-ellipse at the beginning of a price move. As we will later prove via various examples, PHI-ellipses may follow one after the other symmetrically. Small PHI-ellipses may be followed by long PHI-ellipses, or PHI-ellipses may be connected with each other, and so on. The challenge for investors is to correctly interpret price moves and select PHI-ellipses accordingly. Once the appropriate market pattern has been identified, working with PHI-ellipses becomes easier.

To describe the features and parameters of PHI-ellipses in detail, we have divided this section into two parts. We first refer to the shape and the slope of PHI-ellipses, and include approaches for attaching and overlapping PHI-ellipses. In the second part, we address entry and exit rules for trading strategies to be generated from PHI-ellipses.

Typical Features of PHI-Ellipses

Dealing with chart patterns depends a lot on the definition of swings, just as it depends on controlling impulse waves and corrections without losing sight of the main trend picture.

The strength of PHI-ellipses, in this respect, is that no matter how many waves or subwaves we find in a price pattern, we receive a solid overall picture of the total price pattern as long as it can be circumvented by a PHI-ellipse.

Even if the analysis is reduced to a simple 3-swing pattern, there is an indefinite number of possible combinations of impulse waves and corrections. Impulse waves are not difficult to handle, whereas corrections and long sideward periods in the markets can become very tricky.

Long periods of sideward movements are what we consider "noise" in the markets.

PHI-ellipses are the perfect geometrical trading tools when the Fibonacci ratio PHI requires coping with noise and analyzing price moves as entities over time, without having to focus too much on every individual intermediate minor peak or valley that shows up between the starting point and the ending point of the price pattern.

The generation of PHI-ellipses can best be demonstrated by starting with a circle, and then turning the circle into PHI-ellipses (Figure 5.1).

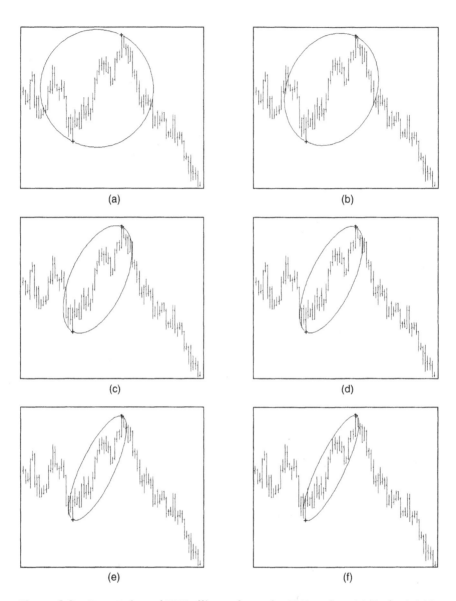

Figure 5.1 Generation of PHI-ellipses from the PHI series. (a) Ratio 1.000; (b) ratio 1.618; (c) ratio 4.236; (d) ratio 6.854; (e) ratio 11.090; (f) ratio 17.944. *Source: FAM Research, 2000.*

A circle is a special kind of PHI-ellipse because the ratio of the major and minor axes is 1.000 from the PHI series. From the circle, ongoing PHI-ellipses can be drawn at alternative axis ratios 1.618, 2.618, 4.236, 6.854, 11.090, 17.944, 29.034, and so on, from the PHI series. According to the mathematical formula for Fischer-transformed PHI-ellipses, the length of the major axis remains unchanged. The minor axis thereby gets shorter and shorter. The resulting PHI-ellipses become narrower and narrower and finally perfectly enclose the entire price move.

It is evident from the sample charts that because ellipses have such special structures, they can be used only as trading tools on computers and only with particular software packages. Fischer-transformed PHI-ellipses, moreover, are unavailable elsewhere and can only be generated by running the WINPHI graphics software that accompanies this book.

PHI-ellipses are interesting as graphical trading tools because their very structure is founded on a 3-wave pattern (Figure 5.2).

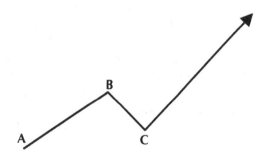

Figure 5.2   General structure of a 3-wave pattern. *Source: FAM Research, 2000.*

After points A, B, and C in the idealized 3-wave swing are identified, we can position the PHI-ellipse around these three points. Wave 1, from A to B, is an impulse wave. Wave 2, from B to C, is the corrective wave to the impulse wave. For wave 3, we expect a second impulse wave in the direction of the first impulse wave. This general pattern follows Elliott's wave principles and can be seen in every traded product, be it commodities, futures, stocks, or cash currencies.

The fundamental structure of the PHI-ellipse allows another way of analyzing price moves. What makes it so unique is the fact that it is dynamic over time and follows price patterns as they develop. That is why we must always be patient and wait—from the very beginning to the very end—until a price move stays within the PHI-ellipse. Action can be taken as soon as the market price moves out of the PHI-ellipse, but only if a price pattern runs completely inside a PHI-ellipse until the final point is reached.

As a general rule, we can say that if the angle of a PHI-ellipse is sloping upward, we can sell at the end of the PHI-ellipse. If the slope of the PHI-ellipse is downward, we can buy at the end of the PHI-ellipse. The exceptions to this rule will be described later.

It is very important to remember that PHI-ellipses are not means of forecasting market moves. We will never know in advance whether a price move will stay within the PHI-ellipse and reach its end so that we can take action. We must always wait to see whether a price move stays inside the borders of the PHI-ellipse, and we cannot take action unless the final point of the PHI-ellipse is met. The rationale behind this waiting principle will become clear in the various examples given later in the section.

Working with PHI-ellipses means watching price action as it progresses. Price action starts with the impulse wave from A to B in Figure 5.2 and is followed by the correction from B to C. In Chapter 3, Elliott's wave principles helped us to determine that the corrective move is not expected to go lower than the low at the beginning of wave 1. Only in exceptional cases did we consider bull traps and bear traps. With PHI-ellipses, however, we consider all sorts of 3-wave moves as long as we can put a PHI-ellipse around it (Figure 5.3).

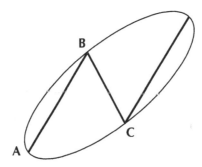

Figure 5.3   PHI-ellipse circumventing a 3-wave pattern. *Source: FAM Research, 2000.*

The 3-swing pattern in Figure 5.3 is an ideal picture of a price move, but, in reality, waves within a PHI-ellipse may have many different forms and magnitudes. As price action progresses, peaks and valleys may touch the outside of a PHI-ellipse several times without destroying the pattern.

We have analyzed and worked with PHI-ellipses for many years, and it has been fascinating to observe the different kinds of price action within PHI-ellipses. Based on the developing price action, PHI-ellipses might need to be adjusted, which is why it takes such discipline to work with PHI-ellipses as investment tools. But once an investor gets used to them, PHI-ellipses are amazing Fibonacci-related trading tools.

There is an indefinite variety of possibilities of price behavior within PHI-ellipses, and PHI-ellipses may be fatter or thinner, longer or shorter, according to the appropriate ratio for drawing a PHI-ellipse chosen from the PHI series. (See Figure 5.1 for a recap.) But these facts should not worry investors too much; price action itself shows up before the final structure of the PHI-ellipse. Tremendous patience and flexibility are required of the investor, for he or she must wait until market pricing reaches the end of the PHI-ellipse. However, the dynamism and flexibility of PHI-ellipses can also be an investor's strength because no other investment tool available can graphically make price patterns as visible.

It is highly probable, but not guaranteed, that the end of a PHI-ellipse will ever be reached. If the final point of a PHI-ellipse is not reached and market pricing leaves the borders of the PHI-ellipse prior to the end, then we have to reevaluate price action and start looking for the next PHI-ellipse to unfold (Figure 5.4).

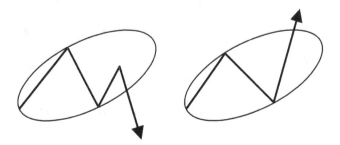

Figure 5.4   Price moves not reaching the final points of PHI-ellipses. *Source: FAM Research,* 2000.

We cannot define a standard PHI-ellipse that suits every product. To work properly with PHI-ellipses as investment tools, we must identify the minimum length and the minimum thickness of relevant PHI-ellipses for every single product, because every product we trade has its own characteristic price behavior. This price behavior expresses itself in typical price patterns that can only be identified on the basis of historical charts.

For the six Fibonacci tools explained in this book, the WINPHI software package is designed to test all the historical data. It would not be enough to analyze just any kind of historical data. It is important that the historical data be analyzed with one and the same price scale. Only when the price scale over the test period does not change can a PHI-ellipse that is specific for a certain product be identified. This has to be done by hand, of course, with the aid of the graphics capabilities of a computer.

When a typical PHI-ellipse for any given product is identified in its length and thickness over 10 years or more with a constant price scale, there is a high probability that this PHI-ellipse can be used as an effective investment tool by a skillful, disciplined, and patient investor.

Working with a PHI-ellipse tells us where we are in the market price action at any point in time. Whenever a market trend reverses at the end of a PHI-ellipse, we can take the final point of an old PHI-ellipse as the beginning of a new PHI-ellipse (Figure 5.5).

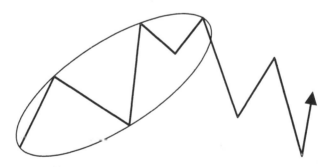

Figure 5.5   Attaching PHI-ellipses. *Source: FAM Research, 2000.*

Often, when cases of price patterns are reaching the end of PHI-ellipses, we see new PHI-ellipses immediately starting to develop. This occurs especially when PHI-ellipses have a steep angle upward or downward. Because PHI-ellipses work best as countertrend investment tools, sideward markets with high volatility and big price swings provide the most favorable price patterns.

Whenever market price action moves out of a PHI-ellipse before the final point of the PHI-ellipse is reached, either to the upside or to the downside, we can assume that we are at the beginning of a new market price pattern that might fit into a new PHI-ellipse. In addition to attaching PHI-ellipses, we may find situations of overlapping PHI-ellipses (Figure 5.6).

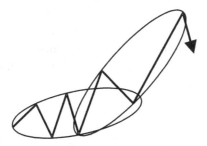

Figure 5.6   Overlapping PHI-ellipses. *Source: FAM Research,* 2000.

The slope of a PHI-ellipse is another parameter that must not be underestimated. It is this slope that first determines the profit potential of countertrend trading signals (Figure 5.7).

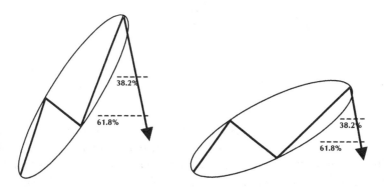

Figure 5.7   Profit potential based on the slope of PHI-ellipses. *Source: FAM Research,* 2000.

In many cases, the slope of a PHI-ellipse is small, as can be expected in sideward markets. In these cases, it is probable that the beginning of a new PHI-ellipse and the end of an old PHI-ellipse will overlap, as was shown in Figure 5.6.

Monitoring the slope of a PHI-ellipse is important. Just as countertrend moves at the end of extensions were described in Chapter 3, we expect retracements of 38.2% or 61.8% at the points of major trend changes in the markets will go back in the direction of the initial impulse wave. The steeper a PHI-ellipse develops, the larger the distance becomes from wave 1 to the final point of the PHI-ellipse. The greater the distance becomes from wave 1 to the final point of the PHI-ellipse, the larger the profit potential in points on 38.2% or 61.8% retracements to this distance.

PHI-ellipses may not only circumvent chart patterns in an actual or short-term trend but may also circumvent the bigger picture in the long-term perspective, which might include a couple of smaller trend changes (Figure 5.8).

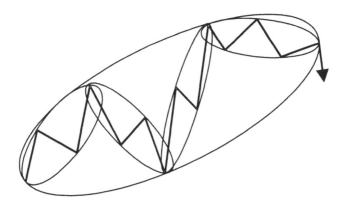

Figure 5.8 Long-term PHI-ellipse circumventing shorter-term PHI-ellipses. *Source: FAM Research, 2000.*

The use of PHI-ellipses requires that price moves be consistently monitored, and this turns out to be a minor problem on weekly and daily data. On intraday data, there will be a lot of pressure to identify and to wait for the end of a PHI-ellipse. Therefore, PHI-ellipses on an intraday basis have to be handled with care and can be recommended only for experienced Fibonacci traders.

Simultaneous analysis of the same product on weekly and on daily data is often very beneficial to the outcome of the analysis. For instance, recognizing a PHI-ellipse with a strong uptrend from weekly data will help to identify the correct trading signals based on daily data.

Figure 5.9 is an illustration of the latter notion.

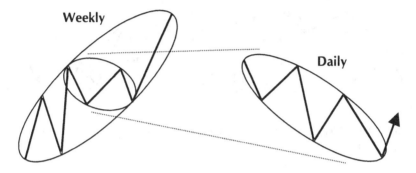

Figure 5.9   Simultaneous analysis on weekly and daily PHI-ellipses. *Source: FAM Research,* 2000.

Identifying the best average PHI-ellipse for any given product requires a software package like our WINPHI program, which allows investors to draw any PHI-ellipse desired on sets of historical data and on a constant price scale.

Once the PHI-ellipse for a particular product is identified, it can be applied to real-time trading. Identifying specific PHI-ellipses is like pattern recognition in the markets, although pattern recognition has an advantage in that stable price patterns detected on historical price moves have a chance of repeating and may become trading indicators for the future.

We have presented a solid overview on key features of PHI-ellipses, and we now proceed to trading strategies and sophisticated entry and exit rules.

Entry Rules and Exit Rules

The basic strategy for trading the markets using PHI-ellipses is: (1) wait for a price move to develop inside the borders of a PHI-ellipse, and (2) act counter to the main trend direction as soon as the end of the PHI-ellipse has been reached and market pricing leaves the PHI-ellipse.

Catching the rhythm of market moves by attaching PHI-ellipses and adding countertrend trades to each other is illustrated in Figure 5.10.

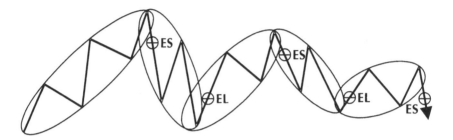

Figure 5.10   Basic scheme of investment using PHI-ellipses. *Source: FAM Research,* 2000.

Selling at the end of a PHI-ellipse is recommended when the PHI-ellipse has an upward slope. Buying at the end of a PHI-ellipse is recommended when the PHI-ellipse has a downward slope.

Trend reversals to the upside or to the downside at the end of a PHI-ellipse are confirmed by an entry rule that is set to the lowest low of the previous one, two, three, or four days for sell signals, and the highest high of the previous one, two, three, or four days for buy signals (Figure 5.11). The choice of an entry rule depends on the risk preference of the investor and how early an investor wants to be invested.

As soon as we are invested on a short position, we define a stop or a stop-reverse point at the highest high of a price bar within the

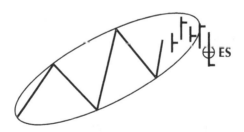

Figure 5.11   Four days' lowest low entry rule on PHI-ellipses. *Source: FAM Research,* 2000.

previous PHI-ellipse. In cases where we are invested long, we protect our position with a stop-loss set to the lowest low of a price bar with in the previous PHI-ellipse.

Figure 5.12 illustrates stop-loss protection on a short position.

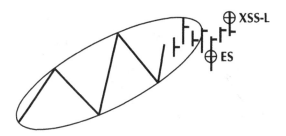

Figure 5.12   Stop-loss protection on a short position. *Source: FAM Research, 2000.*

For an alternative entry point, we may consider the trend channel that touches the relevant PHI-ellipse on either side (Figure 5.13).

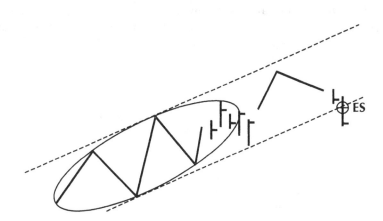

Figure 5.13   Short entry on a combination of PHI-ellipse and trend channel. *Source: FAM Research, 2000.*

By choosing the conservative option of a double confirmation by PHI-ellipse and trend channel, we accept that we might give up some of the profit potential that could have been realized by acting upon a more sensitive entry rule. On the other hand, we might avoid a number of losing trades in strong trending market conditions by staying in the trend channel as long as it lasts.

If the market price leaves the PHI-ellipse at the very end and immediately rises to new highs, we get a buy signal at the level of the highest high made within the PHI-ellipse (Figure 5.14). For sell signals, the correct entry point runs vice versa.

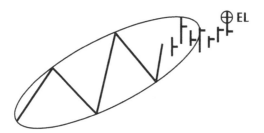

Figure 5.14   Long entry on a runaway market. *Source: FAM Research,* 2000.

The stop-loss or stop-reverse level on this type of buy signal is set to the lowest low of the previous three days. The count starts on the day when the market price reached the end of the PHI-ellipse (Figure 5.15). On sell signals on runaway markets, the stop-loss or stop-reverse level is set to the highest high of the last three trading days inside the PHI-ellipse.

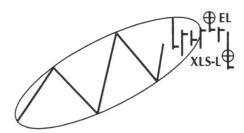

Figure 5.15   Stop protection on runaway long entry. *Source: FAM Research,* 2000.

If a market position is established and the market price moves in the anticipated direction, the investor must decide when to take profits. Several options are available: trailing stop exits, profit target exits, exits on extensions, time exits based on the Fibonacci summation series, and exits on the end of a PHI-ellipse.

The most conservative strategy is to work with a trailing stop set to the high of the previous four days on sells (vice versa on buy signals). In most cases, this option protects at least part of the profits, but it also means giving away open profits that have already accumulated (Figure 5.16).

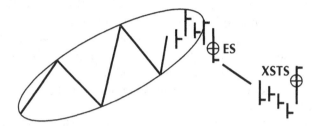

Figure 5.16 **Trailing stop exit on previous four days' high.** *Source: FAM Research,* **2000.**

If we do not want to give up any of our accumulated profits, we can take the risk that the market might move in the direction of our signal after we get stopped out in a profit. In this case, we should predefine a fixed profit target level to cover a position.

We select profit target levels that can be derived from the PHI series (introduced in Chapter 3). The levels we work with are 38.2%, 50.0%, and 61.8% of the total preceding market move, which is measured as the distance from bottom to top of the PHI-ellipse we generated our entry from (Figure 5.17).

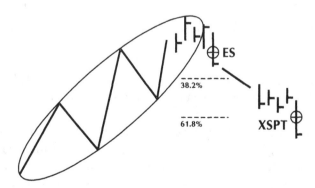

Figure 5.17 **Profit target levels at 38.2% and 61.8%.** *Source: FAM Research,* **2000.**

The profit target level that an investor favors depends not only on the risk preference of the investor, but also on the amplitude of the preceding PHI-ellipse.

If the initial move inside the PHI-ellipse is smaller than a sample of 200 ticks in the Japanese Yen cash currency (e.g., from 110.00 to 112.00), a larger profit target level of 61.8% is preferable. Otherwise, the profit potential is too small. On the other hand, if the total amplitude of the underlying move is 10 full points (e.g., from 110.00 to 120.00) in the Japanese Yen cash currency, a profit target level of 38.2% might be good enough for an investor to minimize risk.

In addition to trailing stop exits and profit target exits, we can wait for a 3-wave swing in the direction of our signal and an extension out of this 3-wave swing.

As explained in Chapter 3, we precalculate the size of an extension by multiplying the amplitude of wave 1 by the Fibonacci ratio 1.618. We liquidate a position as soon as the profit target level in the direction of our signal has been reached at 1.618 times the amplitude of wave 1 (Figure 5.18).

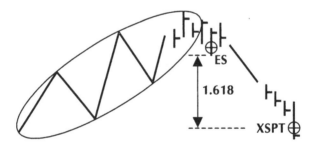

Figure 5.18 Profit target exit on an extension out of a 3-wave move. *Source: FAM Research,* 2000.

Price targets are one solid way of exiting positions, but we can also define targets in time as a means of protecting accumulated gains.

To establish the average standard length of PHI-ellipses on any product with regard to numbers of the Fibonacci summation series, we can use historical data, along with a constant scale supplied by the WINPHI software, and conduct test runs. If we then find out, for a certain product, that the average length of PHI-ellipses is 21 days, we can exit positions that have not been stopped out after 21 days (given that they trade in a profit). The total move in the direction of our signal might continue, but we are content with the profit that we have realized on the basis of the Fibonacci count. Two additional conditions are: (1) there has to be at least one 3-wave move within the 21 days, and (2) the price move must stay within the shape of a PHI-ellipse (Figure 5.19).

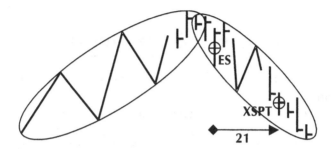

Figure 5.19 Profit target exit on Fibonacci count of 21 days. *Source: FAM Research,* 2000.

If the price move on our established position follows the shape of a PHI-ellipse, a fifth exit rule must be considered: We can wait until the market price reaches the end of the new PHI-ellipse and exit the position at the end of the PHI-ellipse. This exit rule requires the most patience and the strongest discipline, but it takes advantage of the biggest profit potential of all five exit rules in our analysis of PHI-ellipses. Figure 5.20 illustrates how to exit a position on the end of a PHI-ellipse.

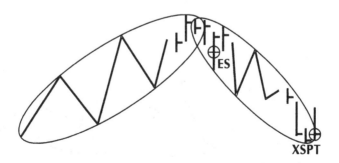

Figure 5.20 Profit target exit on the end of a PHI-ellipse. *Source: FAM Research,* 2000.

Attaching PHI-ellipses, as explained in the last of the five exit rules, is the perfect approach to catching the rhythm of markets, but market rhythms are not always ideal and perfect.

Now that we have presented the basic features of PHI-ellipses and the basic parameters of how to use PHI-ellipses for trading, we will show how to work with PHI-ellipses as geometrical Fibonacci trading tools.

WORKING WITH PHI-ELLIPSES

Working with PHI-ellipses is easy if we understand the rationale behind them.

PHI-ellipses develop over time. The magic of PHI-ellipses is that the perfect form exists inherently from the beginning, but, as users and investors, we only recognize the final form of PHI-ellipses at their very end. Although all PHI-ellipses share a common key-structure, final forms of PHI-ellipses vary, becoming thick or thin, long or short. They are individual manifestations of smaller trend moves, or part of the bigger picture of a circumventing major trend.

The slope of a PHI-ellipse is determined by the high in downtrends and the low in uptrends of the correction wave 2 in our wave count. Considering that we always need three points to be able to draw the first picture of a PHI-ellipse, we then have two possibilities. In the first case, the low of the correction in wave 2 in an uptrend is above the bottom of wave 1 (vice versa for highs instead of lows in downtrends). Depending on whether we have a 38.2%, 50.0%, or 61.8% correction, the slope of a PHI-ellipse will be bigger or smaller (Figure 5.21).

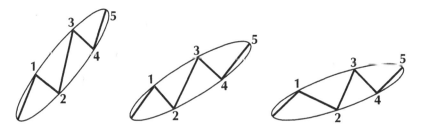

Figure 5.21 Slope of PHI-ellipses upward in relation to correction levels. *Source: FAM Research, 2000.*

The second possibility is that the correction wave 2 goes below (or above) the starting point of wave 1 in an uptrend (or downtrend). In this case, the slope of a PHI-ellipse could turn out very small. A small PHI-ellipse slope indicates a sideward market (Figure 5.22).

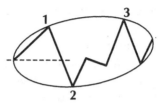

Figure 5.22 **Slope of a PHI-ellipse as an indicator of a sideward market.** *Source: FAM Research,* **2000.**

PHI-ellipses work on monthly, weekly, and daily charts, and those are the data compression rates on which we have conducted our analysis. When it comes to intraday charts, PHI-ellipses will also work on hourly charts. However, to avoid complicating the analysis at this point, we refrain from integrating PHI-ellipses on sets of intraday data into our analysis, and we defer the description of intraday samples until Chapter 8.

The length of the correction in wave 2 after the first impulse wave often determines the length of a PHI-ellipse. We cannot know in advance how long the formation of wave 2 will last, however, so we do not recommend trading as long as the formation of a PHI-ellipse is in progress.

Wave 3, the second impulse wave in our count, has to be at least as long as the first impulse wave. Therefore, we have to adjust the width of PHI-ellipses on multiple sideward patterns (Figure 5.23).

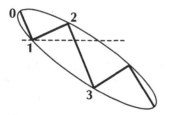 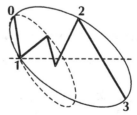

Figure 5.23 **Adjustment of PHI-ellipses based on the duration of corrections.** *Source: FAM Research,* **2000.**

We now focus our analysis on sets of daily charts of the Japanese Yen cash currency and the S&P500 Index. As mentioned in earlier chapters, we have selected these products for reasons of public interest, volatility, and liquidity, and because they especially represent investors' behavior, which is the underlying maxim of our entire Fibonacci analysis. PHI-ellipses, in principle, can be applied to every product traded.

We rely on only an eight-month time span for each of the two products, during which no one PHI-ellipse is like any other. This is similar to the work we have done with extensions and corrections. Even though we apply the ratio 1.618 to different price moves, the size of every price move results in the precalculation of different price targets. The same result occurs when we work with PHI-ellipses. We do not analyze a single swing pattern, but rather, a complete set of swings, smaller ones and bigger ones. Therefore, a major PHI-ellipse will circumvent the complete (and much bigger) price pattern—sometimes with many and sometimes with very few smaller price patterns in between.

PHI-ellipses have their roots in the Fibonacci ratio PHI and the ratios from the PHI series. We can combine PHI-ellipses with other Fibonacci tools, such as the Fibonacci summation series, extensions, and corrections. Doing so allows us to get an early indication of where a PHI-ellipse might end. Because PHI-ellipses develop over time, the combination of Fibonacci tools is helpful in confirming multiple PHI-ellipses in progress. Based on the knowledge we accumulated from the analysis of extensions using the Fibonacci ratio 1.618, we can precalculate a price target from the amplitude of the first impulse wave inside the PHI-ellipse. Independent of any future market move patterns, we can assume that if the market price ever reaches the precalculated price target, it might also mean the end of the progressing PHI-ellipse in price and time.

PHI-Ellipses on Japanese Yen Cash Currency Sample Data

To get started with our applications of PHI-ellipses to market data, Figure 5.24 first shows a plain daily chart of the Japanese Yen cash currency with no added tools. The chart represents just the data stream. Beginning with the plain picture enables an analyst to get a notion of how PHI-ellipses will later fit into the overall picture. The set of O–H–L–C data is contrasted in the second chart of Figure 5.24.

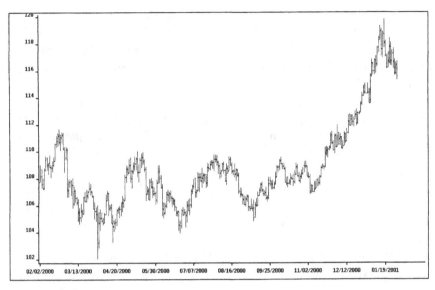

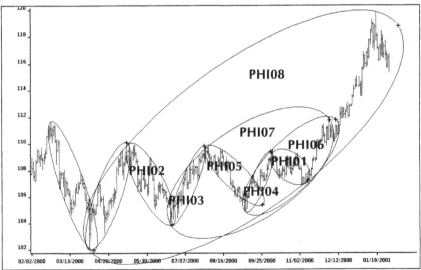

Figure 5.24 Chart of the Japanese Yen cash currency from 02–00 to 02–01.
Plain O-H-L-C price move and price move with PHI-ellipses PHI01 to PHI08.
Source: FAM Research, 2000.

The integrated PHI-ellipses serve as the backbone of our analysis of the relevant market moves (Figure 5.24). Note that the relevant PHI-ellipses have been numbered PHI01 to PHI08. We will refer, consecutively, to all eight PHI-ellipses and demonstrate, in depth, how they were generated.

The basic structure of PHI-ellipses is always the same. To properly draw a PHI-ellipse, at least four points must be defined and touched by the borders of the PHI-ellipse. The four points are: (a) starting point; (b) left side; (c) right side; (d) bottom of the PHI-ellipse.

The starting point is usually the highest or lowest point in a price move. But there are exceptions in patterns such as: (a) irregular tops or bottoms; (b) overlapping PHI-ellipses; or (c) very small angles in a PHI-ellipse.

PHI-ellipse PHI01 (isolated in Figure 5.24) consists of a simple 3-wave pattern, which should be familiar to readers who have dealt with 3-wave patterns on various earlier occasions (Figure 5.25).

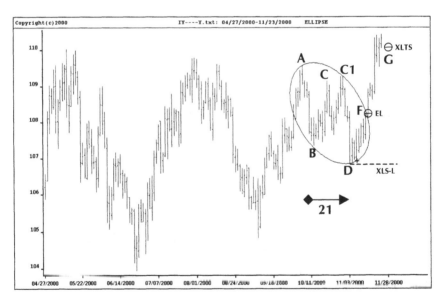

Figure 5.25   Chart of the Japanese Yen cash currency from 04–00 to 11–00. PHI-ellipse PHI01. *Source: FAM Research,* 2000.

The starting point in PHI-ellipse PHI01 is A, and the first of the two side points is B. We can already draw a PHI-ellipse through the peak at point C, but, to complete a PHI-ellipse in a 3-wave pattern, the third wave has to go lower than B. The price move does not go lower than B after C is reached. Instead, it makes a higher high than C, and the side point is changed from C to C1. This may happen at any time when we work with PHI-ellipses.

From C1, the price move goes quickly to point D. However, at valley D, we do not know whether this is the low to watch, for even though we can already draw the PHI-ellipse through point D in its final form, we have to wait for the market price to go outside the PHI-ellipse at point F.

Our Fibonacci count can be used as an additional indicator to distinguish whether point D is actually a significant low point. Valley D occurs one day after number 21 of the Fibonacci summation series (the count begins when starting point A has been reached). 21 is a very important Fibonacci count that is always worth checking.

At point F, where the market price move leaves PHI-ellipse PHI01, a trading signal is generated and executed based on the following three parameters:

1. Entry market as soon as the border of PHI-ellipse PHI01 is broken. No further entry rules apply because the entry level is already far above the previous four days' high.

2. Stop-loss protection set to the valley at point D, which is the lowest low inside PHI-ellipse PHI01.

3. Trailing stop to protect profits, defined as a breakout of a previous four days' low. The trailing stop formation is triggered at point G.

The simple PHI-ellipse PHI01 is a convincing example of how successful trading signals can be derived straight from the core application of PHI-ellipses. From this basic example, we can proceed to much more complex formations that are also subject to analysis on the basis of PHI-ellipses.

PHI-ellipse PHI02 has a form that is much thinner and longer than PHI01. The reason for this shape difference is that the price pattern is a 5-wave move, not a 3-wave move. The first swing—A to B and back to C—is established quickly, but a PHI-ellipse drawn around these swings has no stability at all. After the following waves to the valley at point D and the peak at point E have established side points

that determine the final shape of PHI-ellipse PHI02, we will be able
to correctly draw PHI-ellipse PHI02 to generate a trading signal (Figure 5.26).

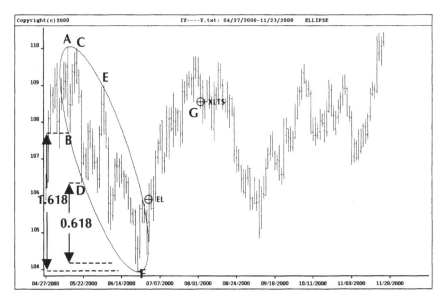

Figure 5.26   Chart of the Japanese Yen cash currency from 04–00 to 11–00.
PHI-ellipse PHI02. *Source: FAM Research,* 2000.

In addition to the shape of PHI02, it is very important to measure the underlying 5-wave swing based on extensions of wave 1 and
wave 3. The amplitude of wave 1 multiplied by the ratio 1.618, and the
amplitude of wave 3 multiplied by the ratio 0.618, point closely to valley F, which then marks the final point of PHI02. (Readers who get
confused here can refer to Chapter 3 for a recap on extensions in
5-wave patterns.)

The day of the lowest low is day 32 (counted from the high of the
first impulse wave of the price move at point A), and that number is
too close to the Fibonacci count of 34 to be ignored. The turning point
in the Japanese Yen cash currency market just below 104.00 JPY is
confirmed through four different methods: (1) the Elliott 5-wave
count; (2) the ratio 1.618 on wave 1; (3) the ratio 0.618 on wave 3; and
(4) PHI-ellipse PHI02. Here, aggressive investors find four good reasons to immediately buy US Dollars and sell Japanese Yen at a level

of 104.00. More conservative investors, however, should wait to get the final confirmation at the point where the market price moves out of the sideline of PHI02. The second approach leads to the following trading outcome:

- Entry on a breakout of a previous four days' high after PHI02 is left by the price move.

- Stop-loss protection set to the valley at point F, which is the lowest low inside PHI-ellipse PHI02.

- Trailing stop to protect profits, defined as a breakout of a previous four days' low. The trailing stop formation is triggered at point G.

As mentioned earlier, a minimum width is required in order to properly work with PHI-ellipses as trading tools. The smaller PHI-ellipses become, the higher the ratios from the PHI series have to be to draw PHI-ellipses around price moves. PHI-ellipse PHI03 is a typical example of a very narrow PHI-ellipse (Figure 5.27).

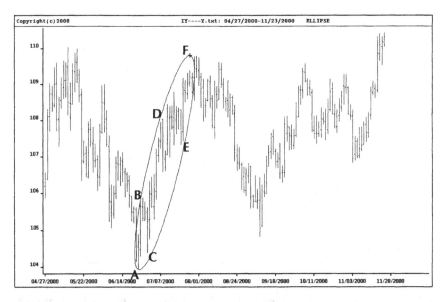

Figure 5.27 Chart of the Japanese Yen cash currency from 04–00 to 11–00. PHI-ellipse PHI03. *Source: FAM Research,* 2000.

Analyzing the 3-wave move from A to B and back to C (Figure 5.27), we find that it takes only five days to complete the entire swing before the market price accelerates sharply above the significant peak at point B of the swing.

Although PHI03 can be drawn after the side points D and E are established, we do not invest in such PHI-ellipses because the width is too narrow. PHI03 is drawn at a ratio 46.979 from the PHI series. This ratio is far beyond the limit of a ratio 17.944, which we consider to be the highest ratio from the PHI series that is appropriate for an application to PHI-ellipses (see Figure 5.1 for a recap).

The same holds true for PHI-ellipse PHI04, which is drawn at ratio 29.034 from the PHI series. (PHI-ellipse PHI04 is part of the overall picture in Figure 5.24.)

The first four examples were selected to introduce readers to trading decisions based on PHI-ellipses. PHI-ellipse PHI05 is now presented to show why trading decisions are not always easy. Various options exist on the entry side as well as on the exit side (Figure 5.28).

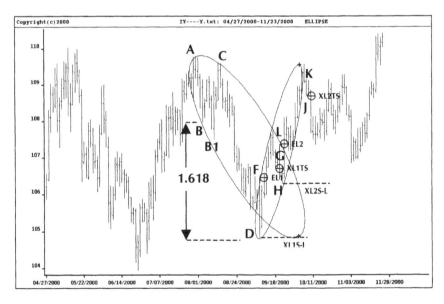

Figure 5.28 Chart of the Japanese Yen cash currency from 04–00 to 11–00. PHI-ellipse PHI05 (combined with PHI-ellipse PHI04 for the exit rule). *Source: FAM Research,* **2000.**

PHI-ellipse PHI05 begins with a strong first wave from the starting point A to point B. Point C becomes the second side point of PHI05 as soon as the market price moves lower than point B. The third wave of the price move goes very quickly from point C to point D (the end of the price move). Market pricing reverses at point D for two possible reasons:

1. Point D does not go lower than the bottom of the PHI-ellipse.

2. Point D is almost exactly the price target of the extension calculated from impulse wave 1, which goes from point A to point B.

Even though point D is confirmed by multiple Fibonacci tools, we need a confirmation of a trend reversal in order to invest. Two options exist for a buy signal. The first option has the following parameters:

• No waiting for PHI05 to be broken to the right side, and entry to the market on a breakout of a previous four days' high. This entry rule is filled at point F in Figure 5.28.

• Stop-loss protection, set to the valley at point D.

• Trailing stop, to protect profits defined as a breakout of a previous four days' low. The trailing stop formation is triggered at point G.

The second option for entering the Japanese Yen cash currency market long works with a different set of parameters:

• Initial buy when the sideline of PHI05 is broken at point L, which is also higher than the previous four days' high.

• Stop-loss protection, set to the swing low at point H.

• Trailing stop, to protect profits defined as a breakout of a previous four days' low. The trailing stop formation is triggered at point J.

Using the second option, we can close out the position by combining PHI-ellipse PHI05 with PHI-ellipse PHI04—the one we do not consider on the entry side because it is drawn at too high a ratio from the PHI series. We exit our position at point K (Figure 5.28) when the market price breaks through the sideline of PHI-ellipse PHI04.

PHI-ellipse PHI06 is an example of capturing a medium-term 3-wave uptrend over three months and generating a short signal from it (Figure 5.29).

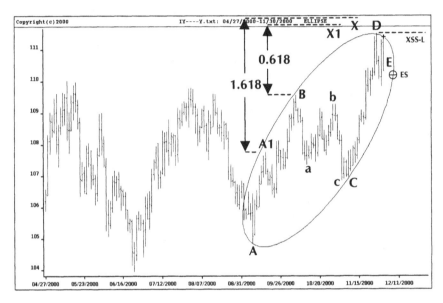

Figure 5.29   Chart of the Japanese Yen cash currency from 04–00 to 11–00. PHI-ellipse PHI06. *Source: FAM Research,* 2000.

PHI-ellipse PHI06 is based on the symmetrical price move from point A to points B, C, and D. The 3-wave swing has an a–b–c correction in wave 2, which, at the same time, gives shape to PHI-ellipse PHI01 (see Figure 5.25).

Our basic investment decision is countertrend at point D. The trend reversal at point D is confirmed by two price goals, X and X1. We reach goal X by multiplying the amplitude of the price move from A to A1 by the Fibonacci ratio 1.618. Price goal X1 is defined by multiplying the amplitude of the market move from point A to point B by the ratio 0.618. Both price targets, X and X1, are close enough together to lead to strong resistance at these price levels and a high probability of a trend reversal as soon the target prices are triggered on the uptrend.

To invest on PHI06, we have two more options. The relevant factors of the first option are:

- Immediate entry short at point D on a previous four days' low, due to the confirmation of the trend reversal by the price goals X and X1, even if the PHI-ellipse PHI06 has not been broken. The entry rule is filled at point E.

- Stop-loss protection set to the highest high at point D.

- Trailing stop to protect profits defined as a breakout of a previous four days' high as long as the short position has not been stopped out in a loss.

- Definition of profit target levels at 38.2%, 50.0%, and 61.8% of the distance measured from points A to D alternatively to the trailing stop-exit rule.

The second option runs a little differently and delays the entry. This happens because we wait conservatively for the final point of PHI06. We use the following set of parameters:

- Entry short on a previous four days' low after the market move left PHI06.

- Stop-loss protection set to the highest high inside PHI06.

- Trailing stop to protect profits, defined as a breakout of a previous four days' high as long as the short position has not been stopped out in a loss.

- Definition of profit target levels at 38.2%, 50.0%, and 61.8% of the distance measured from points A to D alternatively to the trailing stop-exit rule.

The risk preference of investors determines whether an entry on the double confirmation of the trend reversal by two Fibonacci extensions is solid, or whether sticking with the overall rule of first waiting for the final point of PHI-ellipse PHI06 remains preferable.

With PHI-ellipse PHI07, the perspective once again broadens and shifts from midterm analysis to long-term analysis.

PHI-ellipse PHI07 is a splendid example of how pattern recognition can be used for the short term, midterm, and long term, and how different patterns can be identified with PHI-ellipses. Investors' behavior is expressed in both small and big patterns, but, in the end, all are integrated into the same picture (Figure 5.30).

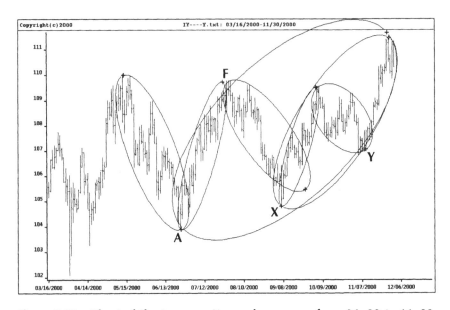

Figure 5.30 Chart of the Japanese Yen cash currency from 04–00 to 11–00. PHI-ellipse PHI07. *Source: FAM Research, 2000.*

PHI-ellipse PHI07 circumvents five of the six PHI-ellipses so far discussed in this section. Only PHI-ellipse PHI02 is not circumvented by PHI-ellipse PHI07.

We have pointed out, several times, that PHI-ellipses develop over time, and it is important to be patient and wait for the total picture to reveal itself. The first critical point in the development of PHI-ellipse PHI07 is point X—the side point of the 3-wave pattern from A to F and back down to X (Figure 5.30). Side point X changes to side point Y at the same moment that PHI-ellipse PHI01 reaches its final point. The final shape of PHI-ellipse PHI07 is realized by the change in side points from X to Y and by when the final point of PHI-ellipse PHI06 is reached and merges with the final point of PHI-ellipse PHI07.

Such a phenomenon does not happen too often and is only documented in a long-term analysis with multiple PHI-ellipses. Our findings demonstrate how important it is to combine the short-term and long-term perspectives of investment strategies. The beauty of Fibonacci trading tools is that they work perfectly together.

According to the general investment rules on PHI-ellipses, the final points of PHI06 and PHI07 provided opportunities for establishing a short position. However, we found that the market in Japanese Yen cash currency did not go lower, as assumed. It went higher (Figure 5.31).

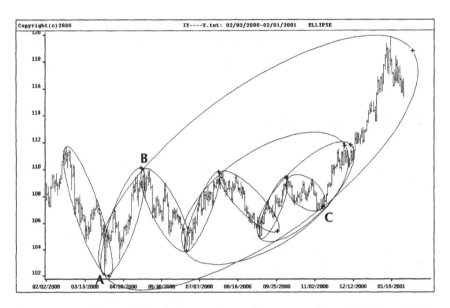

Figure 5.31 Chart of the Japanese Yen cash currency from 02–00 to 02–01. PHI-ellipse PHI08. *Source: FAM Research,* 2000.

An exceptional pattern like the one in Figure 5.31 does not show up very often. It confirms that the end of a PHI-ellipse is an indication of either a trend change in the opposite direction or a breakout in the main trend direction.

In most cases, the market price reverses at the final point of a PHI-ellipse. But the long-term picture in the Japanese Yen cash currency reveals that after selling short at the end of PHI-ellipse PHI06 (or PHI07) and getting stopped out of the short position, it is wise to reverse the position to the long side. There is enough trading potential on the upside, represented by PHI-ellipse PHI08, which is well established and defined by the starting point A and the side points B and C in Figure 5.31.

Examples like the short trades on PHI-ellipses PHI06 and PHI07 make it clear that Fibonacci tools are ordinary trading tools. This means that even on the best looking patterns, trades might yield losses. As long as traders work with a solid stop-loss rule, any harm done by losing trades remains under control. To increase the profitability of investments, we recommend combinations of different Fibonacci trading tools (described in Chapter 8).

Before proceeding with examples of PHI-ellipses on the S&P500 Index, we want to draw readers' attention to the problem of constant scaling when charting data and then applying PHI-ellipses to the charts.

PHI-Ellipses on Constant Scales in the Japanese Yen Cash Currency

It is very important to understand that PHI-ellipses work equally well on daily, weekly, and monthly charts.

Hourly charts are interesting for analysis of intraday data, for they show a very short-term picture. The problem with intraday charts is that entry rules, profit targets, and stop-loss rules may leave investors with a small profit potential. On the other hand, the overall risk (per trade) is limited on an intraday basis.

The risk level is one of the reasons we enjoy working with cash currencies on a daily basis. Cash currencies trade 24 hours a day without gap openings and other inconveniences that may dilute the performance profile.

Long-term historical test runs are necessary to judge the quality of PHI-ellipses for products to be traded. A feature that plots historical data to charts with a constant price scale has already been integrated into the WINPHI software. Two or three years' daily O–H–L–C data are impossible to plot within the width of one screen, and when scrolling the screen, the price scale usually varies according to the highest high and the lowest low of the data being plotted. The WINPHI constant scale feature is a key element because scaling to screen height would otherwise result in distortion of the angles of PHI-ellipses applied to market moves.

We have analyzed more than two years' data of the Japanese Yen cash currency daily bar, from September 1998 to December 2000, and have tested PHI-ellipses historically backward.

The total stream of data over 27 months is divided into two charts in Figure 5.32. By choosing a set of appropriate PHI-ellipses and waiting for market pricing to move out of the PHI-ellipses at their final points, our sample investments follow, with very few exceptions, the price pattern in the Japanese Yen cash currency.

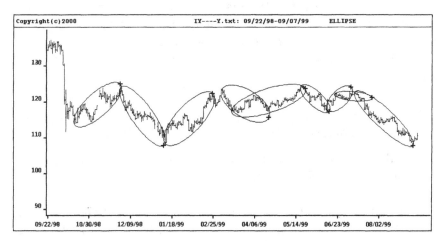

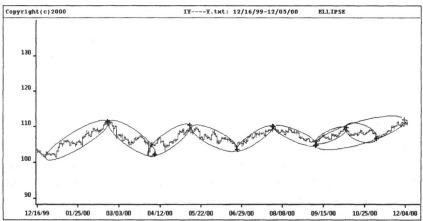

Figure 5.32   Chart of the Japanese Yen cash currency from 09–98 to 12–00. Attached and overlapping PHI-ellipses on a constant scale. *Source: FAM Research,* 2000.

Working with a constant scale feature is the only way to achieve this kind of undistorted picture over such a long period of time.

It is often difficult to believe in the power of the PHI-ellipse. Trading with PHI-ellipses on daily data generates about one trade per month, depending on whether inside PHI-ellipses are found. The pattern of inside PHI-ellipses can be seen in the time period from September 2000 to December 2000 in Figure 5.32, where three smaller PHI-ellipses are contained within one bigger PHI-ellipse.

When we look at the charts, we realize it is necessary to adjust PHI-ellipses dynamically to match market price action. PHI-ellipses are unique; not one PHI-ellipse is exactly like another, even though the shape is always the same. Therefore, working with PHI-ellipses as trading tools is both unique and fascinating.

All PHI-ellipses in our sample calculation have certain elements in common:

1. Both sides of all PHI-ellipses are touched, at least once, during a price move, so there is always a 3-wave pattern.

2. All PHI-ellipses are at least 21 days long and are drawn at a ratio smaller than 17.944 from the PHI series.

In addition, most PHI-ellipses start at the end of the preceding PHI-ellipse. Only in exceptional cases (for example, April 1999 in Figure 5.32), will a PHI-ellipse start when the previous PHI-ellipse is only half finished.

Keeping in mind constant scales and the long-term picture of market price patterns, we can now move to the second sample: the S&P500 Index.

PHI-Ellipses on S&P500 Index Sample Data

The S&P500 Index is the most closely followed and most heavily traded index in the world. It is used not only by large and small traders, but also by hedge funds, to reduce drawdown risk in stock portfolios. The Vanguard S&P500 Index Fund, which has about USD 100 billion under management, is the biggest mutual fund worldwide.

Many analysts and investors believe that the S&P500 Index reflects such an efficient market that trading is not possible in this product anymore. We disagree on this point and will prove why in this section. If PHI-ellipses are reliable trading tools, we propose that they must be able to capture the erratic moves in the S&P500 Index as well as in any other product.

In our opinion, the S&P500 Index suits Fibonacci devices well because investors' behavior is best expressed in this liquid and volatile trading vehicle.

We analyzed two years' S&P500 Index future data, from January 1999 to December 2000. Just as with the analysis of the Japanese Yen cash currency, this is a very short time span. The signals we present herein do not necessarily work as well in other time periods, but they are excellent indicators of what is possible in market analysis on the basis of PHI-ellipses. In addition, more than 10 years' historical data are included with the WINPHI software so that every interested investor can conduct a more detailed self-analysis.

The signals we show might not be the most perfect ones. We try to be consistent in our analysis, which means applying Fibonacci tools all the time, in the same way. Because our signals need to be generated by hand, we might overlook a trading signal or might not apply signals in the most perfect way.

Herein lies a great challenge for every interested and skillful investor. Fibonacci tools are perfect but, as analysts, we might not apply them correctly. Other than Elliott with his wave principles (which rely only on the wave count and the ratios 0.618, 1.000, and 1.618 from the PHI series), we have the chance to introduce previously unknown trading devices—unknown not only to Elliott, but, until now, also unknown to the broader investment community.

We are often asked: Why do we publish our Fibonacci trading tools if they are perfect? First, it would be difficult to fully automate the tools if room was left for interpretation. Second, the worldwide marketplace is so gigantic that no matter what we do, or whatever other traders in our environment do, we will never seriously interfere with each other. In fact, the more investors utilize our strategies, the better investors' behavior finds expression in market patterns, and thus, the better our Fibonacci tools are traded.

January 1999 to December 2000 was probably the most difficult period ever, for analysis of the S&P500 Index. Never before had any stock index gone through a period of such volatility. However, this environment was perfect for working with Fibonacci devices, because volatility is needed to apply these tools successfully.

We conducted our analysis in the same way as we did for the Japanese Yen cash currency. We first showed a plain daily chart of the S&P500 Index to familiarize readers with the overall market pattern. The 11 PHI-ellipses that can be drawn to this price pattern were represented on a second chart (Figure 5.33).

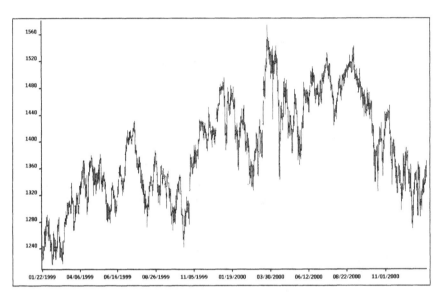

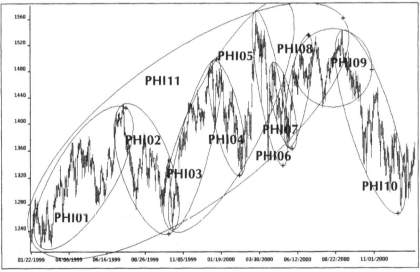

Figure 5.33   Chart of the S&P500 Index from 01–99 to 01–01. Plain daily O-H-L-C price move (top chart) and price move with PHI-ellipses PHI01 to PHI11 (lower chart). *Source: FAM Research, 2000.*

The relevant PHI-ellipses have been numbered PHI01 to PHI11 in Figure 5.33. We will refer to all 11 PHI-ellipses consecutively and demonstrate their generation one-by-one.

PHI-ellipse PHI01 covers the trend move (from around 1,220.00 up to 1,430.00) in the S&P500 Index between January and July 1999 (Figure 5.34).

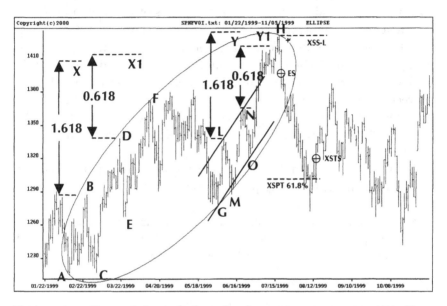

Figure 5.34   Chart of the S&P500 Index from 01–99 to 11–99. PHI-ellipse PHI01. *Source: FAM Research,* 2000.

We generally look for the end of a PHI-ellipse to receive a countertrend entry signal.

The first indication of the possible end of a PHI-ellipse is established with the 5-wave price move from A to B to C to D to E to F. The price goals X and X1, calculated as extensions at ratios 1.618 and 0.618, are not reached at point F. Instead, the market moves into a sideward pattern and corrects back to point G.

We do not want to break down the wave count any further, but another almost perfect 5-wave price pattern starts at point G (below point L) and moves to points M, N, and O. Again, we can project two price targets, Y and Y1, at ratios 1.618 and 0.618, based on the waves from point G to point L, and from point M to point N. These price targets are very close to the previously calculated targets X and X1.

When the market price is in its second 5-wave move, we have the necessary side points F and G for PHI-ellipse PHI01 to project the final point H.

The final point H of PHI-ellipse PHI01 will be a very powerful price target, should the market ever reach it. Point H is confirmed by a regular trend channel, which is drawn as parallels through the valleys at points G and O, and through the peaks at points L and N.

Readers were introduced to regular trend channels in Chapter 4. Trend channels as Fibonacci trading tools can now be integrated into our application of PHI-ellipses. Because the S&P500 Index is so widely referred to by traders, our trend channel analysis is worth considering. We receive an additional confirmation of the trend reversal at H, the final point of PHI-ellipse PHI01. This final point is now confirmed by four price targets—X, X1, Y, and Y1—as well as by the regular trend channel.

As soon as the final point of PHI-ellipse PHI01 is reached, we trade based on the following parameters:

- Immediate entry short on a previous two days' low when point H is triggered, because point H has multiple confirmation by a set of price targets and a regular trend channel.

- Stop-loss protection, set to the highest high before entry.

- Trailing stop, to protect profits defined as a breakout of a previous four days' high.

- Definition of a profit target exit level—61.8% of the total distance, measured from points A to H alternatively to the trailing stop exit rule.

- Because PHI-ellipses often follow each other and can be attached—as we saw in previous examples—another possible exit rule for the signal derived from PHI-ellipse PHI01 (in addition to the trailing stop exit rule and the profit target exit rule) is to wait for the completion of a new PHI-ellipse to the downside that can be attached to PHI-ellipse PHI01.

PHI-ellipse PHI02 on the S&P500 Index is an example of an Elliott 3-wave correction The 3-wave correction is the dominating pattern inside the PHI-ellipse, and it structures the market move of the SP500 Index back to the downside (Figure 5.35).

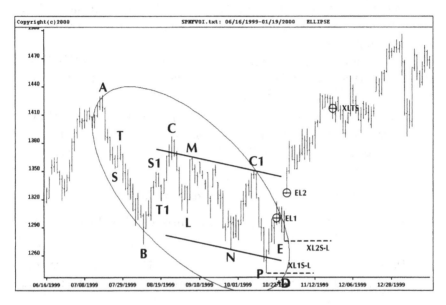

Figure 5.35   Chart of the S&P500 Index from 06–99 to 01–00. PHI-ellipse PHI02. *Source: FAM Research,* 2000.

Wave 1, from point A to point B, corrects in a 3-wave pattern consisting of points S, T, and B. Wave 2, from point B to point C, also corrects in a 3-wave pattern; this time, it consists of points S1, T1, and C. As we have learned from Elliott's wave principles, simple and complex waves alternate in impulse waves and corrections. Wave 3, from point C to point P, is a complex wave with a correction that runs in a 5-wave count from L to M to N to C1 to P.

A PHI-ellipse might be drawn after the two side points, B and C, are established from starting point A. But market pricing does not fall far enough from point M to form a regular bottom of a PHI-ellipse in N.

It is important to wait for market pricing to come very close to the bottom of any PHI-ellipse drawn with two side points established. Point N does not come close to the bottom of a PHI-ellipse drawn from point A through the side points at B and C. Therefore, we have to wait for the peak at C1 to turn out as a new—and final—second side point of PHI-ellipse PHI02.

By using side point C1, PHI02 becomes much shorter and fatter. The final point D of PHI02 is almost reached by the swing from point C1 to point P. Point D, in this respect, has multiple confirmation by a trend channel that runs from peak M to peak C1, with a parallel line drawn through the valley at point N.

Two trading signals can be generated, based on PHI-ellipse PHI02. The first trade runs according to the following parameters:

- Entry long on a previous four days' high breakout after valley P is established. The trend reversal is double confirmed by the final point of PHI02 at point D, and the end of a 5-wave move inside the trend channel at point P.

- Stop-loss protection, set to the lowest low before entry at point P.

- Trailing stop, to protect profits defined as a breakout of a previous four days' low.

- Definition of a profit target exit level—61.8% of the total distance, measured from points A to P alternatively to the trailing stop exit rule.

If there are not at least two combinations of different Fibonacci trading tools to confirm a trend reversal, we must wait until the sideline of a PHI-ellipse is broken. In retrospect, it is always easy to know what would have been the correct decision. Waiting for a breakout of a sideline of a PHI-ellipse is not necessarily the perfect decision, but we strive for a good average entry point because there is no way of always knowing the best turning point in advance.

The second trading signal on a breakout of the sideline of PHI02 is based on a different set of parameters:

- Entry long market on opening after the S&P500 Index moves out of PHI02. This entry point is late, but still profitable.

- Stop-loss protection, set to the valley before entry at point E.

- Trailing stop, to protect profits defined as a breakout of a previous four days' low.

- Alternative exit rule on the final point of PHI-ellipse PHI03, which can be attached to PHI-ellipse PHI02. (PHI-ellipse PHI03 will be described next.)

Working with the S&P500 Index means a large profit potential, but, at the same time, an increased risk on positions. Because of the high volatility in the S&P500 Index, we must not work with too close a stop. We must work with a stop-loss point just in case the market price is running against us. If the stop-loss level is defined too tight, however, the number of losing trades is increased drastically and certain strategies are no longer tradable.

A major problem for making investments profitable occurs when we come as close as possible to the turning points in trending markets. The farther away from turning points we define our market entries, the bigger the drawdown risk becomes on individual positions.

The risk preference of an investor and the amount of trust he or she puts in the investment tools will determine how far away from turning points in the markets the signal entry points finally are. All traders are emotionally involved in every trade they execute. Instinctively, traders will first look for a confirmation of a trading signal before they feel confident with a decision. This means that, in fast-moving markets, the initial move of a trend we want to catch is often already gone.

The whole concept behind using Fibonacci devices is to get closer to the turning points in the market action. If we achieve this aim, the risk of an entry position might still be high because the stop-loss can still be relatively far away, but the chances that we are not stopped out increase dramatically when we work with geometrical Fibonacci trading tools. This is the point where working with Fibonacci trading tools pays off handsomely.

PHI-ellipse PHI03 is an example of a market price move running in a narrow margin inside the PHI-ellipse to its very end, and then sharply breaking out.

The wave count of PHI-ellipse PHI03 does not seem difficult at first glance. We find a midterm 3-wave move to the upside from point A to B to C to D. The final point of PHI-ellipse PHI03 at point D is confirmed by two Fibonacci tools. The first confirmation stems from an extension, calculated at ratio 1.618 on the initial impulse wave from point A to point B. The second confirmation is established by a trend channel based on the two peaks at points L and N, and on a parallel line drawn through point M (Figure 5.36).

Figure 5.36   Chart of the S&P500 Index from 08–99 to 03–00. PHI-ellipse PHI03. *Source: FAM Research,* 2000.

A sample trading signal in the S&P500 Index, based on PHI-ellipse PHI03, can be generated as follows:

- Entry short on a previous four days' low breakout after the final point of PHI03 has multiple confirmation in point D.

- Stop-loss protection, set to the highest high before entry.

- Trailing stop, to protect profits defined as a breakout of a previous four days' high.

- Alternative exit rule on the final point of PHI-ellipse PHI04, which can be attached to PHI-ellipse PHI03.

PHI-ellipse PHI04, which was first introduced as a possible pattern exit for a short trade based on PHI-ellipse PHI03, can also be structured as circumventing a 5-wave move (Figure 5.37).

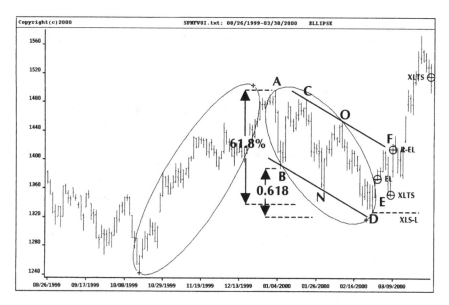

**Figure 5.37   Chart of the S&P500 Index from 08–99 to 03–00. PHI-ellipse
PHI04.** *Source: FAM Research,* 2000.

The side points of PHI-ellipse PHI04 are at B and O. The final
point of PHI04 is almost reached by the 5-wave price move.

Three Fibonacci tools confirm the end of the PHI04:

1. A trend channel is defined by the peaks at points C and O and a
   parallel drawn through the valley at point N. This parallel is almost triggered by the price move at point D.

2. The amplitude of the impulse move from point A to point B, multiplied by 0.618, defines a price target that is reached at point D.

3. PHI-ellipse PHI04 is a correction to the price move covered by
   the PHI-ellipse PHI03. This trend move to the upside is corrected
   at a level of 61.8% at point D, just above the final point of PHI04,
   when the market price reverses its trend direction to the upside
   again.

Tracing the market price move of the S&P500 Index that runs
inside PHI-ellipse PHI04 for more than two months, and considering

the final point of PHI-ellipse PHI04, we can generate a profitable trading signal based on a set of parameters consisting of an entry and a re-entry:

- Entry long on a previous four days' high breakout. The trend reversal has multiple confirmation by different Fibonacci tools, so it is not necessary to wait for a breakout of the sideline of PHI04.

- Stop-loss protection, set to the lowest low before entry at point D.

- Trailing stop rule on a breakout of a previous four days' low. The position is stopped out on a sell at point E in Figure 5.37.

- Re-entry long on a four days' high after being stopped out when the primary entry is confirmed by a correction level of 61.8%. (See Chapter 3 on corrections.) Trailing stop to protect profits set as a breakout of a previous four days' low.

Four examples have been presented in which countertrend moves are captured at the final point of a PHI-ellipse. PHI-ellipse PHI05 runs a little differently (Figure 5.38).

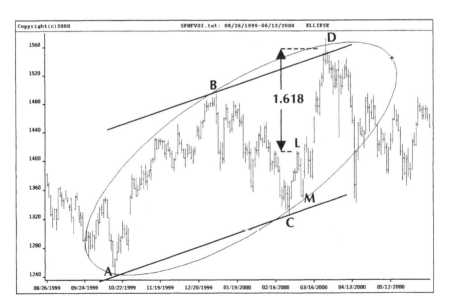

Figure 5.38 Chart of the S&P500 Index from 08–99 to 06–00. PHI-ellipse PHI05. *Source: FAM Research,* 2000.

PHI-ellipse PHI05 circumvents a typical 3-wave pattern formed by points A, B, C, and D. Point D, however, is reached months before the final point of PHI05 by the price move in the S&P500 Index. That is why PHI05 is a good way to illustrate that some PHI-ellipses may look promising, but investors might still refrain from trading.

Two alternatives for speculative investors do, nevertheless, show up in this example. Point D is confirmed by an extension, at ratio 1.618, on the initial move from point C to point L in Figure 5.38. The highest high is also confirmed by a trend channel that is drawn using valleys A and C and a parallel through point B.

Selling short at the peak at point D (based on the rules for extensions described in Chapter 3 and the rules for trend channels explained in Chapter 4) in both cases will open up significant short-term profit potential in the S&P500 Index.

PHI-ellipse PHI06 is one of the more difficult patterns to deal with (Figure 5.39).

The S&P500 Index is always volatile, but what happened between March 2000 and April 2000 has never been seen before. The Index

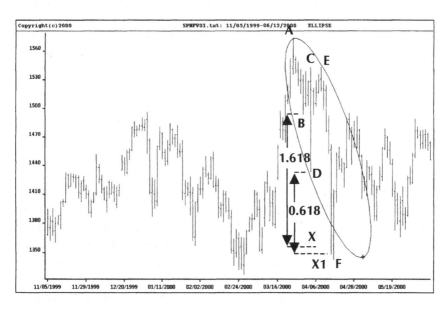

Figure 5.39 Chart of the S&P500 Index from 11–99 to 06–00. PHI-ellipse PHI06. *Source: FAM Research,* 2000.

went from 1,350.00 straight up to 1,560.00 and then corrected, within just two weeks, down to 1,350.00 again.

We cannot catch the up move by PHI-ellipse PHI05, unless it is by an extension and a trend channel. The reversal to the downside becomes visible by PHI-ellipse PHI06. Even in a phase of erratic market swings, we are able to calculate almost perfect price targets. From the wave count A to B in Figure 5.39, we can calculate a price target by multiplying the amplitude of the initial wave by the ratio 1.618. The amplitude of the wave from C to D, multiplied by the ratio 0.618, leads us to price target X1. Both targets, X and X1, meet the bottom of the downswing at point F.

The price move in the S&P500 Index is so fast that it falls out of the steep slope of PHI-ellipse PHI06. The price move stops precisely at the bottom of PHI-ellipse PHI06, which is an important result. As with PHI-ellipse PHI05, trading based on PHI-ellipse PHI06 is questionable because market pricing leaves the PHI-ellipse two weeks before the end of PHI06 is reached, but with the help of the two price targets, the more speculative oriented investor might still have traded.

At this point, it is important to demonstrate the consistency in our analysis. Through a set of convincing examples, we will illustrate the rationale behind trading on the basis of PHI-ellipses. The logic of all trading signals is essentially the same and is repetitive. If an interested investor is able to fight his or her way through all the examples we provide, that investor will gain confidence in the approach and will be able to generate real-time trading signals in a secure manner.

After the huge market swings in March and April 2000, volatility in the S&P500 Index went down significantly. But even though the market moves changed pace rapidly, the quality of the Fibonacci trading tools did not suffer at all.

In relation to the reduced volatility in the S&P500 Index market, the shape of PHI-ellipses changed from the long and narrow examples, such as PHI-ellipse PHI06, to shorter and fatter ones such as PHI-ellipse PHI07. The variation in shape of the PHI-ellipses we analyze is a reflection of a variation in the underlying investment behavior of participants in the market.

PHI-ellipse PHI07 is related to a regular 3-wave price swing that consists of the peaks A and C, as well as valleys B and D. There are

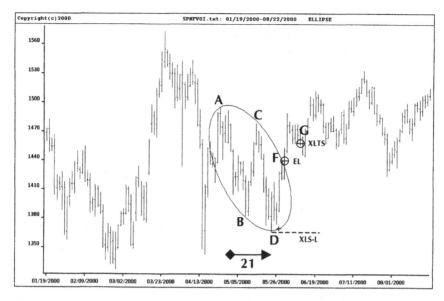

Figure 5.40 Chart of the S&P500 Index from 01–00 to 08–00. PHI-ellipse PHI07. *Source: FAM Research,* 2000.

no special confirmations of trend reversals, although we know that the low at point D is made exactly on day 21 from a Fibonacci count starting at point A (Figure 5.40).

Staying consistent and following every signal that can be generated with a PHI-ellipse, we have to wait for the market price in the S&P500 Index to move out of the sideline of PHI-ellipse PHI07. As soon as the market price leaves PHI-ellipse PHI07 at point F, a trading signal becomes effective and works according to the following parameters:

- Immediate entry long at point F when the sideline of PHI-ellipse PHI07 is broken. No additional entry rule, because the market on the breakout trades is already above a previous four days' high.

- Stop-loss protection, set to the lowest low before entry at point D.

- Trailing stop, to protect profits defined as a breakout of a previous four days' low. This exit rule is filled at point G.

PHI-ellipse PHI08 is an example of how PHI-ellipses, Fibonacci counts, and trend channels can be combined to give multiple confirmation to a trend reversal (Figure 5.41).

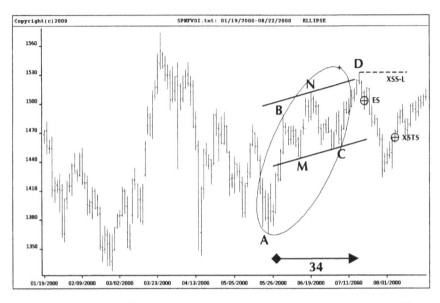

Figure 5.41 Chart of the S&P500 Index from 01–00 to 08–00. PHI-ellipse PHI08. *Source: FAM Research,* 2000.

PHI-ellipse PHI08 is established by the starting point A and two side points, B and C. Even though the market price runs outside the PHI-ellipse, it keeps going higher and stops almost exactly at the high of the PHI-ellipse at point D. The turning point in the S&P500 Index market is confirmed by two Fibonacci tools:

1. The highest high is exactly on day 34 of a Fibonacci count starting at point A.

2. If we connect valleys M and C and draw the parallel through point N, we are able, once again, to project point D out of a trend channel.

The parameters for the resulting trading signal include:

• Entry short on a breakout of a previous four days' low.

• Stop-loss protection, set to the highest high before entry at point D.

• Trailing stop exit on a breakout of a previous four days' high.

PHI-ellipse PHI09 is another one of the few PHI-ellipses that cannot be used for the determination of trend reversals and the generation of trading signals.

Although starting point A and the two side points at peak B and valley C allow us to draw a PHI-ellipse, the resulting PHI-ellipse PHI09 has almost no ascending slope. PHI09 follows the typical pattern of a sideward market. Another indicator that PHI09 is a sideward type of PHI-ellipse: Starting point A of PHI09 lies within the previous PHI-ellipse PHI08.

In Figure 5.42, we present PHI-ellipse PHI09 to complete the overall picture and to demonstrate that there are PHI-ellipses that do

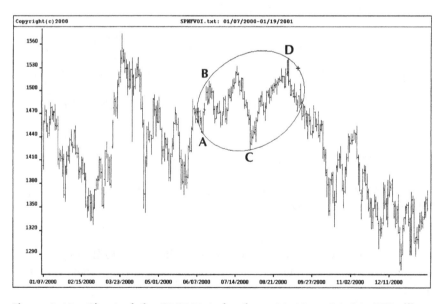

Figure 5.42 Chart of the S&P500 Index from 01–00 to 01–01. PHI-ellipse PHI09. *Source: FAM Research,* 2000.

not fulfill the basic requirements necessary to provide us with relevant trading signals.

The market in the S&P500 Index crashed, but we did not participate in this price move because PHI-ellipse PHI09 had the wrong slope. Missed trades like this can happen if one uses a consistent approach—and there are enough trading opportunities ahead.

PHI-ellipse PHI10, out of an underlying simple 3-wave pattern, has its starting point again at A and its two side points at valley B and at peak C.

The end of PHI-ellipse PHI10 at point D is reached and confirmed by a trend channel that is drawn through peaks M and O with a parallel line running through valley N (Figure 5.43).

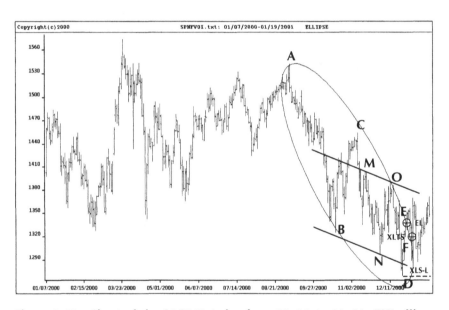

Figure 5.43   Chart of the S&P500 Index from 01–00 to 01–01. PHI-ellipse PHI10. *Source: FAM Research,* 2000.

Following nine other PHI-ellipses in the S&P500 Index, it is not difficult to find parameters for a valid trading signal based on PHI-ellipse PHI10:

- Entry long at point E on a breakout of a previous four days' high as soon as the sideline of PHI10 is broken.

- Stop-loss protection, set to the lowest low before entry at point D.

- Trailing stop, to protect profits defined as a breakout of a previous four days' low. This exit rule is filled at point F.

The final PHI-ellipse in this section on applying PHI-ellipses to the S&P500 Index illustrates the big picture from late in January 1999 to mid-January 2001. Nine of the 10 PHI-ellipses previously described in this section are circumvented by PHI-ellipse PHI11 (Figure 5.44).

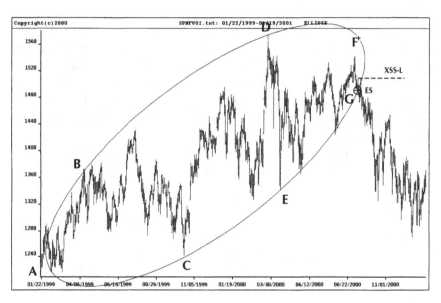

Figure 5.44   Chart of the S&P500 Index from 01–99 to 01–01. PHI-ellipse PHI11. *Source: FAM Research,* 2000.

We find the starting point A of PHI-ellipse PHI11 along with the side points at peaks B and D and at valleys C and E. The final point of PHI-ellipse PHI11 is at point F.

Applying our entry rule (sell on a breakout of the sideline after a market move has reached the end of a PHI-ellipse), we find that the best long-term sell signal is at point G. Depending on the exit rule, a small or a very large profit can be realized. According to a trailing stop rule, profits are limited, but if the position is let go on the definition of a retracement level of 50.0% for a profit target (which is a very likely strategy on a real long-term investment), waiting for the development of PHI-ellipse PHI11 for 18 months will pay off. PHI-ellipse PHI11 is a wonderful example of how symmetrical market price patterns are, even if the beauty in a market pattern might not be obvious at first glance.

A graph like the one in Figure 5.44 can be only drawn with the aid of PHI-ellipses as Fibonacci trading tools. Why does it work like this? Human behavior is actually very predictable, and the PHI-ellipse is one of the best Fibonacci tools ever developed to analyze it. PHI-ellipses as trading tools might be topped only by PHI-spirals, which will be introduced in Chapter 6.

PHI-ellipses confirm what Elliott described some 60 years ago. The markets flow like the tide: up and down and very smoothly. Can we predict these price moves? No, we cannot. But we can draw PHI-ellipses as soon as we have two side points. Although we might have the perfect PHI-ellipse days, weeks, or months ahead of time, we will still never know whether the extreme final point of a PHI-ellipse will ever be reached.

This is where skill, knowledge, and patience become very important. The more Fibonacci tools that suggest the same turning point, the more confidence we can have in our investment.

Before we continue our analysis of Fibonacci trading devices and introduce PHI-spirals, we will take two preliminary steps. We first show PHI-ellipses for the S&P500 Index on a constant scale, as we did for the Japanese Yen cash currency. And then, to prove that the PHI-ellipses on the Japanese Yen cash currency and the S&P500 Index are not just singular events, we present a third trading vehicle: the DAX30 Index.

PHI-Ellipses on Constant Scales in the S&P500 Index

If we can demonstrate that PHI-ellipses work with many products over a longer period of time, we can be confident in our investment. Only on constant scales do we see the similarities of different PHI-ellipses. Each PHI-ellipse varies in shape, length, or width, but the underlying principles based on the Fibonacci summation series and the ratios from the PHI series will never change.

There is no standard PHI-ellipse that is the average fit for every price move. However, the magic of PHI-ellipses lies in their ability to dynamically adjust to ever changing price patterns in the markets.

We have analyzed more than two years' S&P500 Index daily bar data from December 1998 to December 2000, and have tested PHI-ellipses historically backward.

The total stream of data over the 25 months is separated into three individual charts. By choosing a set of appropriate PHI-ellipses and waiting for market pricing to move out of the PHI-ellipses at their final points, our sample investments follow the price pattern in the S&P500 Index with very few exceptions (Figure 5.45).

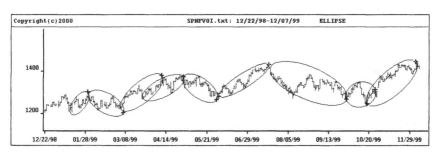

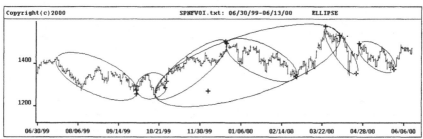

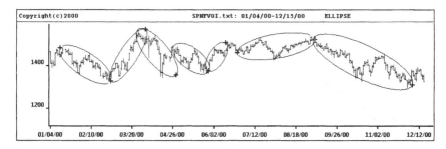

Figure 5.45 Chart of the S&P500 Index from 12–98 to 12–00. Attached and overlapping PHI-ellipses on a constant scale. *Source: FAM Research,* 2000.

Taking into account the 11 PHI-ellipses analyzed in the previous section and the 23 PHI-ellipses from Figure 5.45, the dynamic nature of PHI-ellipses becomes evident.

We get a similar picture if we extend our analysis to two years' DAX30 Index data to complete the chapter on PHI-ellipses as Fibonacci trading tools.

PHI-Ellipses on Constant Scales in the DAX30 Index

The total stream of market data over 27 months, from September 1998 to December 2000, in the DAX30 Index is shown on constant scales on two separate charts (Figure 5.46).

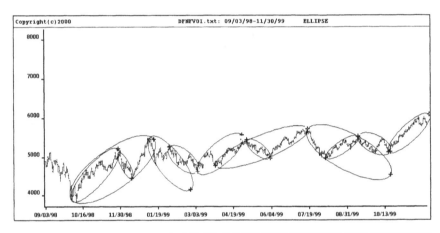

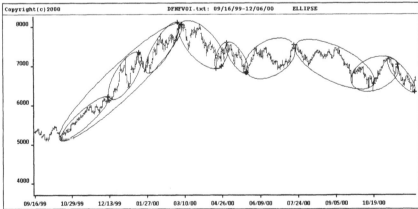

Figure 5.46 Chart of the DAX30 Index from 09–98 to 12–00. Attached and overlapping PHI-ellipses on a constant scale. *Source: FAM Research,* 2000.

Once again, we must find a set of appropriate PHI-ellipses and wait for market pricing to move out of the PHI-ellipses at their final points. PHI-ellipses overlap or are attached to each other and follow the market price pattern in the DAX30 Index.

The change in shape of the PHI-ellipses depends greatly on whether the basic underlying market pattern is a 3-wave move or a 5-wave move. Properly distinguishing between 3-wave swings and 5-wave swings was the key problem that Elliott and his followers were never able to solve. PHI-ellipses as Fibonacci trading tools are the solution to this problem. It does not matter whether we deal with a 3-wave pattern or a 5-wave pattern; the final point of a PHI-ellipse tells us where we are in the market.

Our findings on PHI-ellipses will be summarized before we describe PHI-spirals, next on our list of geometrical Fibonacci trading tools.

SUMMARY

PHI-ellipses as investment devices are special because they make chart patterns visible. When working with PHI-ellipses, investors always know what to look for in the markets—regardless of how confusing daily, weekly, or monthly charts appear. With modern computer high-tech now at investors' fingertips, PHI-ellipses become very valuable.

The basic structure of a PHI-ellipse is simple. PHI-ellipses circumvent a minimum 3-wave swing. To calculate PHI-ellipses, three points are needed: a starting point and two side points. The final point of a PHI-ellipse projects a future market move as the PHI-ellipse develops. The final point of a PHI-ellipse is the decisive point to watch.

In the application of PHI-ellipses, investors are able to master trend patterns and sideward patterns. PHI-ellipses consist of three trading dimensions—price, time, and angle—which, by themselves, are seldom found in a single trading tool. When a solid analysis of all three dimensions precalculates the same turning point in a market, we may invest with confidence.

To make our entry signals safer, we must filter out entry points with a high success rate. This does not mean that every trade will turn out as a winning trade. Getting stopped out on stop-losses and reentering a market while sticking to strict entry rules, stop-loss rules, and re-entry rules, are all part of using Fibonacci tools in volatile markets. The best entry point on PHI-ellipses with the highest rate of profitable trades only happens at the very end of a PHI-ellipse. The investor should then enter the market counter to the main trend direction.

By generating trading signals based on the end of a PHI-ellipse, we sell high or buy low. A countertrend approach, as such, requires a lot of discipline because there is not much support in the markets when a trading signal appears. We will never know whether we meet the highest high or the lowest low at the time we establish a position in a market, but our chances for profitable decisions will be good, at least as far as historical test runs on the Japanese Yen cash currency, the S&P500 Index, and the DAX30 Index are concerned.

In the end, the slope of a PHI-ellipse determines whether we receive a trading signal. We will get sell signals as long as the slope of a PHI-ellipse points upward. We will get buy signals' countertrend as long as the slope of a PHI-ellipse points downward. We will not get any signal in straight sideward markets when a PHI-ellipse runs mainly horizontally. [Readers should check the chart of PHI-ellipse PHI09 on the S&P500 Index (Figure 5.42) for a recap.] Figure 5.47 shows the three main patterns of investment for PHI-ellipses that traders must always remember.

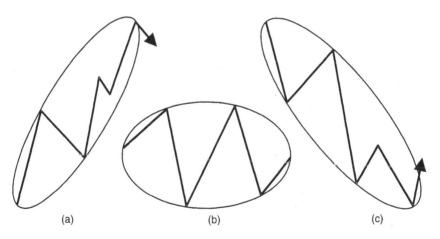

| (a) | (b) | (c) |

Figure 5.47   Main patterns of investment on PHI-ellipses. (a) Sell signal short; (b) no signal; (c) buy signal long. *Source: FAM Research,* 2000.

Our confidence is boosted if trend reversals derived from PHI-ellipses are confirmed by other Fibonacci trading tools. These confirmations come either from price analysis based on corrections and extension, or time analysis based on the numbers of the Fibonacci summation series. Valuable confirmations can also come from the application of trend channels. PHI-spirals and Fibonacci time goal analysis, discussed in the upcoming chapters, will complete our set of Fibonacci tools.

Focus is deliberately directed toward the Japanese Yen cash currency, the S&P500 Index, and the DAX30 Index. These three products were chosen because they are traded worldwide at high volatility and high volume. PHI-ellipses perform well on every product traded, as long as there is enough volatility, volume, open interest, and liquidity. In other words, for a serious analysis based on PHI-ellipses, we need a sample of products in which the international community of investors shows a lot of interest. If investors are interested in a product, there is a very good chance that their behavior will be directly reflected in the product's market patterns.

We are always as precise and complete as possible in the description and analysis of trading tools, and in their application to sets of sample market data. We introduce entry rules and exit rules, stop-loss rules, trailing stop rules and rules for profit targets. However, regardless of our attention to detail, we will never be able to cover the whole spectrum of opportunities and variations that are implied with the analysis of PHI-ellipses.

We do not believe that the entire spectrum of system design, and the development of trading strategies founded on PHI-ellipses, can ever be fully automated and computerized. The dynamic of PHI-ellipses and the three dimension of price, time, and angle would surely be too problematic for programmers. But there is no need for fully computerized trading signals. PHI-ellipses, in combination with other Fibonacci trading devices, open the door for skillful, interested, patient, and determined investors who need basic and reliable trading tools that are guaranteed to work, if handled properly.

Generations of investors have tried to make Elliott's wave principles work and to apply them to successful real-time trading. To the best of our knowledge, no trader has ever succeeded over a longer period of time because Elliott's wave count is not stable. We admire Elliott for his work. His innovative ideas enlightened us and provided the foundation for our work. Given today's computer technology and our accumulated experience over the past 20 years, we strongly believe that we have developed pattern recognition to a higher level.

Four geometrical Fibonacci trading tools have now been described and analyzed: Fibonacci summation series; corrections and extensions; PHI-channels; and PHI-ellipses. Two more Fibonacci trading tools are still missing. PHI-spirals will be dealt with in Chapter 6, and Fibonacci time goal analysis will follow in Chapter 7.

6

PHI-SPIRALS

PHI-spirals provide a link between price and time analysis and are the answer to a long search for a solution to **forecasting** both time and price. If we really want to link patterns of investor behavior—expressed in the price swings of cash currencies, stocks, and commodities—to nature's law, we must look to PHI-spirals. Any point on a spiral represents the optimal relationship of price and time.

The only mathematical curve to follow the pattern of natural growth is the spiral, expressed in natural phenomena such as *Spira mirabilis,* or, more commonly, the nautilus shell. Geometrical key features of spirals were presented in the first chapter. At this point, we will only review some of the most striking aspects before analyzing PHI-spirals as Fibonacci trading tools.

The PHI-spiral is the most beautiful of mathematical curves. This type of spiral has been a common occurrence in the natural world for millions of years. The Fibonacci summation series and the golden section, introduced in Chapter 1 as the geometrical equivalent of the Fibonacci summation series, are very well associated with this remarkable curve.

The successive chambers of the nautilus shell develop in the framework of a PHI-spiral. As the shell grows, the size of its chambers increases but the shape remains unaltered. Two segments of the spiral may be different in size, but not in shape. The spiral has no terminal point. Figure 6.1 shows a radiograph of the shell of the chambered nautilus. The chambers of the nautilus shell grow according to "the divine proportion," which is Fibonacci's PHI (the ratio 1.618).

Figure 6.1 The PHI-spiral represented in the nautilus shell. *Source: The Divine Proportion,* by H. E. Huntley (New York: Dover, 1970), p. iv. Reprinted with permission.

The greatest challenge of PHI-spirals comes in their development in extreme market situations when behavioral patterns of investors are the most evident.

The October 1987 stock market crash is an example of a market situation that was a strong manifestation of investors' behavior. At a stage where most other methods of market analysis fail desperately, the correct use of a PHI-spiral pinpoints the bottom of the sharp market move. The exactness with which PHI-spiral analysis captured the crash pattern as of October 1987 can be demonstrated on a sample chart, using the S&P500 Index as the role model for the crash in stock prices. With the center of the PHI-spiral at point X and the starting point at A, the spiral is penetrated by the S&P500 Index at the lowest low—point P (Figure 6.2). Points X and A are definitive and could have been selected by any investor.

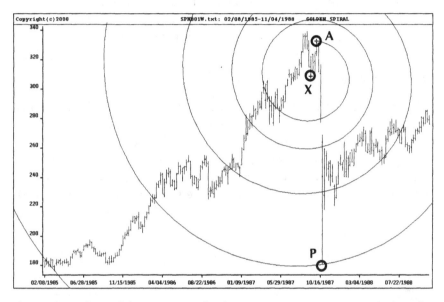

Figure 6.2   Chart of the S&P500 Index from 02–85 to 11–88. PHI-spiral to pinpoint exactly the low of the stock market crash in October 1987. *Source: FAM Research,* 2000.

The structure of the current chapter is similar to that of Chapter 5. We will go into detail on basic features and key parameters of PHI-spirals before we present examples of how to apply PHI-spirals to real-time trading.

BASIC FEATURES AND PARAMETERS OF PHI-SPIRALS

PHI-spirals as geometrical Fibonacci trading tools are easy to understand and conceptually simple to apply to the markets.

PHI-spirals identify trend reversals in the markets. Trading signals based on PHI-spirals, therefore, require investment action against the main trend direction. Valid investment countertrend

decisions require exceptional discipline, accuracy in executing trading signals, and trust in the trading strategy.

We will prove that if the correct center is chosen, PHI-spirals
pinpoint turning points in the markets with an accuracy seldom before seen. Investing based on PHI-spirals is neither a black-box approach nor an overfitted computerized trading system. It is a simple
universal geometrical law applied to different sorts of products such
as futures, stock index futures, stocks, or cash currencies.

Market Symmetry

PHI-spirals show that there is a stunning symmetry in price patterns.
The existence of this symmetry provides evidence that market moves
are not random, but follow a clear behavioral pattern.

We regard symmetry in the markets as an expression of investor
behavior and nature's law. Figure 6.3 is an illustration of a symmetrical sample downtrend price move in the Euro cash currency against
the US Dollar.

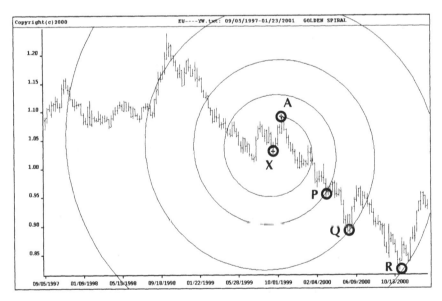

**Figure 6.3 Chart of the Euro cash currency from 09–97 to 01–01. Market sym-
metry captured by a PHI-spiral.** *Source: FAM Research,* **2000.**

In Figure 6.3, the center of the PHI-spiral on the move in the Euro cash currency is set to point X. Point X is chosen because it marks a significant valley. As we will see later, any significant valley or peak can be chosen for analysis with PHI-spirals. With the center at point X, we choose the peak at point A as the starting point of the PHI-spiral.

The PHI-spiral is turned clockwise. With remarkable accuracy, the market price in the Euro cash currency has a mild correction down to where the PHI-spiral is penetrated at point P. There is an even stronger correction when the PHI-spiral is penetrated at point Q. But the strongest correction is seen at the valley at point R, when the fourth ring of the PHI-spiral is penetrated.

The Euro cash currency move is presented to demonstrate how PHI-spirals can be applied to reveal the symmetry in price patterns. The same symmetrical market price patterns can be found in many different products as long as PHI-spirals are drawn correctly. The secret lies in the investor's ability to choose the correct center of the PHI-spiral and to select an appropriate starting point.

The center of a PHI-spiral can be set either in the middle of a market pattern or at one of the extreme points—a peak or a valley. The use of daily or weekly data does not affect the overall accuracy of a PHI-spiral, but the data compression rate determines which of the spiral rings will be penetrated.

Future research will show how reliable PHI-spirals work on intraday charts. The greater number of swings intraday makes it much more difficult to properly locate the center of a PHI-spiral.

Rule of Alternation

The rule of alternation runs hand in hand with the Fibonacci summation series and the Fibonacci ratio. The rule of alternation can be applied equally well to price patterns in futures or cash currencies.

The rule of alternation in relation to PHI-spirals is best described by Jay Hambridge, who uses the example of a sunflower: "In the sunflower, two sets of equiangular spirals are superimposed or intertwined, one being right handed and the other a left handed spiral, with each floret filling a dual role by belonging to both spirals."*

---

* Jay Hambridge, *Practical Applications of Dynamic Symmetry* (New York: Dover Publications, 1970), pp. 28, 29.

Elliott knew about the rule of alternation. This rule made it possible for him to claim that he was able to forecast future price moves based on formations in wave 2 and wave 4 of 5-wave patterns. (See Chapter 1 for a recap of Elliott's wave principles.)

The rationale behind the rule of alternation in relation to PHI-spirals will be explained by using a Crude Oil chart (Figure 6.4).

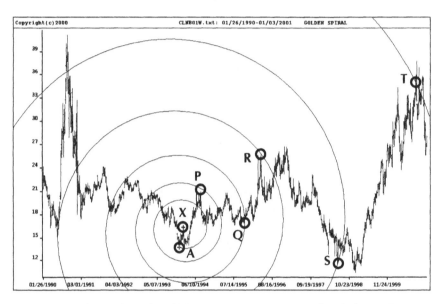

Figure 6.4 Chart of Crude Oil from 01–90 to 01–01. Rule of alternation represented by a PHI-spiral. *Source: FAM Research,* 2000.

With the center at point X, the PHI-spiral has its starting point in A. The PHI-spiral is rotated counterclockwise. The first peak is reached at point P on the second spiral ring. The following valley is marked when the third spiral ring at point Q is penetrated. The valley is followed by a peak at point R once the fourth spiral ring is penetrated. The peak alternates with a valley at point S on the fifth spiral ring. The valley at point S alternates with another significant peak at point T when the sixth spiral ring is penetrated.

Does this almost perfect example of the rule of alternation on the Crude Oil chart mean that PHI-spirals are proficient forecasting instruments, and that the rule of alternation will tell us when there will be a high or low in a market? The rule of alternation still has to pass a final test. The reason we hesitate to judge the quality of PHI-spirals is that, after identifying a low with a spiral ring, the next spiral ring might identify either a new peak or a new valley that is lower than the previous valley (Figure 6.5).

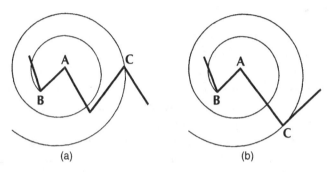

(a)   (b)

Figure 6.5   Identification of peaks and valleys based on PHI-spirals. (a) Definition of a new high; (b) definition of a new low. *Source: Fibonacci Applications and Strategies for Traders,* by Robert Fischer (New York: Wiley, 1993), p. 138. Reprinted with permission.

In addition to the uncertainty as to whether a new high or low is defined when a PHI-spiral ring is penetrated, the rule of alternation offers the option of turning PHI-spirals either counterclockwise or clockwise, beginning with the same center and starting point (Figure 6.6).

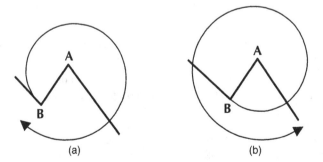

(a)   (b)

Figure 6.6   Rotation of PHI-spirals. (a) Clockwise; (b) counterclockwise. *Source: Fibonacci Applications and Strategies for Traders,* by Robert Fischer (New York: Wiley, 1993), p. 140. Reprinted with permission.

Research shows that in order to catch every major turning point in the markets, it is necessary to work with both options for rotating PHI-spirals. The productive combination of the rule of alternation and the direction of rotation gets the most out of the application of PHI-spirals.

Swing Sizes

The swing size calculated from significant peaks and valleys determines the size of a PHI-spiral.

A minimum swing size is needed for practical purposes because a PHI-spiral needs a minimum radius for proper rotation. Finding appropriate swing sizes on daily or weekly charts is mechanical and can be easily undertaken by every investor.

Choosing a wrong swing size has immediate repercussions. If the swing size is too small, there is a lot of noise in the market and the PHI-spirals become unreliable. In addition, corrections on small swings do not offer enough profit potential. If the swing size is too large, the PHI-spiral rings are too far away from each other and have no value for the analysis.

To find the best swing size for a product, historical data and a constant scale are of immense value. Because every product has its own character and special market behavior, swing sizes vary from product to product. Some useful swing sizes for a variety of products are listed in Table 6.1.

Table 6.1 Sample Swing Sizes, Daily and Weekly

Product	Daily Swing Size in Points	Daily Sample Move	Weekly Swing Size in Points
S&P500 Index	40.00	1,300.00 to 1,340.00	80.00
DAX30 Index	100.00	6,400.00 to 6,500.00	200.00
Crude Oil	2.00	20.00 to 22.00	4.00
Soybeans	20.00	520.00 to 540.00	40.00
Pork Bellies	2.00	50.00 to 52.00	4.00
Euro	0.02	0.92 to 0.94	0.04
Japanese Yen	2.00	110.00 to 112.00	4.00

Source: FAM Research, 2000.

Swing highs and swing lows are confirmed in two steps. The first step is to check for the minimum swing size measured on the distance from lowest low to highest high on swing highs, and from highest high to lowest low on swing lows. The second step is to confirm a swing high. We may find at least two closing prices on either side of the day with the highest high lower than the low of the highest day, or we may find two closing prices that are lower than the close of the highest day (vice versa for confirmations of swing lows). This rule is the same as the one introduced in Chapter 2 (see Figure 2.2).

Specifications of PHI-Spirals

Finding the center of a PHI-spiral and the appropriate starting point is the most crucial part of the analysis. Almost every major turning point can be pinpointed if the correct PHI-spiral is chosen.

3-wave moves running as a-b-c corrections are the basic patterns we look for when setting up PHI-spirals. 3-wave patterns of this type include everything needed for solid forecasts of turning points in the markets. Four different combinations of 3-wave patterns exist. They are differentiated in Figure 6.7.

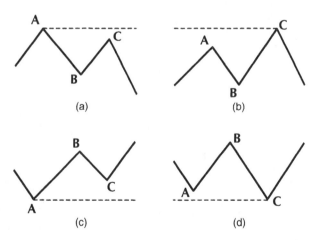

Figure 6.7   3-swing relations of A, B, and C. (a) Downtrend with high in A; (b) downtrend with high in C; (c) uptrend with low in A; (d) uptrend with low in C. *Source: Fibonacci Applications and Strategies for Traders,* by Robert Fischer (New York: Wiley, 1993), p. 142. Reprinted with permission.

Whenever we use a 3-swing pattern, we have the option of locating the center of a PHI-spiral at point A, B, or C. Our research shows that the best results are achieved by using point B as the center for the generation of PHI-spirals. However, there is no fixed rule that centers of PHI-spirals have to be set to point B. Points A and C may be valid, too. A, B, and C are also the three points to select from when starting points of PHI-spirals are designated.

In addition to the central point and the starting point of PHI-spirals, the clockwise or counterclockwise direction in which PHI-spirals are rotated is a decisive parameter.

Depending on whether the chosen centers or starting points of PHI-spirals are A, B, or C, and whether PHI-spirals are rotated clockwise or counterclockwise, we distinguish a set of options out of which four cases shall be described.

The first of the four cases is a combination of center at point B of a 3-swing pattern, starting point at A, and clockwise rotation of the PHI-spiral. This case is demonstrated on a chart of the DAX30 Index from December 1999 to January 2001 (Figure 6.8).

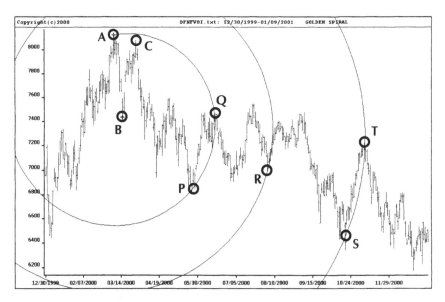

Figure 6.8   Chart of the DAX30 Index from 12–99 to 01–01. PHI-spiral rotated clockwise with the center at point B and the starting point at A. *Source: FAM Research,* 2000.

The main trend direction in the DAX30 Index changes when the first PHI-spiral ring is penetrated at point P, and this is followed by a new high on the same PHI-spiral ring at point Q. The second PHI-spiral ring is penetrated at the valley at point R. At point R, we can expect the market pricing to climb to a new high in accordance with the rule of alternation. But the DAX30 Index market will make a new low at point S, once the third PHI-spiral ring is penetrated and before a strong rally is able to lift the market to a peak at point T, on the third PHI-spiral ring.

It is always possible for two valleys or two peaks to show up in a row. On those occasions when two consecutive peaks or two consecutive valleys do appear and contrast the rule of alternation, chances are especially good that the upcoming price move will run strongly in the opposite direction.

The second of our sample combinations (PHI-spiral center, starting point, and direction of rotation) shows the center of the PHI-spiral again at point B, and the starting point once more in A, but this time the rotation of the PHI-spiral is counterclockwise. This constellation is illustrated on a chart of the S&P500 Index (Figure 6.9).

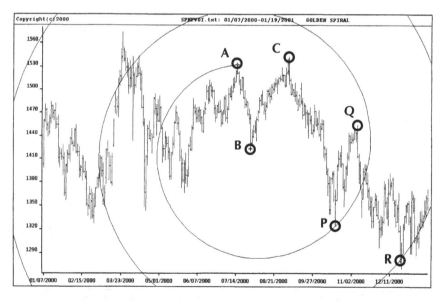

Figure 6.9   Chart of the S&P500 Index from 01–00 to 01–01. PHI-spiral rotated counterclockwise with the center at point B and the starting point at A. *Source: FAM Research, 2000.*

The main trend direction in the S&P500 Index changes on the day when the market price gets to the first PHI-spiral ring at point P. A rally is initiated from there, up to the peak at point Q. This peak is followed by a new valley at point R on a penetration of the second PHI-spiral ring. Again the market reacts with a strong rally after the valley at point R is made.

It is important to watch the swing size of the PHI-spiral. The swing size—which is the distance from the center of the PHI-spiral in B at 1,420.00 to the starting point of the PHI-spiral in A at 1,535.00—is very large: more than 100 full S&P500 Index points. The resulting PHI-spiral on such a large swing size is, therefore, very big as well, which means that peaks and valleys can most likely be found on the second and the third PHI-spiral ring.

The third of the four options is the combination of the center of the PHI-spiral at point C instead of point B, and the starting point at point B instead of point A, while the PHI-spiral is still rotated counterclockwise. The PHI-spiral is applied to a sample daily chart of the DAX30 Index (Figure 6.10).

The total distance from point A to point B in the DAX30 Index is 600 points with no smaller swing size in between. In Elliott's terms,

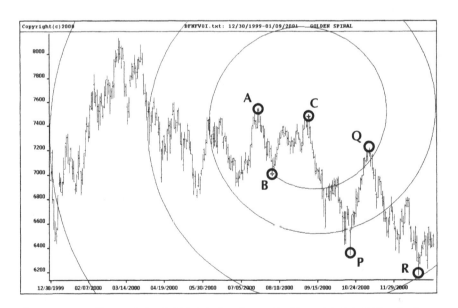

Figure 6.10   Chart of the DAX30 Index from 12–99 to 01–01. PHI-spiral rotated counterclockwise with the center at point C and the starting point at B. *Source: FAM Research, 2000.*

this is a regular move. The price move from point B to point C has a smaller a–b–c correction in between, which Elliott would call an irregular correction.

PHI-spiral rings, which create strong support or resistance, are most likely followed by corrections that go back to the previous PHI-spiral ring. In the case of the DAX30 Index, the market price finds support at the second PHI-spiral ring at point P and starts a rally that comes close to the first PHI-spiral ring at point Q. From the peak at point Q, the market collapses again and reaches the third PHI-spiral ring at point R.

Another rule to remember: Whenever the price action goes to the next PHI-spiral ring, we can expect the following counterswing to be stronger. What starts as a correction—against the main trend—turns into a complete trend reversal because the greater the number of PHI-spiral rings reached by a market move, the more likely a stronger correction will result.

In the fourth case, the center of the PHI-spiral is at point B and the starting point is at C, and these are combined with a clockwise rotation of the PHI-spiral. The S&P500 Index serves as our chart sample (Figure 6.11).

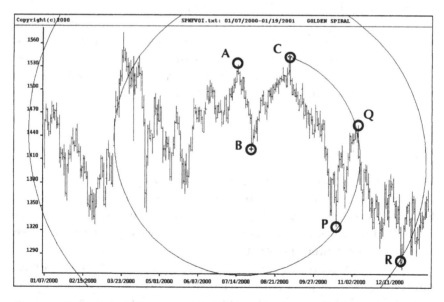

Figure 6.11 Chart of the S&P500 Index from 01–00 to 01–01. The PHI-spiral is rotated clockwise with the center at point B and the starting point at C. *Source: FAM Research, 2000.*

Our first reference is the valley at point P, when the first PHI-spiral ring is penetrated. From here, the market price strongly rallies back to the peak at point Q, which is still inside the first PHI-spiral ring. What is interesting is that the strong price moves from points C to P and back to the significant peak at point Q all occur within the first PHI-spiral ring. The reason for this lies in the long distance between the center of the PHI-spiral and the starting point. The next price move gets the market down to a new valley at point R, where the second PHI-spiral ring is penetrated.

The second and fourth options of combining the center point, starting point, and direction of PHI-spiral rotation proves that different PHI-spirals may have multiple confirmation trend reversals in the markets. In both cases, the PHI-spirals are penetrated on the second PHI-spiral ring by the valley at point R.

Whenever a peak or a valley penetrates two different PHI-spirals at the same time, there is a high probability that the main trend will change to the opposite direction. The multiple confirmation of a trend reversal by two PHI-spirals is as valuable as a multiple confirmation by two individual Fibonacci tools. Multiple confirmations of turning points are what we try to detect in the markets. As soon as we discover a crossover of two PHI-spirals on one market move, we have reached the main goal of PHI-spiral analysis.

The four ways of combining center, starting point, and rotation of PHI-spirals demonstrate downtrend configurations in cases (a) and (b) in Figure 6.7. PHI-spirals can be applied—identically—to uptrends; therefore, we will not present separate examples for them. Uptrends will, however, be used in examples in the section that follows.

Rotation of PHI-Spirals and the Rule of Alternation

Up to this point, we have seen that, in most cases, peaks and valleys alternate between different spiral rings. Peaks are followed by valleys, and vice versa. The rule of alternation is applied here as well, because PHI-spirals can be turned either clockwise or counterclockwise from the same center and starting point.

There is no rule as to which rotation is the more important one, but if a significant peak is identified with a PHI-spiral turned clockwise, it is probable that by changing the rotation to counterclockwise and maintaining the same center and the same starting point, the market will make either a significant valley or a significant peak once the following PHI-spiral ring is reached. Figure 6.12 shows the S&P500 Index weekly from June 1998 to January 2001.

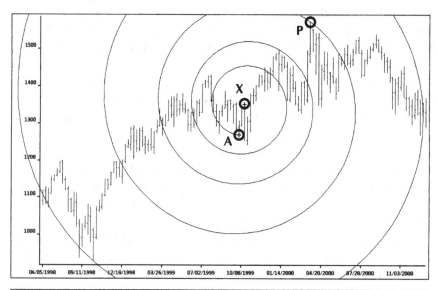

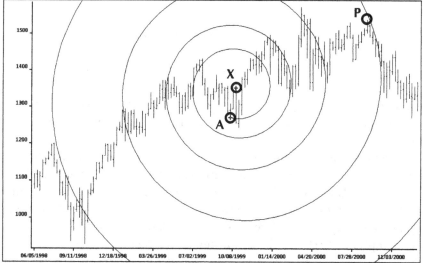

Figure 6.12   Chart of the S&P500 Index from 06–98 to 01–01. Rotation of PHI-spirals and the rule of alternation. *Source: FAM Research,* 2000.

The center of the PHI-spiral in the upper chart in Figure 6.12 is at X, the starting point is at A, and the rotation is clockwise. The market price reaches its highest high when the second PHI-spiral ring is penetrated at the significant peak at point P.

On the lower chart in Figure 6.12, the center of the PHI-spiral is also at point X, and the starting point is again at valley A, but this time the PHI-spiral is rotated counterclockwise. Once the market price penetrates the third PHI-spiral ring at the peak at point P, the S&P500 Index starts its major straight correction from 1,574.00 to 1,280.00 as an intermediate lowest low.

A strategic search for resistance or support points by changing the direction of rotation from clockwise to counterclockwise is not enough for reliable results, but it is an important addition when working with PHI-spirals. This becomes relevant when dealing with the confirmation of support or resistance points.

Regardless of how we get crossovers of PHI-spirals—whether from changing the rotation or from varying central points or starting points—the crossover of PHI-spirals reveals the potential turning points in major markets.

The general features and key parameters of PHI-spirals have been revealed. We will now present examples of how beneficial the application of PHI-spirals can be to pinpoint trend reversals.

WORKING WITH PHI-SPIRALS

PHI-spirals can be applied to any product traded, but, in our experience, PHI-spirals have worked best on products with high open interest and high liquidity, such as financial futures or cash currencies. These products have sufficient liquidity to enter and exit the positions we want to trade.

It is important to understand that swing sizes must not be too small because the smaller the swing size, the more PHI-spiral rings we receive. To properly deal with long term trend reversals, it is important to look for turning points on third PHI-spiral rings. However, this is not a strict rule. Exceptions are possible, as we will see.

Applying PHI-spirals to market moves means investing against the main trend. The strategy is to identify major trend reversals in advance and to act accordingly as soon as PHI-spiral rings are penetrated.

For successful trading on PHI-spirals, we need at least two or more PHI-spirals that identify the same significant peak or valley in the stream of market data. These PHI-spirals can come from: (a) the selection of one center and starting point, but with the PHI-spirals turned clockwise or counterclockwise; (b) different PHI-spirals with different centers and starting points; or (c) PHI-spirals on weekly and daily data.

Different PHI-spirals do not necessarily have to come from earlier and nearby swings. Significant peaks or valleys may also be discovered by PHI-spirals using swing formations weeks or months earlier.

The simultaneous application of at least two PHI-spirals means that we end up with a lot of PHI-spiral rings on our sample charts. This might be irritating at the beginning for some readers. To provide readers with a clearer picture, we show the individual PHI-spirals on small charts, and the combination of PHI-spirals, including the crossover points, on one large-scale chart.

When conducting a PHI-spiral analysis, the investor will not know which PHI-spirals are the correct ones at the beginning of a market move. Only future market action can tell. Therefore, it takes a lot of patience and discipline to wait for a crossover point of PHI-spirals and, thus, indication that it is the appropriate time to invest. Being patient and waiting for the crossover will pay off. We have not analyzed a single significant turning point in our tested products that could not have been identified by a crossover of two PHI-spirals.

With this book's WINPHI software, readers can follow, consider, and easily reproduce all our examples to get a feeling of how PHI-spirals can be applied to charts. We are currently in the final stages of developing a professional version of the WINPHI software. It is designed as an online trading device available on the Internet, on a registered membership basis, at www.fibotrader.com. The online version allows us to permanently update weekly, daily, and intraday data automatically and to include a wide range of trading vehicles from major international markets.

We have chosen three liquid and volatile sample products for purposes of demonstrating the general use of PHI-spirals. These products are: the S&P500 Index, the Euro cash currency, and the DAX30 Index.

To make our PHI-spiral analysis easier to understand, we first pinpoint turning points in the S&P500 Index on weekly data. Then we analyze the same turning points in the S&P500 Index on daily data. By identifying significant turning points, using a combination of PHI-spirals derived independently from weekly and daily data, we gain additional evidence of the stability of investors' behavior in market patterns. Examples on charts of the Euro cash currency and the DAX30 Index follow in separate sections.

S&P500 Index Weekly

The potential of our PHI-spiral analysis can best be demonstrated by going through a series of significant peaks and valleys, one after the other, and showing how PHI-spirals can be applied to historical data.

Before we go into detail on the major turning points of weekly bar data D–O–H–L–C in the S&P500 Index, we would like readers to appreciate the incredible symmetry that can be found in price patterns (Figure 6.13).

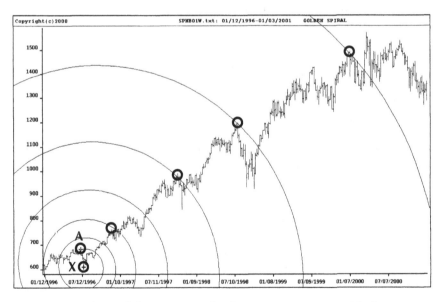

Figure 6.13 Chart of the S&P500 Index from 01–96 to 01–01. Market symmetry reflected in a PHI-spiral. *Source: FAM Research,* 2000.

Figure 6.13 shows a PHI-spiral applied to a bar chart of weekly S&P500 Index data from January 1996 to January 2001. It is a perfect example of nonrandom price moves that are symmetrical, based on nature's law and investors' behavior.

In the S&P500 Index in July 1996, the center of the PHI-spiral is at point X, and the starting point is at A. The PHI-spiral is turned clockwise. Four major peaks can be identified on the third, fifth, sixth, and seventh PHI-spiral rings. The problem with applying only one PHI-spiral to a chart is that, back in 1996, there was no way of knowing that, out of the many spirals possible, this one would be the most stable and therefore the best to correctly identify significant peaks. That is why we now look primarily for crossovers of PHI-spirals as confirmations of significant trend reversals.

Now, back to the S&P500 Index trend reversals in detail. To explain changes in trend direction, we identify relevant peaks (P) and valleys (V) in the S&P500 Index weekly chart as P#01 to V#12. Figure 6.14 covers the same time span as the previous chart, but this time, 12 significant peaks and valleys have been distinguished.

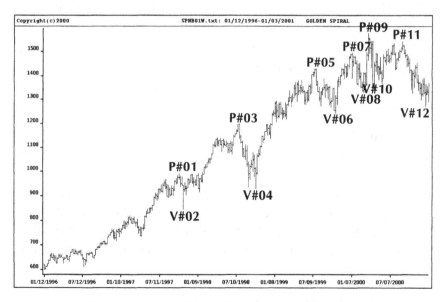

Figure 6.14 Chart of the S&P500 Index from 01–96 to 01–01. Significant peaks and valleys P#01 to V#12. *Source: FAM Research, 2000.*

Each of the 12 trend reversals will be described individually in this section. We will explain how the significant turning points can be identified based on a PHI-spiral analysis.

To focus directly on peaks and valleys and to avoid confusion, we will not repeat entry and exit rules on every trading signal that can be generated from the 12 peaks and valleys. The same entry and exit rules that were introduced in Chapter 3 ("Applying the Fibonacci Ratio to Corrections and Extensions") are also valid for investments based on a PHI-spiral analysis.

A set of eight fundamental underlying parameters applies to every PHI-spiral analysis:

1. At least two PHI-spirals, from different swings, are needed for the confirmation of a trend reversal.

2. On the chart, every swing with the appropriate swing size may be a valid initial swing.

3. The two PHI-spirals that are used to confirm a trend reversal must differ in starting point and center.

4. PHI-spirals can be turned in either a clockwise or a counter-clockwise direction.

5. Crossovers of the two PHI-spirals need to be close to the turning points in order to make them valid trend reversals.

6. Market moves are required to penetrate both PHI-spirals in the area of the crossover point.

7. Generally, crossover points of third or higher PHI-spiral rings are considered. Only in exceptional cases are crossovers of second PHI-spiral rings relevant.

8. Peaks are considered when the price levels of the centers of corresponding PHI-spirals are equal to the peak levels or below the peaks. Valleys are considered when the price levels of the centers of corresponding PHI-spirals are equal to the valley levels or above the valleys.

The fact that PHI-spirals pinpoint peaks and valleys is not the issue; many other analytic tools can do this, too. What is a major issue, however, is whether PHI-spirals are able to identify all significant turning points on historical data, in sequence, as shown in the S&P500 Index. A major issue is whether PHI-spirals confirm turning points identified on weekly and on daily data. This is why we conduct our analysis in a two-step approach: weekly data first, and then again on daily data.

Do we always have to wait for the third PHI-spiral ring in order to receive a proper confirmation of a trend reversal? Certainly not. But waiting for the third PHI-spiral ring prevents us from jumping into the market too fast.

There is much room for improvement on the rules we prescribe, but our goal is to provide a conservative and profitable long-term strategy. Investors with other risk preferences may be able to modify our rules and come out with even better results. The beauty of all Fibonacci tools is that there is plenty of room for creativity. Aided by the book's WINPHI software package, traders can generate PHI-spirals by themselves. The historical database on the CD-ROM can be updated, and additional ASCII O-H-L-C data can be used to get to an almost unlimited scope of options for PHI-spiral analysis.

We present three charts for each of the 12 significant peaks and valleys. Each of the major charts consists of the sample price move in the S&P500 Index and the PHI-spirals that define the crossover point. Two minor charts illustrate the two individual PHI-spirals that point at the respective peaks or valleys. Presenting three charts per trend reversal is the best way of showing how our PHI-spiral analysis matches the peak and valley configurations.

Working with PHI-spirals is not easy. PHI-spirals by themselves are not the problem; one mouse-click designates the center and another mouse-click designates the starting point. The computer itself then draws a PHI-spiral.

But locating centers and starting points of PHI-spirals must be done by hand. Therefore, it is technically possible that some small mistakes may be made in drawing PHI-spirals. However, the importance and the quality of PHI-spiral analysis as an investment device should not be affected by subtle inaccuracies.

Let us now begin our analysis of the significant peaks and valleys, P#01 to V#12.

Peak P#01 is defined by a crossover of two PHI-spirals with centers and starting points in December 1996 and March 1997

(Figure 6.15). Using these reference points, our goal is to get an idea of where the next turning point in the S&P500 Index might be.

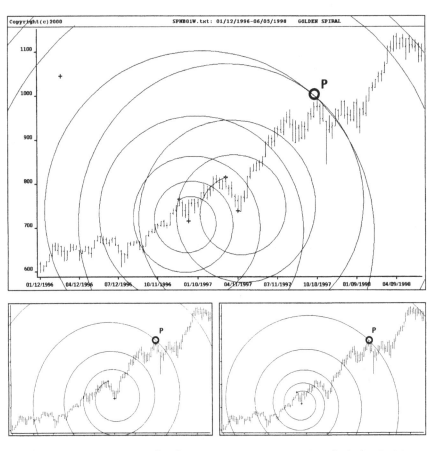

Figure 6.15   S&P500 Index from 01–96 to 06–98. PHI-spirals for P#01.

The PHI-spiral on the left minor chart is turned counterclockwise; the PHI-spiral on the right minor chart is rotated clockwise. The centers of both PHI-spirals are valleys, and the starting points in both cases are peaks. Both PHI-spirals are penetrated separately at peak P#01 on the minor charts. The penetration occurs on the third PHI-spiral ring on the first chart and on the fifth PHI-spiral ring on the second chart. The major chart shows the total picture of the two PHI-spirals combined. Peak P#01 is met almost exactly at the crossover point P.

Valley V#02 is the next trend reversal to be analyzed (Figure 6.16).

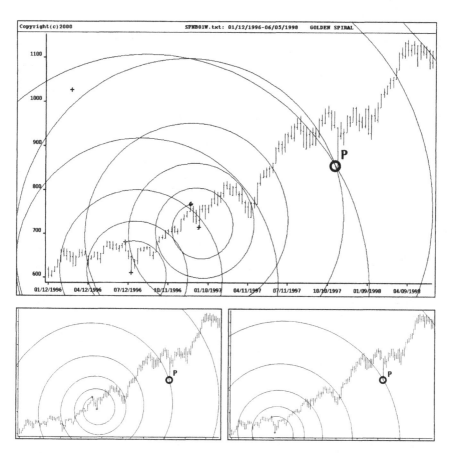

Figure 6.16   S&P500 Index from 01–96 to 06–98. PHI-spirals for V#02.

PHI-spirals act as resistance points for peaks and support lines for valleys. Turning point V#02 is a significant valley. The market correction in the S&P500 Index stops exactly at the crossover of the two PHI-spirals at point P.

The problem with weekly charts is that, compared to daily charts, we have fewer swings to work with. Therefore, it is even more astonishing that the PHI-spirals drawn from different swings cross

over at point P, where the correction stops. In addition, we have found
that five of the 10 PHI-spiral rings on the minor charts in Figure 6.16
define excellent support levels for corrections in the S&P500 Index.

Peak P#03 is the third trend reversal on our list (Figure 6.17).

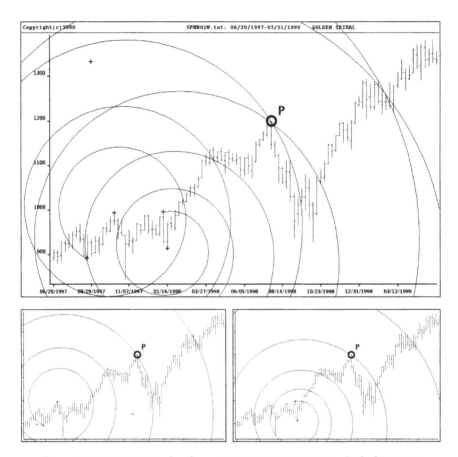

Figure 6.17   S&P500 Index from 06–97 to 05–99. PHI-spirals for P#03.

The first PHI-spiral is rotated clockwise and is penetrated at
point P on its third PHI-spiral ring. The market price stays within
the PHI-spiral ring and runs along it during the correction. The second PHI-spiral also turns clockwise and is penetrated by the market
price on its fourth PHI-spiral ring at point P. From there, the market price retraces toward the second PHI-spiral ring and finds support there.

The correction down from P#03 brings us to the significant valley V#04 (Figure 6.18).

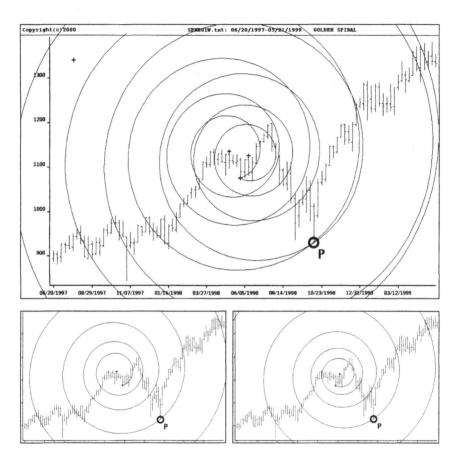

Figure 6.18   S&P500 Index from 06–97 to 05–99. PHI-spirals for V#04.

PHI-spiral analysis of valley formations considers those starting points and centers that are above the respective valleys and generate a crossover on, at least, a third PHI-spiral ring. If we do not find PHI-spirals that meet this condition, we go to a lower level and use those PHI-spirals that generate a crossover point on a lower PHI-spiral ring. If, under these conditions, no PHI-spirals are available, we can check for PHI-spirals with centers below the level of the valley in question, as shown in the example of valley V#02.

Both PHI-spirals shown in the minor charts in Figure 6.18 rotate counterclockwise and are penetrated by the market move on a fourth PHI-spiral ring. Both PHI-spirals are support lines at point P for valley V#04, from which a new impulse wave rises to new highs.

We find a further major trend reversal at peak P#05 (Figure 6.19).

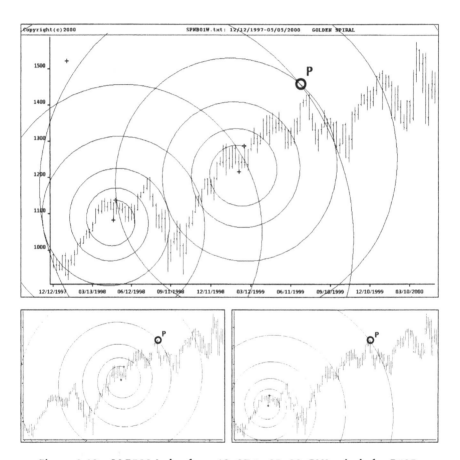

Figure 6.19   S&P500 Index from 12–97 to 05–00. PHI-spirals for P#05.

The peak we identify is at the end of an uptrend that lasts for several months and has a couple of major and minor corrections in between.

Two PHI-spirals are chosen, with different centers and starting points on smaller corrections and penetrations of peak P#05 on the third and sixth PHI-spiral ring. It is important to remember that there are other PHI-spirals pointing exactly at the same peak. We will not present them here, but will return to this issue later in the chapter.

As the market price gets close to the crossover in point P, both PHI-spirals act as support lines for the price move to the downside to follow peak P#05.

Valley V#06 is the next significant point of a major trend reversal (Figure 6.20).

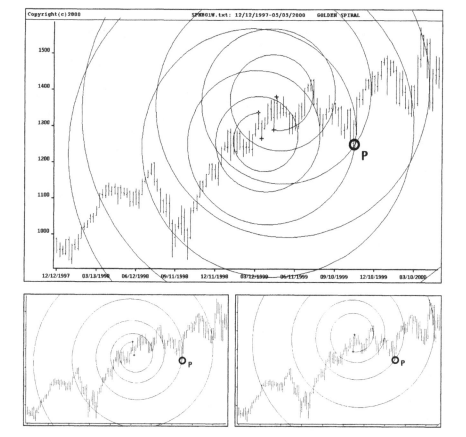

Figure 6.20   S&P500 Index from 12–97 to 05–00. PHI-spirals for V#06.

Drawing PHI-spirals as support lines of corrections works best if the corrections run as a-b-c swing patterns, with wave c being stronger than wave a, and wave a being used to draw the PHI-spiral.

This is not the case in the market price pattern of valley V#06. The correction from peak P#05 to valley V#06 is relatively small, and the intermediate swings are of little use for drawing PHI-spirals. We use two earlier swings to generate a pair of PHI-spirals in which the centers are only slightly above the level of the crossover point. The crossover of the two PHI-spirals at a point P is the end of the correction. Both PHI-spirals turn counterclockwise and are penetrated on their third PHI-spiral rings.

From V#06 on, the market rises up to peak P#07 (Figure 6.21).

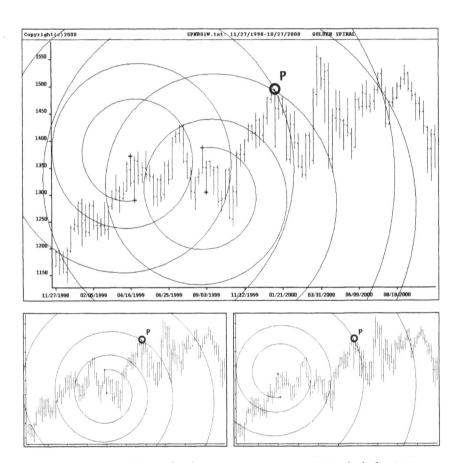

Figure 6.21   S&P500 Index from 11–98 to 10–00. PHI-spirals for P#07.

The two sample PHI-spirals on the minor charts have centers and starting points in April and in August of 1999. Both PHI-spirals are rotated clockwise. They cross over on their third PHI-spiral ring at peak P#07 (point P).

It is also possible to draw a PHI-spiral that reaches the crossover point on its fifth PHI-spiral ring. We do not show the alternative here because, if we have the option, we prefer PHI-spirals closer to the crossover point. Again, it is clear that correct PHI-spirals do not depend on the distance they are drawn from the crossover. The first PHI-spiral has its center and starting point about eight months before the third PHI-spiral ring is penetrated by the S&P500 Index at peak P#07.

The sharp correction to follow from peak P#07 runs down to valley V#08 (Figure 6.22).

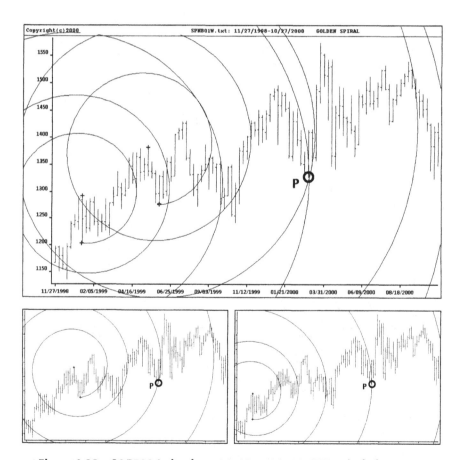

Figure 6.22   S&P500 Index from 11–98 to 10–00. PHI-spirals for V#08.

It is difficult to find swings in strong bull markets that allow us to draw PHI-spirals to generate crossovers as support levels for major lows. It is even more difficult to find centers and starting points of PHI-spirals that are higher than the support areas of the correction.

The correction in the S&P500 Index ends at valley V#08. Both PHI-spirals that identify V#08 are turned counterclockwise. The market price stops exactly at point P, where the two PHI-spirals cross over. However, the center of the PHI-spiral on the left minor chart, and the center and the starting point of the PHI-spiral on the right minor chart, are below the crossover point. This is an exception to the general rule.

Peak P#09 is the all-time high in the S&P500 Index (Figure 6.23).

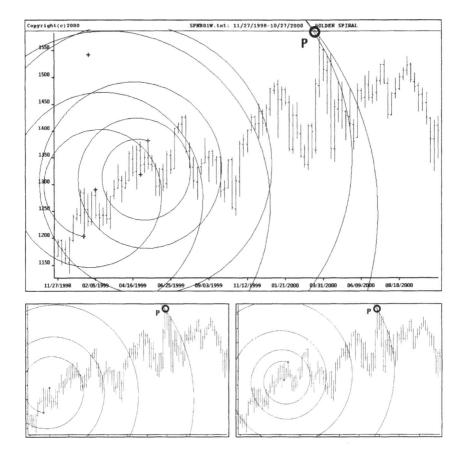

Figure 6.23 S&P500 Index from 11–98 to 10–00. PHI-spirals for P#09.

Not surprisingly, peak P#09 is identified by a nearly perfect crossover of two PHI-spirals. To demonstrate the power of PHI-spirals, we select two PHI-spirals that have their centers and starting points back in January and March of 1999. The left chart of the two PHI-spirals turns clockwise, and the right one turns counterclockwise. The fourth PHI-spiral ring is penetrated at peak P#09 in both cases.

There is no magic in PHI-spirals, but one soon realizes that crossover points of PHI-spirals on a third or higher PHI-spiral ring are always powerful indications of trend reversals. In Chapter 8, we will describe how to achieve multiple confirmation trend reversals and make the analysis even safer. For now, we turn to valley V#10 (Figure 6.24).

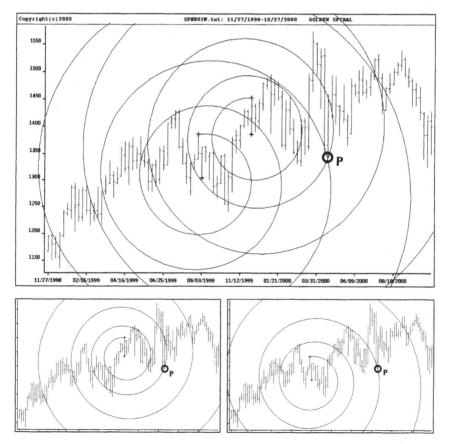

Figure 6.24 S&P500 Index from 11–98 to 10–00. PHI-spirals for V#10.

As mentioned earlier, it is difficult to identify short-term corrections on PHI-spirals with weekly data because there are not enough swings to analyze. Accuracy diminishes because we cannot wait for a crossover to penetrate a third (or higher) PHI-spiral ring. Readers will thus be surprised that two PHI-spirals identify valley V#10 on a crossover after a very short-term correction from peak P#09. The PHI-spiral on the left turns counterclockwise; the one on the right turns clockwise. What is unexpected is that the crossover point lies on a second and a third PHI-spiral ring; in both cases, the center and the starting point of the PHI-spirals are almost parallel to valley V#10.

A little more midterm is the up move to peak P#11 (Figure 6.25).

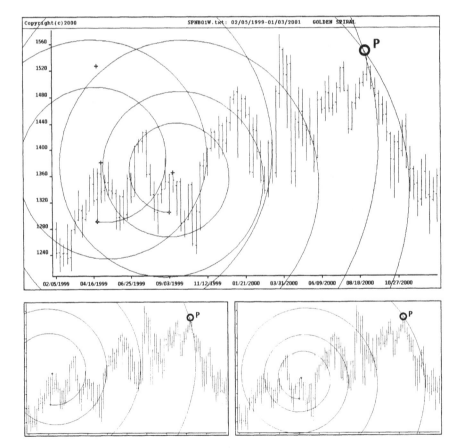

Figure 6.25 S&P500 Index from 02–99 to 01–01. PHI-spirals for P#11.

The two selected PHI-spirals pinpoint the trend reversal when both fourth PHI-spiral rings cross over at point P. In both cases, the center and the starting point of the PHI-spirals are lower than the crossover point.

Several minor peaks and valleys are made before peak P#11 occurs. The secret of PHI-spiral analysis is to wait for the next trend change to develop after peaks and valleys are identified. We can project future crossover points from existing swings, but we still have to wait for a confirmation by market price action. PHI-spirals cannot forecast final price levels of trend changes, but they can suggest targets of possible trend reversals.

The final sample trend reversal is at valley V#12 (Figure 6.26).

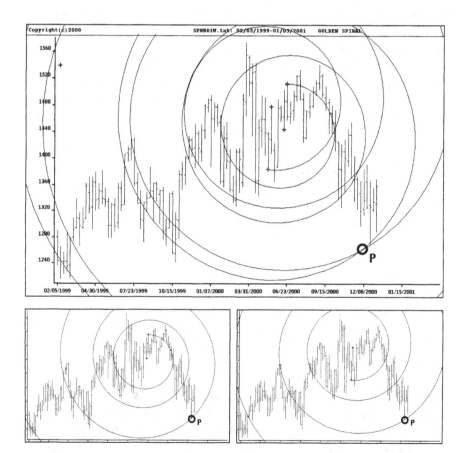

Figure 6.26   S&P500 Index from 02–99 to 01–01. PHI-spirals for V#12.

Valley V#12 is the lowest low of the first major correction in the S&P500 Index since 1996.

Therefore, it is not unusual that a great number of major and minor swings appear from which we can generate different PHI-spirals and various crossovers of PHI-spirals.

Two PHI-spirals with different centers and starting points have been selected for the confirmation of valley V#12. The PHI-spiral on the left chart rotates clockwise, and the one on the right rotates counterclockwise. Centers and starting points of both PHI-spirals are way above the crossover point at P. The crossover point in both cases is on the third PHI-spiral ring.

The trend reversal at valley V#12 is confirmed by the crossover at P and at points into the future. There is no way of knowing whether the crossover will mark a significant turning point in the S&P500 Index on its way to a new significant peak. Time will tell, but odds are in favor of our PHI-spiral analysis.

The most fascinating discovery of PHI-spirals is that major trend reversals can be separated from minor and intermediate trend changes by a solid PHI-spiral analysis. The more PHI-spirals that independently pinpoint one, single, significant peak or valley, the more important the trend reversal.

We cannot change the structure and the mathematical formula that define a PHI-spiral. We can use different swing sizes. We can also vary the direction of rotating PHI-spirals from counterclockwise to clockwise. Some people might see optimization in this, but overoptimization can backfire by adding too many technical indicators to trading strategies that do not improve future trading results. In contrast, increasing the number of PHI-spirals that pinpoint the same turning point in a market provides us with very valuable information instead of worthless overoptimized parameters.

To further clarify this important point, we present eight PHI-spirals (see Figure 6.27) that pinpoint the same all-time high in the S&P500 Index (already illustrated as peak P#09) on different PHI-spiral rings.

The first of the eight PHI-spirals is drawn from a center and a starting point in 1996. The all-time high in the S&P500 Index penetrates the PHI-spiral on the seventh PHI-spiral ring. All other examples follow the same principle with individual centers, starting points, directions of rotation, and PHI-spiral rings that are penetrated. Instead of putting all eight PHI-spirals on one chart, we have opted for eight smaller charts with individual PHI-spirals.

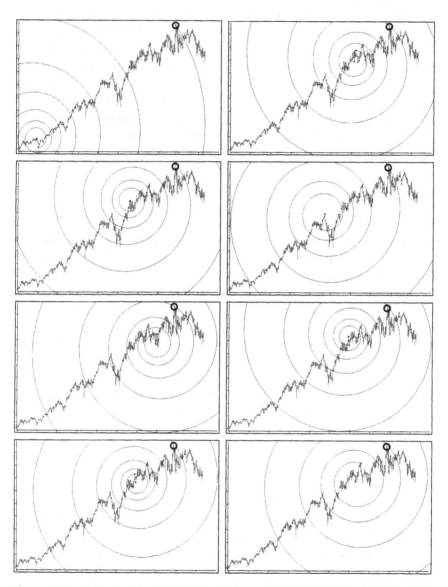

Figure 6.27   Chart of the S&P500 Index from 01–96 to 01–01. Multiple PHI-spiral confirmations of the all-time high at peak P#09. *Source: FAM Research, 2000.*

Working with PHI-spirals is not easy; we always have to select the center and the starting point of a PHI-spiral by hand. Even on large computer displays, it is very difficult to match exactly the swing high or low we want to apply. Another difficulty is that the extension of PHI-spirals in a third, fourth, fifth, or higher PHI-spiral ring gets bigger so quickly that even the smallest inaccuracy in a center or starting point selection can affect the correct identification of a peak or a valley. However, considering the results shown in the past section, we know it cannot just be coincidence that so many different PHI-spirals convincingly identify peaks and valleys on their crossovers.

The outlook is promising. The analysis shall now be extended to sets of daily O-H-L-C data in the S&P500 Index.

S&P500 Index Daily

The analysis of daily data is probably more practical than the application of weekly data alone. Most investors are impatient and do not want to wait until the end of a week for updates of their databases and the generation of trading signals.

Nature's law is of great relevance for market action, no matter what data compression rate we choose, be it daily or weekly. If we find evidence that crossovers of PHI-spirals pinpoint major peaks and valleys simultaneously on daily and on weekly data, we increase the significance and the safety level of our analysis.

The problem with PHI-spirals lies not in finding perfect combinations of PHI-spirals, but in the initial choice of swings for centers and starting points from which to draw PHI-spirals. As soon as daily and weekly crossovers of PHI-spirals point to the same trend reversals, we can fine-tune our PHI-spiral analysis.

We will not go into the same detail on daily data that we did on weekly data. All relevant charts are stored in our database, and if readers are interested, they can request additional information on important centers and starting points to get to crossovers of different PHI-spirals through our Web site.

In this section, we concentrate our analysis on a total of two sample peaks and three sample valleys, starting with the peak at the highest high in the S&P500 Index in March 2000. Readers will see how PHI-spiral analysis can be applied to daily data in the same way—and as easily and profitably—as weekly data.

The all-time high in the S&P500 Index on a daily bar chart can be identified by a number of PHI-spirals. Because there are many more swings to work with on daily charts than on weekly charts, it is a lot easier to find crossover points of different PHI-spirals.

Figure 6.28 is a convincing illustration of a crossover of two PHI-spirals out of the universe of possible PHI-spirals at the highest high in the S&P500 Index.

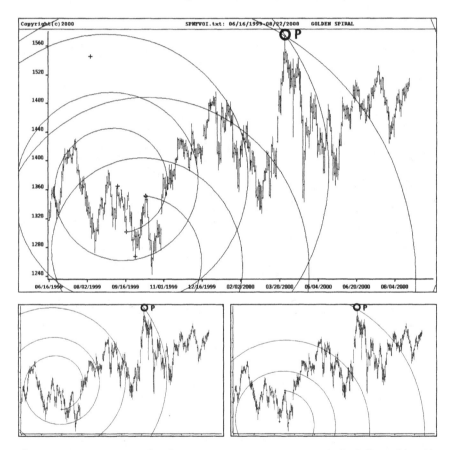

Figure 6.28   S&P500 Index from 06–99 to 08–00. PHI-spirals daily to identify the all-time high in March 2000.

Both PHI-spirals in Figure 6.28 have different centers and starting points. The left PHI-spiral turns counterclockwise, and the one on the right is rotated clockwise. Both PHI-spirals are penetrated by the highest high in the S&P500 Index on their fourth PHI-spiral rings. The crossover of the two PHI-spirals is a perfect confirmation of the peak that was identified by several PHI-spirals on a weekly basis in the previous section.

Only three weeks after the most prominent all-time high occurs, an erratic move in the S&P500 Index creates a very significant valley that is closely identified by two PHI-spirals (Figure 6.29).

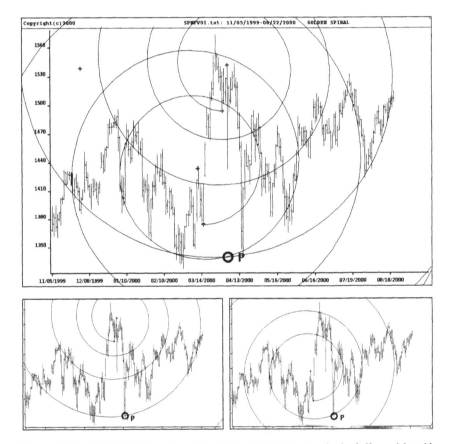

Figure 6.29   S&P500 Index from 11–99 to 08–00. PHI-spirals daily to identify a significant valley.

The short-term correction in the S&P500 Index is interesting and important because it illustrates how Fibonacci tools perform in extreme market situations. Compared to the PHI-spirals in Figure 6.29, no other analytic tools available get so close to a sharp trend reversal with such precision on daily (and weekly) charts.

The two PHI-spirals are rotated clockwise on the left and counterclockwise on the right of the two minor charts. The penetration of the PHI-spirals by the market's down move is on the third PHI-spiral ring in the left minor chart, and on the second PHI-spiral ring in the right minor chart.

The recovery of the S&P500 Index market brings us to a new peak (Figure 6.30).

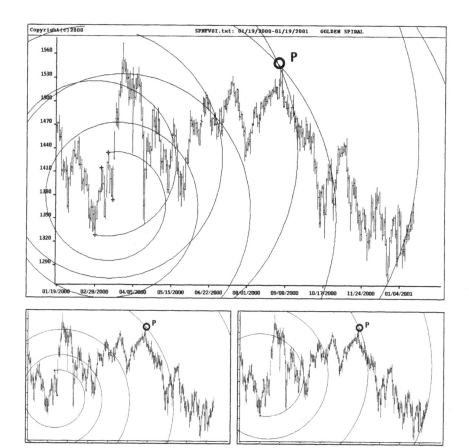

Figure 6.30   S&P500 Index from 01–00 to 01–01. PHI-spirals daily to identify a significant peak.

The major peak in Figure 6.30 is a very clear one. It is identified by several PHI-spirals on both a daily and a weekly basis. A vast number of PHI-spirals with different centers and starting points give early notice that if the market price ever reaches this level, a significant turning point is expected. We will never know the size of a trend change in advance, but we do know that as soon as significant points like this are triggered, strong corrections may last for weeks or even for months.

More than two months later, at the end of the down move in the S&P500 Index, the following valley shows every feature of a striking trend reversal on a daily basis (Figure 6.31).

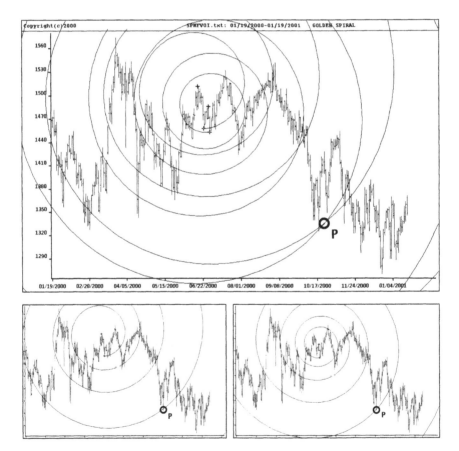

Figure 6.31   S&P500 Index from 01–00 to 01–01. PHI-spirals daily to identify a significant valley.

We find a pair of PHI-spirals crossing over on the fourth PHI-spiral rings right at the valley. The PHI-spiral in the left minor chart is turned counterclockwise, and the one in the right minor chart rotates clockwise. However, this is only a short-term trend reversal. The market moves back up for 15 days and then changes direction to the downside again.

Recalling the peak-and-valley formations on weekly charts, we realize that this valley is not confirmed weekly. It is an intermediate turning point between peak P#11 weekly and valley V#12 weekly, and is not a significant long-term trend reversal. The next significant valley to watch is identified nine weeks later (Figure 6.32).

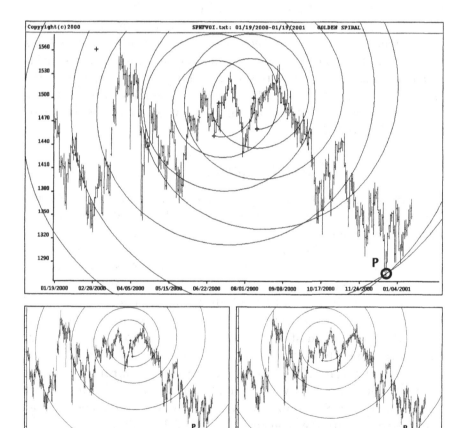

Figure 6.32 S&P500 Index from 01–00 to 01–01. PHI-spirals daily to identify a significant valley.

The valley analyzed here corresponds with valley V#12 in the previous section. This significant valley is an indication of a major trend reversal because it is possible to generate crossover points independently from at least two PHI-spirals on weekly as well as on daily data. On weekly data and on daily data, the market price in the S&P500 Index reverses on the crossover of the PHI-spirals. This is the strongest type of trading indication we can get, based on our PHI-spiral analysis.

Early in 2001, we do not yet know how the market in the S&P500 Index will develop. Time will tell, and by the time readers work their way through this chapter, they will be able to check for new trend reversals in the S&P500 Index market within a few months, and will know the latest price bars from an updated database.

Fibonacci tools can best be applied to volatile products such as cash currencies, stocks, and stock index futures. The S&P500 Index is therefore a good trading vehicle to demonstrate the use of PHI-spirals on a stock index future. Now that we have proven the relevance of PHI-spirals for the most intensively watched aggregate of the American stock market, we will conduct a similar analysis for the Euro cash currency against the US Dollar.

Euro Cash Currency Weekly and Daily

After its start with 11 participating countries in January 1999, the Euro cash currency quickly became the world's third major reserve currency, next to the Japanese Yen and the US Dollar.

In contrast to the analysis of the S&P500 Index, where we discussed PHI-spirals on weekly and daily data, the Euro cash currency is first analyzed on weekly data in general and in principle. If crossovers of at least two PHI-spirals on weekly data are not found (due to a lack of swings in the market that are required to define appropriate centers and starting points of PHI-spirals), we shift our perspective to daily data in order to fine-tune the analysis.

We will now illustrate the application of PHI-spirals to the Euro cash currency on a weekly bar chart. Seven major trend reversals are marked between September 1997 and January 2001. These seven trend reversals are the relevant points we will analyze.

The peaks and valleys of interest are numbered consecutively from peak P#01 to peak P#07. We find a total of four peaks—P#01,

P#03, P#05, and P#07—along with another three valleys—V#02, V#04, and V#06 (see Figure 6.33).

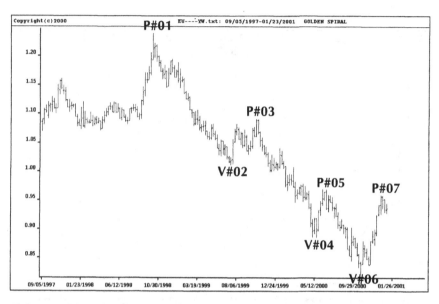

Figure 6.33   Chart of the Euro cash currency from 09–97 to 01–01. Significant peaks and valleys P#01 to P#07. *Source: FAM Research,* 2000.

Once again, we define pairs of PHI-spirals whose crossovers pinpoint the significant peaks and valleys at the turning points. As should be clear by now, we do not forecast these turning points. We must always wait for the market price to develop until the price pattern matches the precalculated crossovers of different PHI-spirals with different centers and different starting points.

As with our presentation for the S&P500 Index, we present three charts for every major peak and valley in the Euro cash currency. The major chart shows the two PHI-spirals in combination and the crossover point of the two PHI-spirals. The two minor charts show the PHI-spirals separately, to give readers a clear idea of where the starting points and centers of the different PHI-spirals are located. Knowing exactly where centers and starting points are is very important. Readers will be able to redraw all of our PHI-spirals with the WINPHI software package.

We begin our analysis of major trend reversals with the high in the Euro cash currency in October 1998, at peak P#01 weekly (Figure 6.34).

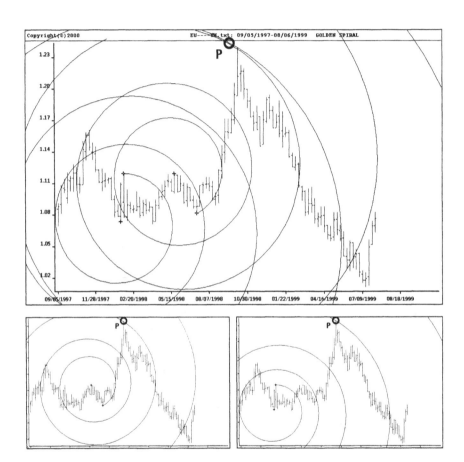

Figure 6.34   Euro cash currency from 09–97 to 08–99. PHI-spirals for P#01.

Two PHI-spirals with different centers and different starting points cross over when the market reverses its trend direction at peak P#01. The PHI-spiral in the left minor chart turns counterclockwise and is penetrated by the price move on its third PHI-spiral ring at point P. The right PHI-spiral of the minor charts is rotated clockwise and is penetrated on its fourth PHI-spiral ring. Both PHI-spirals meet the basic requirement for a major trend change of crossovers on a third or higher PHI-spiral ring.

From the analysis of the S&P500 Index, we have learned that the best turning points are established on a double confirmation of weekly and daily data. Peak P#01 in the Euro cash currency is a good example in this respect. The trend reversal from the weekly chart is confirmed by a pair of PHI-spirals on a daily basis (Figure 6.35).

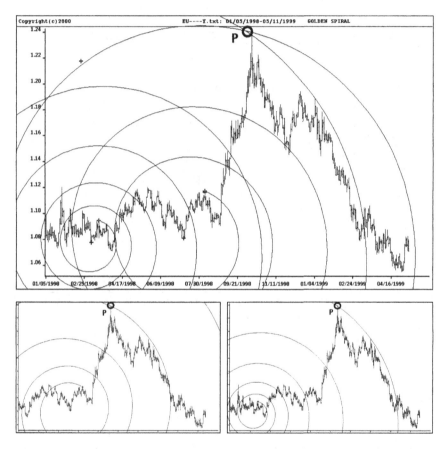

Figure 6.35   Euro cash currency from 01–98 to 05–99. PHI-spirals for P#01.

The PHI-spiral on the left is turned counterclockwise. The penetration by the peak occurs on its third PHI-spiral ring. The right PHI-spiral is rotated clockwise and is penetrated on its sixth PHI-spiral ring. The crossover of the two PHI-spirals matches the previously described crossover of the PHI-spirals on a weekly basis.

PHI-spirals other than the two presented in Figure 6.35 would also have confirmed P#01. Interested readers working with the WINPHI software package and the enclosed sets of historical data can create these PHI-spirals themselves.

Valley V#02 weekly in the Euro cash currency is also confirmed by a crossover of two PHI-spirals (Figure 6.36).

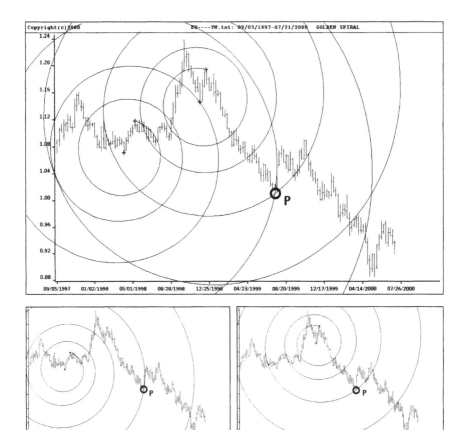

Figure 6.36   Euro cash currency from 09–97 to 07–00. PHI-spirals for V#02.

The market in the Euro cash currency moves steadily downward and penetrates the PHI-spirals on the fourth and the third PHI-spiral ring. A trend reversal is expected and occurs when the market price reaches the crossover of the two PHI-spirals.

The corresponding daily confirmation of valley V#02 is based on two PHI-spirals (see Figure 6.37).

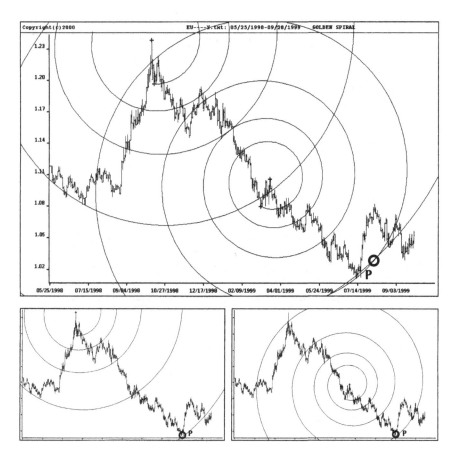

Figure 6.37   Euro cash currency from 05–98 to 09–99. PHI-spirals for V#02.

Up to this point on the Euro cash currency, we have been able to pinpoint two significant trend reversals with PHI-spirals on weekly and daily data. On both occasions when a pair of PHI-spirals weekly and daily had the same crossover point, there was a significant change in the trend in the marketplace.

The trend reversal at valley V#02 happens as expected, but the correction that follows is not strong enough to generate swings on a weekly basis. We are not able to find a pair of appropriate PHI-spirals that confirms peak P#03 in a crossover weekly. However, there are two PHI-spirals in the daily data and its crossover is penetrated by the market move at peak P#03 (Figure 6.38).

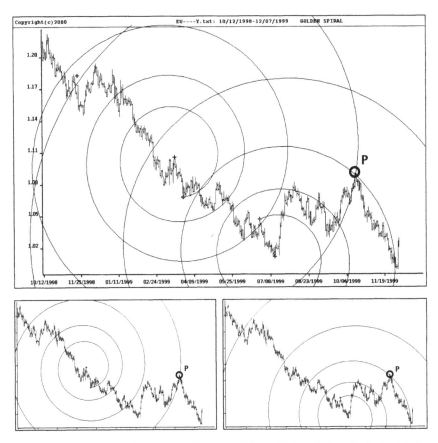

Figure 6.38   Euro cash currency from 10–98 to 12–99. PHI-spirals for P#03.

The PHI-spiral in the left minor chart is rotated counterclockwise and is penetrated on its fourth PHI-spiral ring. The right PHI-spiral is turned clockwise with a penetration on the third PHI-spiral ring. The penetration of the crossover by the market move at peak P#03 is one of the nearest—and is the best in the examples—seen so far.

We do not have a double confirmation of crossovers on weekly and daily data; therefore, it is uncertain as to whether the turning point is significant and the market really will go higher. This example is similar to the second of the three valleys in the section on the S&P500 Index daily, for it too is not confirmed weekly. It is only an intermediate short-term correction, not a significant trend reversal.

After the market reverses to new lows, valley V#04 is (in contrast to peak P#03) again double-confirmed on a weekly and a daily basis. Figure 6.39 shows the weekly pattern.

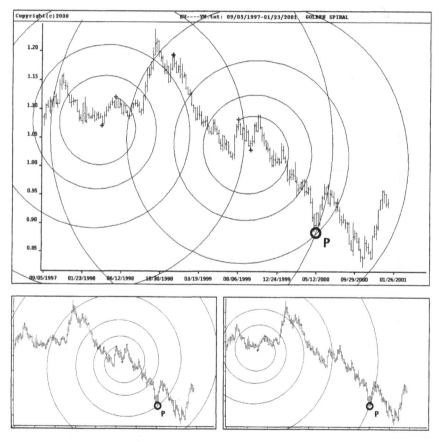

Figure 6.39   Euro cash currency from 09–97 to 01–01. PHI-spirals for V#04.

Valley V#04 is a significant valley. Two PHI-spirals on weekly and daily data identify the same major turning point. In this case, we concentrate our analysis on the set of weekly data to avoid becoming repetitive. Readers can easily generate the crossover points on daily data themselves, using the WINPHI software.

Peak P#05 is more interesting than valley V#04, because here we experience the same situation as with peak P#03. After the significant valley V#04 is confirmed by PHI-spirals on weekly and daily data, the correction that follows to the upside in the Euro cash currency is not strong enough to provide us with a swing pattern that is relevant for a weekly PHI-spiral analysis. However, a pair of PHI-spirals applied to the set of daily data gives a valid crossover point for the confirmation of peak P#05 (Figure 6.40).

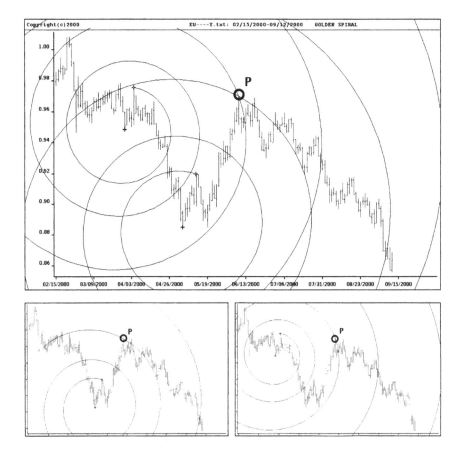

Figure 6.40   Euro cash currency from 02–00 to 09–00. PHI-spirals for P#05.

There is no definite distinction between intermediate turning points that are short-term and confirmed only once, and significant trend reversals that are double-confirmed by pairs of PHI-spirals weekly and daily.

From peak P#05, the market drops sharply to lower lows and finally to an all-time low at valley V#06. The weekly pattern for this market move is covered by Figure 6.41.

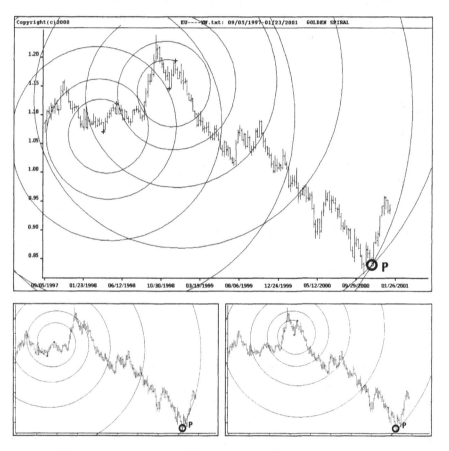

Figure 6.41   Euro cash currency from 09–97 to 01–01. PHI-spirals for V#06.

Valley V#06 is one of the significant trend reversals that can be pinpointed with many different PHI-spirals drawn from different centers and starting points months and years ahead. The left PHI-spiral has a center and starting point from the second quarter of 1998. The PHI-spiral on the right has a center and starting point from late in 1998, shortly after the highest high is made.

Although we were able to draw the crossover point at 0.84 USD per EUR by the end of 1998, there was no way of knowing that the market price would ever go that low. The indication that valley V#06 might be a significant trend change is the crossover double-confirmed by an additional pair of PHI-spirals on daily data.

The final trend reversal in the Euro cash currency to be analyzed is peak P#07. We first show the results of our analysis on weekly bar charts (Figure 6.42).

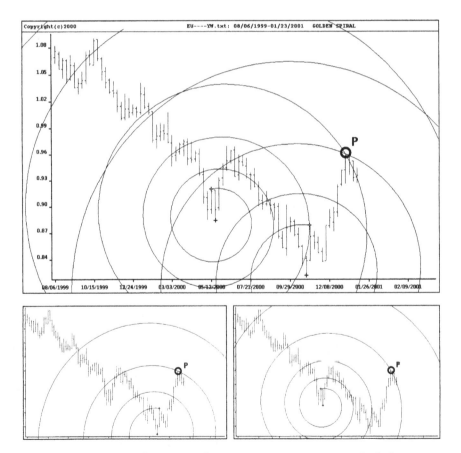

Figure 6.42   Euro cash currency from 08–99 to 01–01. PHI-spirals for P#07.

Peak P#07 on a weekly basis is pinpointed by various PHI-spirals with different centers and starting points. The two PHI-spirals we present in Figure 6.42 are penetrated by the uptrend in the Euro cash currency on the third and fourth PHI-spiral ring. To clarify the picture and check peak P#07 for its significance as a major trend reversal, we look for additional PHI-spirals, on a daily basis, that are also penetrated by the market move at peak P#07. And we do find a pair of PHI-spirals daily that turns out to be a perfect confirmation of peak P#07 (Figure 6.43).

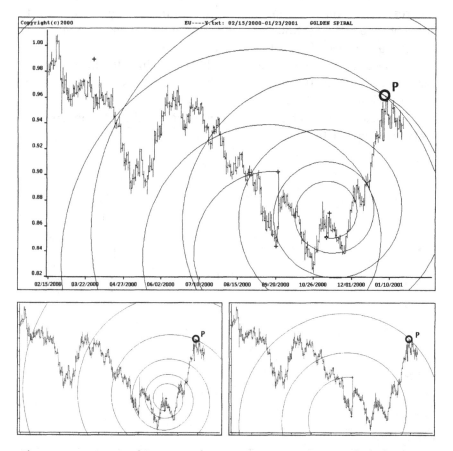

Figure 6.43   Euro cash currency from 02–00 to 01–01. PHI-spirals for P#07.

Multiple confirmations are what we try to receive by analyzing the markets based on geometrical Fibonacci devices, such as pairs of

PHI-spirals. In Chapter 8, we will see how this convincing approach can be fine-tuned even more by combining different geometrical Fibonacci trading tools.

We now leave the Euro cash currency and consider the possibilities of successfully applying PHI-spirals to the DAX30 Index.

DAX30 Index Weekly and Daily

The DAX30 Index is one of the major European benchmarks, and—next to the S&P500 Index—one of the most heavily traded stock index futures in the world. As far as volume, liquidity, and marketability are concerned, the DAX30 Index is suitable for Fibonacci analysis in general, and especially for PHI-spiral analysis.

From January 1996 to January 2001, we find 10 major trend reversals in the DAX30 Index that are worth discussing in the context of our PHI-spiral analysis.

The 10 significant turning points are numbered from P#01 to V#10 in Figure 6.44.

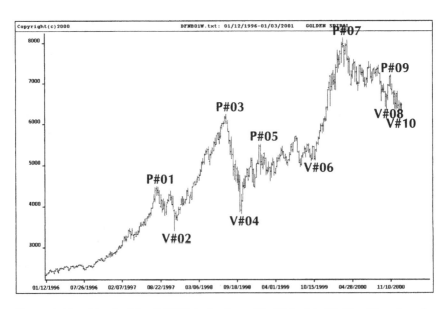

Figure 6.44   Chart of the DAX30 Index from 01–96 to 01–01. Significant peaks and valleys P#01 to V#10. *Source: FAM Research, 2000.*

All five valleys and four out of five peaks are double-confirmed by pairs of PHI-spirals weekly and daily. These nine trend reversals can be considered significant. Peak P#09 is the only exception; it is an intermediate peak for which we cannot find a crossover of PHI-spirals weekly. Therefore, we present the charts for the daily crossover of PHI-spirals at peak P#09 and contrast it with the other peaks and valleys in the DAX30 Index. To show PHI-spirals and relevant crossovers, we present examples of two striking peaks—P#03 and P#07—and two valleys—V#04 and V#10—in detail on weekly data.

Peak P#03 on a weekly O-H-L-C bar chart is illustrated in detail in Figure 6.45.

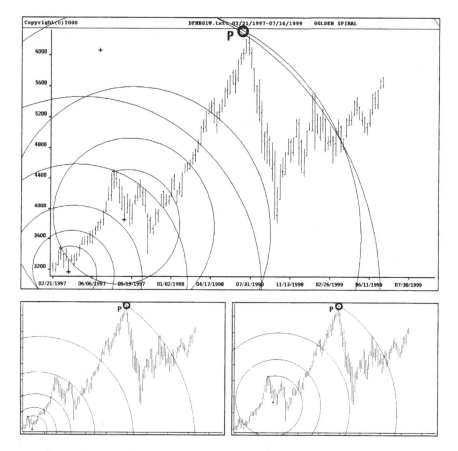

Figure 6.45 DAX30 Index from 02–97 to 07–99. PHI-spirals for P#03.

Peak P#03 is a schoolbook example of a solid PHI-spiral analysis. Both PHI-spirals are rotated clockwise. The PHI-spiral in the left minor chart is penetrated by the market move in the DAX30 Index on its sixth PHI-spiral ring. The PHI-spiral in the right minor chart is penetrated on its third PHI-spiral ring.

The most difficult part for investors is to wait until the market price touches the crossover point. Apart from having to correctly analyze the data, having the discipline to stick to the rules and not become impatient is the biggest challenge when working with all Fibonacci tools.

Valley V#04 weekly is not much more complicated than peak P#03 (Figure 6.46).

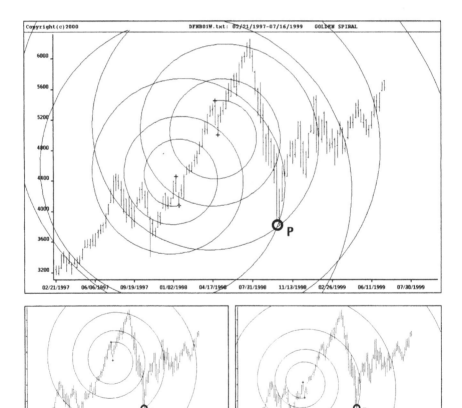

Figure 6.46   DAX30 Index from 02–97 to 07–99. PHI-spirals for V#04.

The DAX30 Index market collapses so fast from peak P#03 that there is hardly a trading tool available to tell where the bottom is. Often, in these extreme situations, Fibonacci tools perform best.

The market price penetrates the PHI-spirals at the crossover of the third PHI-spiral rings of both PHI-spirals. In both cases, the centers of the PHI-spirals are above the crossover point. This fact makes the crossover reliable. In short corrections, if the centers of PHI-spirals are below the analyzed valley, a crossover will be generated with fewer PHI-spiral rings, or the market price will penetrate the relevant PHI-spiral rings from outside to inside (which is a less reliable pattern).

From here, we jump directly to peak P#07 weekly (Figure 6.47).

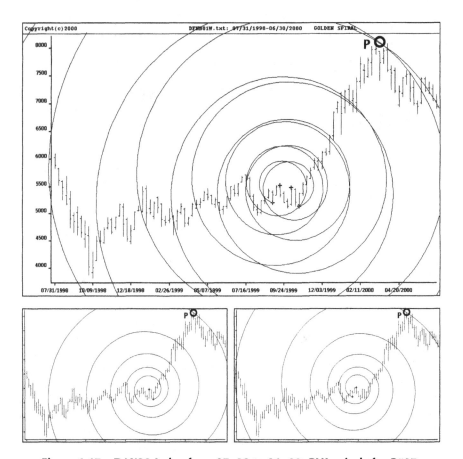

Figure 6.47   DAX30 Index from 07–98 to 06–00. PHI-spirals for P#07.

Peak P#07 marks the end of an extremely strong market trend. At a time when few media sources hint at a trend change, the crossover of the PHI-spirals will give a significant indication that a major trend change is imminent. The beauty of geometrical Fibonacci tools is that they indicate trend changes when almost no one else is aware of what is about to happen. It is, of course, very difficult to stay disciplined if the odds are against oneself, but investors can look for additional confirmations of reversals (as will be described in Chapter 8, "Combining Fibonacci Tools").

We will next analyze peak P#09, which is the only exceptional peak or valley in the DAX30 Index that leaves us without a weekly crossover of two PHI-spirals. Figure 6.48 shows P#09 daily.

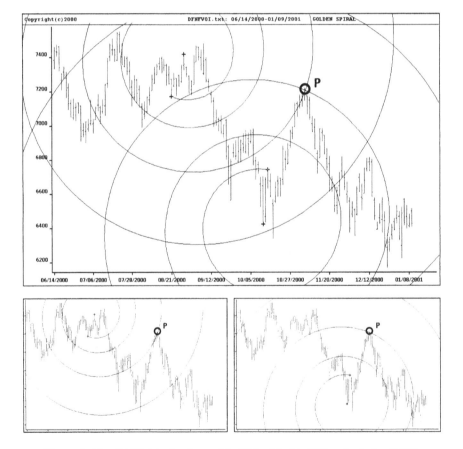

Figure 6.48 DAX30 Index from 06–00 to 01–01. PHI-spirals for P#09.

Peak P#09 cannot be identified as a significant peak by a double confirmation of pairs of PHI-spirals weekly and daily, because there is no crossover of two PHI-spirals on a weekly basis.

Here, we acknowledge a drawback in our weekly analysis of PHI-spirals. Major trend changes can be identified based on PHI-spirals only when there are swing highs and lows to work with. If there is only a very strong short-term rally without a swing in between (as we see for three weeks from valley V#08 to peak P#09), it is unlikely we will get valid PHI-spirals.

However, as with several examples of the S&P500 Index and the Euro cash currency, we are able to draw a pair of PHI-spirals on the daily chart of the DAX30 Index.

Both daily PHI-spirals turn counterclockwise and are penetrated at the crossover on their third PHI-spiral rings. One PHI-spiral center is below the peak, the other is above the peak. Here, we find a special case in that one PHI-spiral provides some support for the market move and the other one acts as a resistance level. These cases are the most difficult ones to analyze. Additional trading tools can further confirm peak P#09 as a major turning point.

Confirmations by two PHI-spirals on a daily basis can be exploited by short-term-oriented investors who want to participate in the profit potential of sharp trend changes. The type of confirmation an investor takes as a decision to enter the market depends on the risk preference of that individual. For example, an investor may decide that a crossover—confirmed multiple times by a crossover of two PHI-spirals on a daily basis, but not by two crossovers daily and weekly—is sufficiently confirmed. Our research shows, however, that, for long-term investments, it pays to wait for a multiple confirmation of trend reversals daily and weekly.

Readers now know how to conduct a solid PHI-spiral analysis and should be able to create the weekly and daily PHI-spirals for the peaks and valleys that are not already described in detail on charts. Those missing PHI-spirals can be created using the WINPHI software.

The last valley to be described in detail is valley V#10. We are unable to predict the market move in the DAX30 Index that will develop from the low starting in January 2001. However, we are able to identify pairs of PHI-spirals weekly and daily that meet exactly the same low. Therefore, we are optimistic that valley V#10 can be featured as a significant valley.

Figure 6.49 covers the weekly pattern that leads to a crossover of two PHI-spirals at valley V#10. The daily counterpart, as we have said, is easy for readers to create themselves.

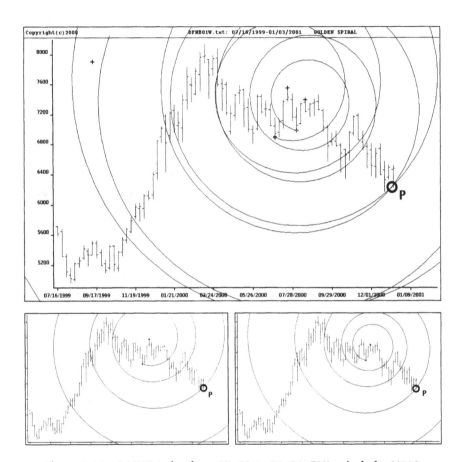

Figure 6.49   DAX30 Index from 07–99 to 01–01. PHI-spirals for V#10.

The PHI-spiral of the left minor chart is rotated counterclockwise; the right PHI-spiral is turned clockwise. Both PHI-spirals are penetrated by the market move in the DAX30 Index at their third PHI-spiral rings. Valley V#10 is a turning point where other PHI-spirals, drawn months earlier, have also had their crossover points.

To conclude this chapter, we demonstrate one more time how the overall significance of a trend reversal may be strongly increased, depending on the number of PHI-spirals that identify the same peak or valley.

On a daily chart of the DAX30 Index, we choose three PHI-spirals that have the same crossover point at valley V#10. Special market configurations like this do not occur often; therefore, we feel this price pattern is worth presenting. See Figure 6.50.

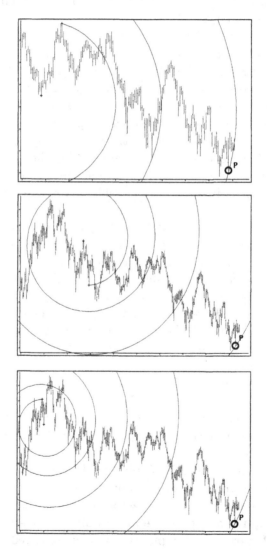

Figure 6.50   DAX30 Index from 01–00 to 01–01. PHI-spirals for V#10.

Our findings on PHI-spirals are detailed and complex, so we will summarize them before introducing readers to Fibonacci time goal days, which is the last of our six Fibonacci trading tools.

SUMMARY

PHI-spirals provide the missing analytical link between geometrical price and time analyses.

PHI-spirals, considered the most beautiful of all mathematical curves, have occurred in nature for millions of years. To link human behavior—expressed in the price swings of financial futures, stock index futures, stocks, and cash currencies—to nature's law, expressed in its purest form in the nautilus shell, we must look to the PHI-spiral.

PHI-spirals give evidence that market price patterns are not random, for there is a stunning symmetry in each major product traded. Each product follows a clear behavioral pattern. The forces that direct price moves also allow investors to take advantage of trading opportunities, as long as investors are capable of correctly applying PHI-spirals.

The rule of alternation, along with market symmetry, can also be applied to analyze price patterns. Elliott deserves a great deal of credit because he knew about these rules, back in his era, without being able to enlist computer support for his calculations.

PHI-spirals are simple to work with and easy to understand. Only one center and one starting point has to be chosen per PHI-spiral. However, PHI-spirals cannot be drawn by hand, and it takes a software package like our WINPHI computer program to put PHI-spirals on charts.

Precision is another element that determines the quality of the outcome of PHI-spiral analysis. The less accurately the centers and starting points of PHI-spirals are marked, the more off-target PHI-spiral rings become, because PHI-spirals then circle farther away from their center points.

The main challenge in PHI-spiral analysis is actually rather simple: Just believe in it. Crossovers of PHI-spirals occur at extreme points in the markets and are always counter to the main trend direction. Discipline and patience are required. Investment decisions based on PHI-spirals, by design, are long-term oriented. They let markets develop instead of trying to exploit every minor up or down.

The most profitable trend reversals can be identified by working with weekly data. But because the number of possible swings is limited on weekly bar charts, crossovers of PHI-spirals on weekly data are not frequent. That is why we favor a combination of PHI-spiral analysis weekly and daily. It is incredible to watch significant peaks or valleys being pinpointed by crossovers of different PHI-spirals—spirals that differ not only in centers and starting points, but also in weekly and daily data compression rates.

Our analysis of three sample products—the S&P500 Index, the Euro cash currency, and the DAX30 Index—has led us to the conclusion that whenever we identify a significant turning point on both weekly and daily data, we can expect a strong market reaction to follow.

However, a correctly identified trend change is not always followed by another significant trend change. In these cases, especially in the Euro cash currency, significant peaks and valleys do not alternate. A significant peak follows a significant peak, and a significant valley follows a significant valley, with only minor corrections in between. These minor corrections, or intermediate peaks or valleys, can be identified on daily data but not on weekly data. Although such cases are rare, it is very important to understand that these patterns do show up.

Interestingly, examples in which significant highs or lows appear in line, without alternation, indicate a high probability that the second peak or valley will have a stronger correction than the peak or valley that preceded it.

All charts presented and all PHI-spirals shown have been created with the greatest accuracy possible. All sample PHI-spirals can easily be redrawn with the WINPHI software package and the historical database included with the CD-ROM.

Readers may ask why we have presented so many charts and examples in this chapter if PHI-spirals are so easy to apply. The reasons are:

1. It is very difficult to believe that a tool like the PHI-spiral exists but is virtually unknown in a world where everything seems to have been discovered already.

2. We want to show how crossovers of PHI-spirals point to possible trend reversals far before significant peaks or valleys materialize. There are always alternative swings available from which

PHI-spirals can be drawn. We must wait for the market itself to confirm a crossover at a peak or valley.

3. We want readers to understand the level of precision required for a successful application of PHI-spirals. Working with a tool like the PHI-spiral is heightened if significant peaks and valleys are identified in sequence on examples over more than five years in heavily traded products.

The best analysis will not help if an investor does not believe in it and does not have the discipline to wait for an ideal entry point. On the other hand, sometimes a turning point is missed because a market price move does not reach an expected crossover point. For newcomers to Fibonacci analysis, it might be best to wait for opportunities where several Fibonacci tools give multiple confirmation of one and the same turning point. This will be the subject of Chapter 8.

We realize that we have not answered *all* remaining questions regarding PHI-spirals and their proper applications. Readers should feel free to contact us through our Web site for comments and further information.

7

FIBONACCI TIME-GOAL ANALYSIS

In 1983, Robert Fischer, in a series of seminars held in the United States, introduced for the first time the ways the Fibonacci ratio could fruitfully be applied to time-goal days.

The Fibonacci time-goal analysis is similar to the time analysis based on the Fibonacci summation series described in Chapter 2. But instead of using the count of the Fibonacci summation series to forecast turning points in the markets, Fibonacci time-goal analysis makes use of the ratios 0.618, 1.000, and 1.618, which result from the Fibonacci summation series.

Fibonacci time-goal days are days on which a price event is supposed to occur. Being able to anticipate the exact day on which a price trend will change direction is helpful in our daily and weekly analysis, and is very much in line with the analysis we performed on PHI-ellipses and PHI-spirals. Fibonacci time-goal analysis is not lagging but is of forecasting value. Trades can be entered or exited at the price change rather than after the fact. The concept is dynamic. The distance between two highs or two lows is seldom the same, and precalculated Fibonacci time-goal days vary, depending on larger or smaller swing sizes of the market price pattern.

Readers were introduced to Fibonacci time-goal analysis in principle in Chapter 1. To properly calculate Fibonacci time-goal days, we draw upon the work of the Greek mathematician, Euclid of Megara, and his invention of the "golden cut" (also called golden section) that links nature's law to geometry.

In accordance with Euclid's findings, we take the distance between two peaks or two valleys as the basis for calculating Fibonacci time-goal days. The distance from peak to peak or from valley to valley is multiplied by one of the ratios—0.618, 1.000, or 1.618—to identify the point in the future at which a major trend reversal can be expected. (Readers who need a quick review should see Figure 1.3 and Figure 1.15 in Chapter 1.)

We cannot predict whether a market price will be high or low on the day when a Fibonacci time goal is reached. Fibonacci time-goal days forecast trend changes simply as events.

Figure 7.1 is an illustration of Fibonacci time-goal days out of peak-to-peak formations.

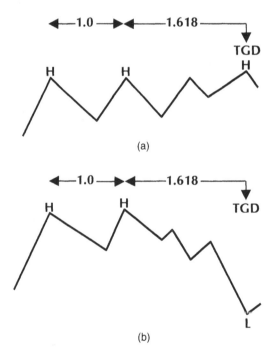

Figure 7.1 Fibonacci time-goal days. (a) Market price is high on time-goal day out of a peak-to-peak formation; (b) market price is low on time-goal day out of a peak-to-peak formation. *Source: FAM Research, 2000.*

Fibonacci time-goal days can be measured on weekly, daily, or intraday data series using the three ratios 0.618, 1.000, and 1.618. Fibonacci time-goal days can also be confirmed by higher ratios from the PHI series, but the following examples will concentrate on the three fundamental ratios because they stem directly from the Fibonacci summation series.

The structure of this chapter is similar to that of the two preceding chapters. We first describe features and parameters of Fibonacci time-goal days, and then present sample applications of Fibonacci time-goal days to market data.

BASIC FEATURES OF FIBONACCI TIME-GOAL DAYS

Fibonacci time-goal days work as independent investment devices, just like the five geometrical Fibonacci trading tools we have described so far.

Trading signals on Fibonacci time-goal days appear by design as countertrend entries, and the media will often recommend opposite trading strategies in respective situations. As with trading signals on corrections and extensions (Chapter 3), investors must wait until a clear timing signal is determined before entering the market.

Having patience is the toughest part of trading, because signals come when least expected.

Fibonacci time-goal analysis forecasts changes in trend direction. Therefore, traders must be prepared to buy when the price is high and sell when the price is low. This strategy sounds simple, but it is difficult to execute because emotion usually drives traders to buy on uptrends in expectation of further rising prices, and to sell on downtrends in expectation of lower lows.

Rules for calculating Fibonacci time-goal days and corresponding entry rules, exit rules, stop-loss rules, and re-entry rules were described in detail in the earlier book, *Fibonacci Applications and Strategies for Traders*.

We will not repeat the rules here because our main goal is to teach readers how to detect and forecast trend reversals in the markets. We want to reveal the power of pattern analysis and introduce our geometrical approach. Readers who wish to add entry and exit rules to this concept should use the rules described in Chapter 3. They are reliable and can safely be combined with PHI-channels, PHI-ellipses, PHI-spirals, and Fibonacci time-goal days.

The key-parameter is the size of the initial swing that defines valid peaks and valleys from which Fibonacci time-goal days are calculated. Each product we analyze has a specific minimum swing size. Swing sizes vary, not only from product to product, but also depending on the data compression rate that is chosen (monthly, weekly, daily, or intraday). The number of trades is directly proportional to the swing size. If the swing size is too small, we will receive too many Fibonacci time-goal days and too many potential trend changes. If the swing size is too large, there will be very few signals, and important price moves are likely to be missed.

Readers will find sets of historical data for various products and various data compression rates on the WINPHI CD-ROM. These datasets can be used to find appropriate minimum swing sizes for different products. The WINPHI software includes a feature that charts historical data on a constant scale and allows users to go back to historical data and search for minimum swing sizes for every product they desire. The WINPHI charting feature works with ASCII D–O–H–L–C data, so files from any major data vendor can be loaded into the program once they are converted to plain ASCII format.

No matter how closely we look for the best minimum swing size, there will be situations, especially in strong trending markets, where the minimum swing size is not available. "Not available," in this case, means that we do not find valid swing highs or swing lows in a market move for a longer period of time.

As a general rule, valid swing highs and valid swing lows must occur at least every 15 days on daily data or every 10 weeks on weekly data. If swing highs and lows occur less frequently, the Fibonacci time-goal days are so far apart that trend reversals can no longer be captured. This problem is solved by reducing the swing size below the level of the optimal swing size. We simply select the highest peak or the lowest valley of 15 days or 10 weeks, and then receive a new measurement for a valid swing to calculate a Fibonacci time-goal day.

A reformulation of the swing definition may also become necessary when there is a strongly increased number of swing highs or lows in only a few days or a few weeks (the opposite case to what we just discussed). Too high a frequency of swing highs or swing lows means increased noise in the market and is a major problem in volatile market conditions.

Excessive noise can be eliminated by a simple amendment to the general definition of filter swings. There must be at least three days between the highs and lows of two swings that satisfy the minimum swing size. This applies to both top and bottom formations.

Successful Fibonacci time analysis depends on the correct identification of peaks and valleys. The standard swing size is chosen based on test runs on historical data, but this minimum swing size is only the first way to identify the correct peaks and valleys. The amendments added to those cases of too low and too high frequencies of swing highs and swing lows make the rule workable and also make Fibonacci time-goal days tradable.

Whenever we look at a chart of any time span, we find market price patterns expressed in big and small swing sizes. These swings rarely represent the wave structure that Elliott defined, because most market patterns are irregular. As discussed earlier, irregular market patterns are the result of complex corrections and extensions.

Applications of Fibonacci time-goal days do not require the use of the wave count. In the Fibonacci time analysis, it is not important if there is an uptrend, downtrend or sideward market. The Fibonacci ratios can be applied to any predefined market swings.

Fibonacci time-goal days forecast events in time. We never know whether a market price will be high or low by the time a Fibonacci time-goal day is reached. Our primary objective is to sell on the Fibonacci time-goal day if the market price is high, and to buy on the Fibonacci time-goal day if the market price is low.

In our Fibonacci analysis, we strive for multiple confirmations of trend reversals, which are the most solid basis for investment decisions. This principle also holds true for Fibonacci time analysis.

Market entries in our Fibonacci time analysis are based on double confirmations of Fibonacci time-goal days. A trend reversal must be confirmed by one Fibonacci time-goal day that is calculated from two peaks (valleys), and a second Fibonacci time-goal day that is calculated from two valleys (peaks). On daily data, at least one of the calculations, either from high to high or from low to low, has to use the Fibonacci ratio 1.618. The second calculation can use any of the three ratios: 0.618, 1.000, or 1.618. On weekly data, this additional condition for calculating valid Fibonacci time-goal days is not necessary.

The perfect case, of course, occurs when one Fibonacci time goal, calculated from two peaks, and another Fibonacci time goal, calculated from two valleys, point at exactly the same day (Figure 7.2).

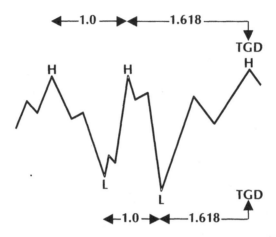

Figure 7.2 Fibonacci time-goal days coincide based on a peak-to-peak and a valley-to-valley formation. *Source: FAM Research,* 2000.

Having a pair of Fibonacci time goals is an exception to the rule that Fibonacci time-goal days are interspersed.

To receive a valid multiple confirmation of a trend reversal, Fibonacci time-goal days must be close together; the precalculated Fibonacci time goals must not differ for more than two days or two weeks. If this does not happen, we do not act at all; we must wait for a future time when two Fibonacci time goals are confirmed closer together.

In most cases, the first of the Fibonacci time goals points to a day or a week shortly before a peak or valley. The second Fibonacci time goal often points right at the peak or valley, or at one day or week after the peak or valley. We receive a narrow time band for the appearance of a trend reversal; it is similar to the price bands for corrections and extensions, described in Chapter 3. Whenever a Fibonacci time goal points to three or more days, or three or more weeks after a peak or valley, it should be ignored as long as we do not find another possible minimum filter swing from which to calculate.

The basic features of Fibonacci time goals are easy to understand in theory and not much more difficult to apply to market data.

Once more, we will use the S&P500 Index, the DAX30 Index, and the Euro cash currency to demonstrate the use of Fibonacci time-goal analysis in practical terms.

APPLICATIONS OF FIBONACCI TIME-GOAL DAYS

In the chapters on PHI-ellipses and PHI-spirals, we showed how weekly analysis and daily analysis support each other and must be considered together in order to get a clear overall picture of the market strategy.

The advantage of using weekly data is that a lot of smaller swings are eliminated, and analysis can be concentrated on major trend changes. But this does not mean that trend changes analyzed with daily data have no value at all.

Daily trend changes are of great importance for investors who focus on smaller swings short-term and trade more frequently. Trend changes on daily data are also very important for day-traders who are in search of confirmations of their intraday signals.

In this section, we will analyze the S&P500 Index, the DAX30 Index, and the Euro cash currency on sample sets of weekly and daily data.

S&P500 Index Weekly

We will first analyze the S&P500 Index on weekly data, and look for confirmations of trend reversals where Fibonacci time-goal days are not more than two price bars apart. All Fibonacci time goals are calculated exclusively, based on high-to-high connections and/or low-to-low connections.

1.618 is the best ratio for calculating Fibonacci time-goal days, although weekly data compression often does not provide enough swings to work with. Sometimes we must change the ratio to 1.000 for the first Fibonacci time-goal day. To create the time band, the calculation of the second Fibonacci time-goal day can be based on all three ratios—0.618, 1.000, and 1.618—as long as no more than two weeks pass between the first Fibonacci time-goal day and the second.

Often, alternative calculations from different highs or lows, and by using different ratios, point at the same peaks or valleys. The more Fibonacci time-goal days point at the same trend change, the better. It is likely that the use of higher ratios from the PHI series will provide additional Fibonacci time goals that point at already identified peaks or valleys. Higher ratios from the PHI series can be applied to increase the number of confirmations per trend reversal.

Ten major trend reversals in the S&P500 Index are marked from peak P#01 to valley V#10 (Figure 7.3). These 10 significant peaks and valleys are in accordance with the trend changes analyzed in the previous chapter. Highs and lows serving as the basis for our calculations of time targets are numbered consecutively from #1 to #28. Highs are marked with uneven numbers, and lows with even numbers. Low #16 and low #18 are used twice because there is no valid swing to calculate from, between valley V#04 and valley V#06.

Readers are asked to create the same Fibonacci time-goal days with the WINPHI computer program, for it will increase their understanding of Fibonacci time-goal analysis.

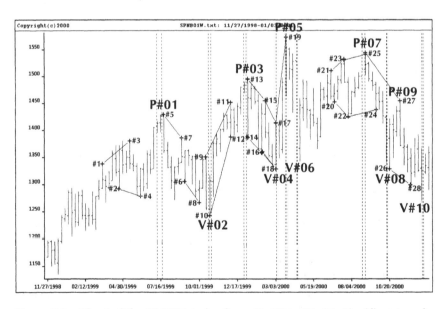

Figure 7.3   Chart of the S&P500 Index from 11–98 to 01–01. Significant peaks and valleys P#01 to V#10. *Source: FAM Research,* 2000.

From the chart in Figure 7.3, we conclude, with one exception, that all significant peaks and valleys are identified by a price band of two Fibonacci time-goal days less than two price bars apart. On all sample signals, Fibonacci time-goal days are either before, or exactly at, the peaks or valleys.

Peak P#09 is the only exception that is not identified by a pair of Fibonacci time-goal days, yet this result does not come as a surprise. The price move between peak P#07 and valley V#08 has no valid swing of an appropriate swing size. Peak P#09 is an example of the rare cases in which a trend reversal is missed on a weekly basis, although the significant peak is easily captured on daily data.

S&P500 Index Daily

Fibonacci time-goal days on daily data occur much more frequently than on weekly data. If we limit analysis to the ratio 1.618 for the first Fibonacci time-goal day, and then use all three ratios (0.618, 1.000, and 1.618) to confirm Fibonacci time-goal days, we can identify every major trend reversal daily, while staying very close to the market action.

It is very important to have the time band between two Fibonacci time goals no wider than two days. This rule filters out many time targets.

We show our analysis of the S&P500 Index on daily data from March 2000 to January 2001. This time span was chosen because (1) it is the closest period to the writing of this book, and (2) it was one of the most difficult periods the S&P500 Index ever went through.

Our Fibonacci time-goal analysis covers 14 major trend changes in the S&P500 Index. They are numbered consecutively from valley V#01 to valley V#14. We have marked the swing highs and lows used for the calculation of the Fibonacci time-goal days from #1 to #43, enabling readers to perform similar calculations with the WINPHI software.

The only critical trend change is at valley V#09. Without an entry rule, more aggressive investors get a straight buy signal. As the market drops rapidly from valley V#09, we realize how important it is to work with a stop-loss rule, no matter how promising a signal for a trend reversal might look. On the other hand, the trend reversal at valley V#10 shows how far away from the entry point stop-loss levels can be set if a conservative entry rule is applied after the Fibonacci time target is triggered.

All 14 significant trend changes in the S&P500 Index, as well as the highs and lows used to calculate the Fibonacci time-goal corridors, are shown in Figure 7.4.

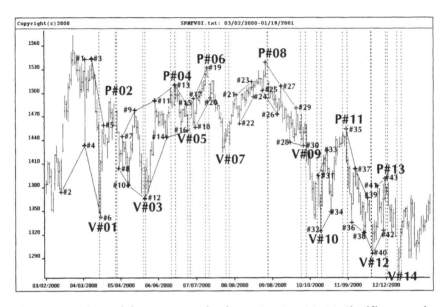

Figure 7.4   Chart of the S&P500 Index from 03–00 to 01–01. Significant peaks and valleys V#01 to V#14. *Source: FAM Research,* 2000.

To identify the safest points to invest, we recommend a combination of weekly and daily chart analysis. If we use the S&P500 Index as an example, start with a weekly chart analysis, and then add the daily confirmation, we find that some of the Fibonacci time-goal days are already eliminated. When the remaining Fibonacci time-goal days are combined with PHI spirals, the total number of multiple confirmed trend changes is reduced to as few as four.

Sophisticated investors will decide how they want to make the best use of the Fibonacci time-goal analysis, depending on individual risk preference. The Fibonacci time-goal analysis works well as a stand-alone Fibonacci trading tool, but is more complex because there are more signals to observe. On the other hand, a skillful investor might welcome this geometrical device, for, in combination with intraday data, Fibonacci time-goal analysis can be most beneficial.

Our overall findings on the forecasting potential of Fibonacci time-goal days in the S&P500 Index are promising. We want to analyze the DAX30 Index in the same way and see whether we find some convincing results in this trading vehicle, too.

DAX30 Index Weekly

The rules for applying our Fibonacci time-goal analysis to the DAX30 Index are identical to those for the S&P500 Index.

We always look for a Fibonacci time-goal day based on the ratio 1.618, calculated from the previous distance of swing high to high or swing low to low. The confirming second Fibonacci time-goal day can be calculated using any of the three ratios: 0.618, 1.000, or 1.618. We do not consider higher ratios from the PHI series.

The analysis is first conducted on weekly data. An application to daily bar charts will follow in the next part of the section. Figure 7.5 provides us with 13 major trend reversals in the DAX30 Index between March 1997 and January 2001.

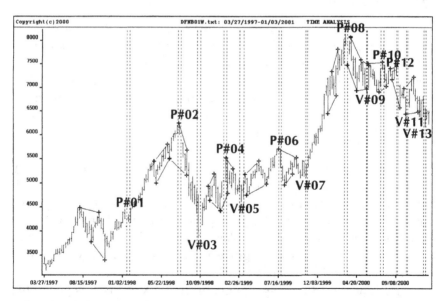

Figure 7.5   Chart of the DAX30 Index from 03–97 to 01–01. Significant peaks and valleys P#01 to V#13. *Source: FAM Research,* 2000.

Peak P#01 is a perfect example of a false trend reversal. Although two Fibonacci time-goal days give a clear signal for a trend change, the momentum of the market price is so strong that if an investor goes short at peak P#01, he or she has to reverse the position on new highs in the DAX30 Index. Losing trades occur in any trading approach, and Fibonacci time-goal days are no exception. However, the approach will not be affected as long as the percentage of profitable signals remains high.

When analyzing weekly data, there is always a danger of not having a sufficient number of swing highs or swing lows to stay close to the market action. This is illustrated by peak P#10 and peak P#12, which are both trend changes for a sell signal. There are only six weekly bars between the two peaks; therefore, not enough time is available for a valid swing low, in between the two sell signals. The same price pattern occurs between valleys V#11 and V#13, where time is too short on a weekly basis to come up with a swing high for a sell signal according to the rule of alternation.

The problem of not having a sufficient number of valid swings can be addressed by analyzing daily data.

DAX30 Index Daily

Our Fibonacci time-goal analysis (over 13 months, on daily data) leads us to 16 major trend reversals in the DAX30 Index. Sixteen main trend changes in 13 months translate to a little more than one signal per month. This frequency might be perfect for an active trader but too high for conservative investors. Because Fibonacci time-goal analysis relies on the frequency of valid swing highs and lows according to the predefined swing size, many more signals are generated daily than weekly.

The only way to reduce the number of trades is to combine daily analysis with either the signals generated on a weekly basis, or with additional Fibonacci tools. The preferred method will depend on the investor's risk preference and his or her ability to live with bigger equity swings. The overall drawdown risk and the average setback in equity on losing trades are significantly larger on weekly data than on weekly and daily data combined.

Each of the 16 trading signals in the DAX30 Index is generated according to the same rules as the S&P500 Index and the DAX30 Index weekly. Figure 7.6 covers all trend reversals in the DAX30 Index daily. All swing highs and lows used for the analysis are marked on the chart by connecting lines. The highs and lows do not overlap. They are all used in sequence. The span between the two Fibonacci time goals in each time band is never more than two days.

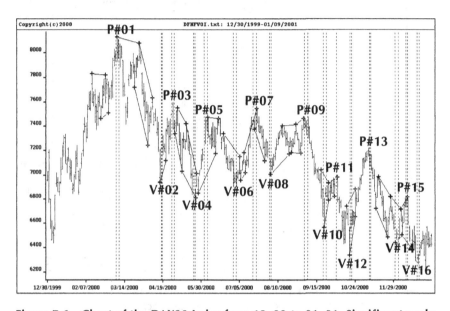

Figure 7.6 Chart of the DAX30 Index from 12–99 to 01–01. Significant peaks and valleys P#01 to V#16. *Source: FAM Research,* 2000.

The S&P500 Index and the DAX30 Index are volatile products related to the stock markets, but Fibonacci time-goal days can solidly capture trend changes in cash currencies, too, as demonstrated with the Euro cash currency versus the US Dollar.

Euro Cash Currency Weekly

Cash currencies are some of the best products to analyze and trade. If cash currencies trend, they usually maintain trend directions for significant periods of time.

Eight major trend reversals as trading signals can be identified in the Euro cash currency for the period from January 1998 to

January 2001 on weekly data. Four significant peaks and four significant valleys, over the three years, are captured by pairs of Fibonacci time-goal days (Figure 7.7).

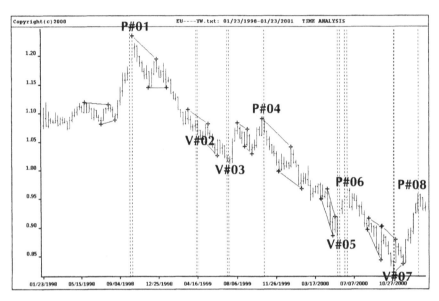

Figure 7.7   Chart of the Euro cash currency from 01–98 to 01–01. Significant peaks and valleys P#01 to P#08. *Source: FAM Research, 2000.*

Once again, there is a sequence of two significant valleys that do not alternate with a significant peak. There is no valid swing to interrupt the downtrend that runs from valley V#02 to valley V#03. If investors use valley V#02 as an indication of a major trend change and invest long at that point, they will either get stopped out in a loss, or will reverse the position and wait for the coming trend change, which occurs at the buy signal at valley V#03.

The frequency of the trend changes in the Euro cash currency (confirmed by Fibonacci time-goal days) demonstrates that trading signals can either be farther apart in trending markets, or close together in sideward markets. This distance between the signals peak P#04 and valley V#05, in a trending state of the Euro cash currency, is 32 weeks, whereas valley V#05 is followed by peak P#06 in a sideward market condition after just six weeks.

The calculation of pairs of Fibonacci time-goal days from high-to-high formations or low-to-low formations will normally create a time band, but sometimes these calculations fall perfectly together. This can be seen on the signals at peak P#04 and peak P#08, where we find a single line for the two Fibonacci time-goal day calculations.

We close this chapter with a presentation of the Euro cash currency on daily data.

Euro Cash Currency Daily

The key parameters for daily analysis of the Euro cash currency regarding Fibonacci time-goal days are the same as for the S&P500 Index and the DAX30 Index.

We find a total of seven significant peaks and eight major valleys in the Euro cash currency daily, over a test period of 17 months from September 1999 to January 2001. All are doubly confirmed by pairs of Fibonacci time-goal days (Figure 7.8). The total width of the time bands is never more than two price bars.

The 15 significant trend changes in the Euro cash currency, based on our Fibonacci time-goal analysis, are regular. Peaks and

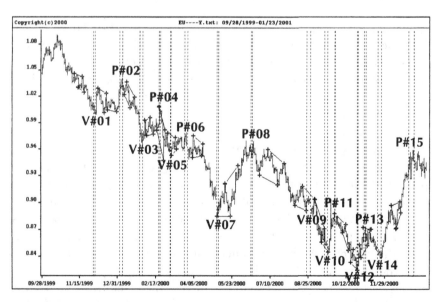

Figure 7.8 Chart of the Euro cash currency from 09–99 to 01–01. Significant peaks and valleys V#01 to P#15. *Source: FAM Research,* 2000.

valleys alternate from turning point to turning point, with the exception of valley V#09 and valley V#10.

Valley V#09 and valley V#10 show up in sequence when the Euro cash currency is in a strong trending condition to the downside. Similar price patterns have been analyzed for the S&P500 Index and the DAX30 Index. It is important to make investors aware of the exceptions to the rule of alternating peaks and valleys, and the need to always protect positions with a stop-loss. When signals based on Fibonacci time-goal analysis are stopped out in a loss, the best strategy is to not only go flat, but also to reverse the position. This is because markets continue to run in a previous trend direction that has been interrupted but does not have a valid swing.

Readers have now been introduced to all six geometrical Fibonacci tools on our list. In the next chapter, we will present the safest ways of investing, according to Fibonacci principles. We will point out that combinations of different Fibonacci tools are, by far, the most promising of our Fibonacci approaches to multiple confirmation of major turning points in the markets.

SUMMARY

Fibonacci time-goal analysis is similar to time analysis based on the Fibonacci summation series (described as the first of our Fibonacci tools in Chapter 2), but instead of using the count of the Fibonacci summation series to forecast trend reversals, we calculate Fibonacci time-goal days from swing highs and swing lows and from the three ratios 0.618, 1.000, and 1.618.

A Fibonacci time-goal day is a price bar in the future on which a market price pattern might change its trend direction.

Compared with other trading strategies, the geometrical approach of Fibonacci time-goal days has the advantage of forecasting the markets rather than lagging them as most technical indicators do.

In addition to the forecasting quality of Fibonacci time-goal days, the concept is dynamic. The distance between two swing highs or two swing lows from which a Fibonacci time-goal day is calculated is seldom the same. Therefore, Fibonacci time-goal days will be closer together or further apart as soon as the distance from high to high or low to low is multiplied by the Fibonacci ratio 1.618, or one of the two alternative ratios: 0.618 or 1.000.

Successful Fibonacci time analysis depends on the correct identification of peaks and valleys. The standard swing size is chosen based on test runs on historical data, but this minimum swing size is just the first way to find the correct peaks and valleys.

The swing size is reduced below the level of the optimal swing size in those exceptional cases where a market remains without swing highs and swing lows for more than 15 days or 10 weeks, respectively. We must then simply select the highest peak or lowest valley of 15 days or 10 weeks, thereby receiving a new measurement for a valid swing from which to calculate a Fibonacci time-goal day. Excessive noise in a market is eliminated by an amendment to the general definition of filter swings: there must be at least three days between the highs and lows of two swings that satisfy the minimum swing size. This amendment applies to both top and bottom formations.

Whenever we look at a chart of any time span, we find market price patterns expressed in big and small swing sizes. These swings rarely represent the wave structure that Elliott defined, because most market patterns are irregular. As discussed, irregular market patterns are the result of complex corrections and extensions.

Applications of Fibonacci time-goal days do not require the use of a wave count. In the Fibonacci time analysis, having an uptrend, downtrend, or sideward market is not important. The Fibonacci ratios can be applied to any predefined market swings.

Fibonacci time-goal days only forecast events in time. We will never know whether a market price will be high or low by the time a Fibonacci time-goal day is reached. Our primary objective is to sell on the Fibonacci time-goal day if the market price is high, and to buy on the Fibonacci time-goal day if the market price is low.

In Fibonacci analysis, we strive for multiple confirmations of trend reversals, because they are the most solid basis for investment decisions. This principle holds true for our Fibonacci time analysis as well.

Market entries in our Fibonacci time analysis are based on double confirmations of Fibonacci time-goal days. A trend reversal must be confirmed by one Fibonacci time-goal day that is calculated from two peaks (valleys), and a second Fibonacci time-goal day that is calculated from two valleys (peaks), using the ratios 0.618, 1.000, and 1.618. On daily analysis, it is necessary to have at least one of the calculations based on the ratio 1.618. This rule does not apply to weekly data.

If the double confirmation of a trend reversal is perfect, the two Fibonacci time goals will coincide exactly on the same price bar. However, Fibonacci time goals are usually a bit before or somewhat after the anticipated peak or valley. As long as the distance between the first and the second Fibonacci time-goal day does not exceed two price bars, the time bands of the Fibonacci time goals we receive will be valid for our calculations. Otherwise, we have to wait for new swing highs or swing lows in order to start another calculation.

Fibonacci time-goal days, calculated at ratios 0.618, 1.000, or 1.618, can be applied to monthly, weekly, daily, or intraday charts. The more Fibonacci time-goal days that point at the same trend reversal, the higher the chance that a trend reversal will occur at the precalculated target.

We do not explicitly impose entry rules, exit rules, stop-loss rules, or re-entry rules into the analysis of Fibonacci time-goal days, because our focus has been on multiple confirmations of significant trend reversals based on our Fibonacci time analysis. Readers who wish to try trading strategies in detail can use the rules described in Chapter 3 for corrections and extensions.

Fibonacci time-goal days are an interesting stand-alone investment tool. In Chapter 8, we will see that the relevance of Fibonacci time-goal days is increased when they are applied in combination with PHI-channels, PHI-ellipses, and PHI-spirals.

8

COMBINING
FIBONACCI TOOLS

Can the trading strategies based on our six geometrical Fibonacci tools be improved by combining them? Can Fibonacci trading become even safer and more profitable? These are the key questions we will tackle in this chapter.

Timing is the most crucial element in trading. It is important to know what to buy, but it is more important to know when to buy. In the previous six chapters, we have pointed out that each Fibonacci tool, by itself, can serve investors as a profitable stand-alone trading solution. All trading signals result from geometrical interpretations of market price patterns. All six geometrical Fibonacci trading devices are based on the understanding of investors' behavior expressed in peak and valley formations.

The most important discovery in this book is that, in certain instances, more than one of the Fibonacci tools can forecast trend changes in price and time. This is a unique finding that has never been presented before. Forecasting in this way does not mean we can say in advance whether a turning point is going to be triggered, but if a precalculated price target is reached, we can safely act according to the rules given for the different geometrical Fibonacci trading tools.

Working with our set of Fibonacci trading tools takes nothing more than swing highs or lows and the Fibonacci ratio (or the ratios from the PHI series). The greatest difficulty is choosing correct swing highs or lows. On weekly price data, we cannot always apply Fibonacci trading tools because of a lack of valid swings from which to calculate turning points. On daily data, in contrast, we receive enough swing highs and swing lows, but we might get too many signals. A strong increase in the number of trading signals can be even worse on intraday data.

Using the six Fibonacci tools will not ensure that we never suffer losing trades, but we can expect the majority of trades to be profitable as long as the geometrical Fibonacci tools are applied correctly.

For appropriate executions, geometrical Fibonacci trading tools require patience, discipline, and computer skills, because all trading tools can be applied only by using our WINPHI software package. The User Manual in the Appendix instructs readers in how to use the computer program.

In addition to multiple confirmations of trend reversals by at least two Fibonacci tools, we recommend a double confirmation of turning points on two sets of data. Investors who trade mainly on daily charts should also consider weekly data, and traders who favor intraday data must not neglect a supplementary analysis on daily data. Double confirmations at different data compression rates reduce trading signals to the most reliable ones.

This chapter is subdivided into four sections. We first introduce readers to different combinations of geometrical Fibonacci trading tools. We then present examples of combinations of Fibonacci tools on stock index futures daily. The third section deals with examples on stock index futures intraday, and the final section covers Fibonacci trading tools on stocks weekly and daily.

SORTS OF COMBINATIONS OF FIBONACCI TOOLS

All six geometrical Fibonacci trading devices are, to a certain degree, based on 3-wave patterns.

PHI-ellipses work well as graphical trading devices because they circumvent 3-wave patterns. PHI-ellipses adjust dynamically to changing price patterns and work as filters for noise in erratic markets. Therefore, in our opinion, PHI-ellipses are best suited to start the analysis of price moves.

All other Fibonacci trading devices work, to some degree, within the framework of PHI-ellipses (Figure 8.1).

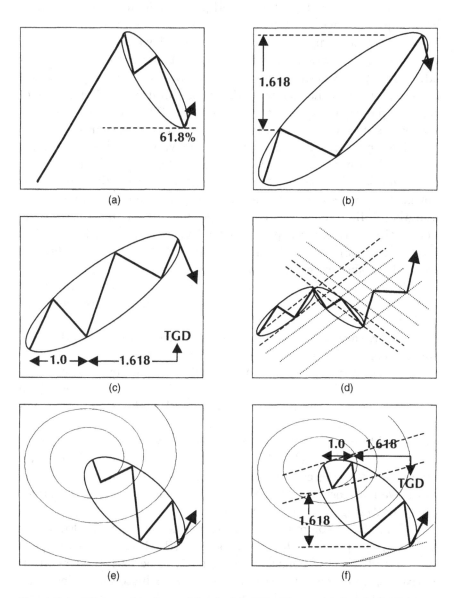

Figure 8.1   Fibonacci tools combined with PHI-ellipses. (a) Correction; (b) extension; (c) time-goal day; (d) PHI-channels; (e) PHI-spiral; (f) multiple. *Source: FAM Research, 2000.*

PHI-ellipses are unique because they are dynamic over time and they follow price patterns as they develop. This is why we must always be patient and wait to see whether the market price stays, from beginning to end, within a PHI-ellipse. We can take action as soon as the market moves out of the PHI-ellipse *only if* the final point of a PHI-ellipse is reached. PHI-ellipses work almost universally and can be applied to monthly, weekly, daily, or intraday data.

The six combinations of Fibonacci trading tools with PHI-ellipses (Figure 8.1) illustrate the basic investment principle that we have explained in the course of this book. Multiple confirmations of turning points by at least two geometrical Fibonacci tools give investors a safe way to follow the ups and downs of the markets.

Ever since Elliott structured market swings with his wave count, legions of analysts have tried, unsuccessfully, to apply Elliott's wave count to real-time trading. Although—after the fact—the wave count appears obvious and definitive, there is no way to predict today what a market will do tomorrow. Nor is it possible to say that future market pricing will reach a precalculated price target (which is what many Elliott followers claim they can do). Elliott's wave count fails to correctly predict waves in sideward markets.

It is possible, however, to make visible, and to measure, investors' behavior as expressed in price patterns. This analysis is done with PHI-ellipses.

The reliability of PHI-ellipses as the core analytical Fibonacci instrument can be improved by integrating additional Fibonacci tools. Even though PHI-ellipses can be applied to almost any price pattern, other Fibonacci tools are not always valid devices. In other words, a market price move might extend within a PHI-ellipse up to a precalculated Fibonacci time-goal day, but, pricewise, might not reach a price goal that is precalculated based on an extension.

On the weekly and daily data that have been presented so far, all significant turning points can be pinpointed with several Fibonacci tools. We must now combine all Fibonacci trading tools in one single analytic strategy.

Some basic computer skills are needed to apply the Fibonacci tools to price patterns, but the book's WINPHI software package is user-friendly. Any Fibonacci trading tool can be used to show alternative combinations of Fibonacci devices on historical price data. Readers who have worked their way through the previous chapters will be able to comfortably use the WINPHI computer program and repeat all examples on individual Fibonacci trading tools and combinations of those tools.

STOCK INDEX FUTURES AND CASH CURRENCIES DAILY

The first applications of geometrical Fibonacci trading tool combinations will be on stock index futures and cash currencies daily.

Sample charts are presented for the DAX30 Index, the S&P500 Index, and the Japanese Yen cash currency. We begin each case analysis with one or more PHI-ellipse(s) capturing the market price pattern, and we then add other Fibonacci tools to the PHI-ellipse(s).

DAX30 Index Daily

The DAX30 Index is analyzed on a daily bar chart from June 2000 to February 2001 (Figure 8.2).

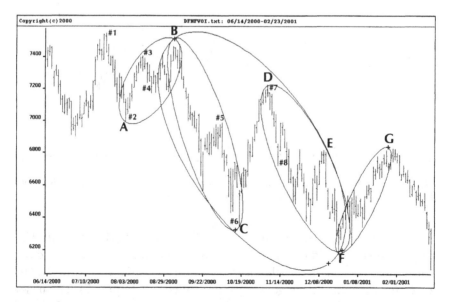

Figure 8.2   Chart of the DAX30 Index from 06–00 to 02–01. PHI-ellipses and significant peaks and valleys. *Source: FAM Research,* 2000.

PHI-ellipses are considered the most important analytic tools available to make investors' behavior visible in the marketplace. Five PHI-ellipses were drawn during the nine months we analyzed the DAX30 Index (Figure 8.2).

To demonstrate successful combinations of different Fibonacci trading tools, we focus on the trend reversal at point F. Point F is not just the final point of the PHI-ellipse based on the peaks B and E and the valleys C and F; it is also the final point of a smaller PHI-ellipse that starts in D and has a side point in E.

Fibonacci time-goal days, another geometrical Fibonacci device, can easily be integrated into the bar chart of the DAX30 Index with PHI-ellipses (Figure 8.3).

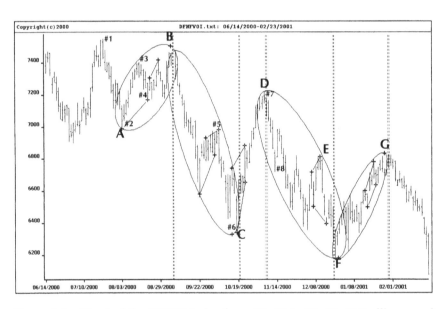

Figure 8.3   Chart of the DAX30 Index from 06–00 to 02–01. PHI-ellipses and Fibonacci time-goal days. *Source: FAM Research, 2000.*

The valley, F, at the final point of the third PHI-ellipse in Figure 8.3, is confirmed by a pair of overlapping Fibonacci time-goal days. The time corridor is one day and is therefore valid according to the rules for Fibonacci time-goal days (described in Chapter 7). The other four major turning points in B, C, D, and G are also confirmed by valid time targets.

It is very difficult for investors to act counter to the main trend direction and sell when prices are high and buy when prices are low. The Fibonacci time-goal analysis, in connection with PHI-ellipses, is a valuable investment approach because it makes decisions easier for investors.

The overall picture varies only slightly when an extension and a PHI-spiral are added to the DAX30 Index chart. These third and fourth geometrical Fibonacci trading devices give multiple confirmation of the valley at point F (Figure 8.4).

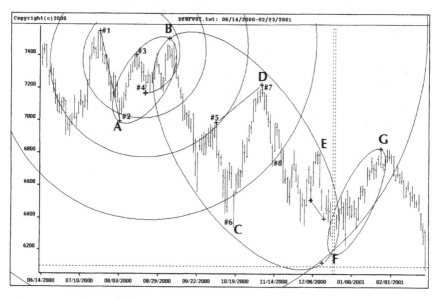

Figure 8.4 Chart of the DAX30 Index from 06–00 to 02–01. PHI-ellipses, Fibonacci time-goal days, PHI-spiral and extension. *Source: FAM Research,* 2000.

The PHI-spiral in Figure 8.4 has its center at point #3 and its starting point at valley #4. The PHI-spiral is penetrated by the market move in the DAX30 Index on its fifth PHI-spiral ring.

In Chapter 6, we explained that valid confirmations of trend reversals require a crossover of at least two PHI-spirals, but, to avoid confusion, we do not draw a second PHI-spiral onto the chart. Readers who feel it necessary to check the second PHI-spiral are directed to the WINPHI software and the DAX30 Index database on the CD-ROM, which will allow them to add the missing PHI-spiral themselves. The center of the second PHI-spiral is at point #1, the starting point at valley #2. The PHI-spiral must be rotated clockwise and must cross over the first PHI-spiral exactly at the significant valley in F.

The extension (represented by the vertical dotted line in Figure 8.4) is performed from point #1, which is the highest high in this price pattern. The distance between peak #1 and valley #2 is multiplied by the ratio 1.618. The price target out of the extension misses the market price by a small margin, but the price target is almost identical to the low point of the PHI-ellipse.

Although the valley at F is not exactly met by the precalculation out of the extension, it is safe for investors to invest long at point F. Three Fibonacci trading tools are sufficient to solidly confirm a trend reversal, even if the fourth confirmation misses by a slim margin.

PHI-channels (described in Chapter 4) are another essential part of our Fibonacci analysis. PHI-channels (Fibonacci trend channels) could easily have been integrated into Figure 8.4, but we prefer to present an example of a PHI-channel in combination with the relevant PHI-ellipses (see Figure 8.5).

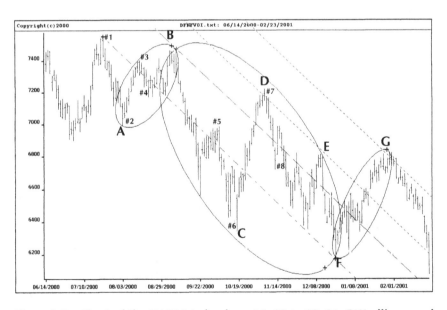

Figure 8.5   Chart of the DAX30 Index from 06–00 to 02–01. PHI-ellipses and PHI-channel. *Source: FAM Research,* 2000.

Our PHI-channel analysis starts at the highest high: point #1. The PHI-channel baseline intersects the distance from point A to point B and has its final point at the valley in F. The outside parallel PHI-channel line is drawn through the peak at point B.

The width of the PHI-channel is multiplied by the ratios 0.618 and 1.618 to establish two lines that run parallel to the baseline of the PHI-channel. The power of PHI-channels as Fibonacci trading tools is proven by our example at the peak at point G. The PHI-channel parallel line at point G confirms the final point of the PHI-ellipse that has its starting point in F. The peak at point G is another significant trend reversal in the DAX30 Index. It receives multiple confirmation via geometrical Fibonacci trading tools.

Our examples in the DAX30 Index show how useful the combination of geometrical Fibonacci tools can be. Should investors wait until all Fibonacci trading tools pinpoint, in advance, one and the same target in price and in time?

We strongly believe that the more Fibonacci trading tools confirm a turning point, the safer it is to invest. The main reason we prefer multiple confirmations is that they filter out a lot of minor trades, but this preference is not a rule. Trading signals derived from only one Fibonacci tool, or a combination of only two Fibonacci tools, can be very profitable. Decisions on the number of confirmations, and which confirmations of Fibonacci trading devices to use, will depend on the risk preference of each investor.

S&P500 Index Daily

The S&P500 Index, on a daily basis, is analyzed in a similar way. Because the S&P500 Index has been analyzed intensively and over longer periods of time in the previous chapters, we will cover here only the seven months between late August 2000 and late February 2001.

The PHI-ellipse again serves as our basic geometrical Fibonacci trading tool. Four PHI-ellipses with varying shapes cover the market segments in different periods of time.

The last downtrend is not analyzed because the database is insufficient in late February 2001. We must have a starting point and at least two side points to properly draw a PHI-ellipse. PHI-ellipses develop over time. At the beginning of a market move, we do not know the final shape of a PHI-ellipse.

Figure 8.6 represents the PHI-ellipses that can be found in the S&P500 Index over the respective six months. Significant turning points, besides the peaks and valleys that are used to draw the PHI-ellipses, are marked in the chart as well.

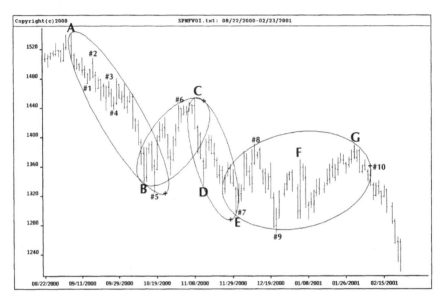

Figure 8.6   Chart of the S&P500 Index from 08–00 to 02–01. PHI-ellipses and significant peaks and valleys. *Source: FAM Research,* 2000.

Although we get trading signals based on PHI-ellipses and on combinations of PHI-ellipses with other Fibonacci trading tools, we do not know how strong a market will move in our favor after the trend reversal. This is clarified when we look at the fourth PHI-ellipse.

The best description of a sideward market pattern is: a PHI-ellipse that has no slope. Investors must be aware that Fibonacci devices discover major trend reversals, but they cannot forecast the strength of changes in the major trend direction.

Fibonacci time analysis is a great way to identify trend changes. In connection with PHI-ellipses, Fibonacci time-goal analysis ensures that investors sell high or buy low. There is no guarantee that each signal will be at the highest high or the lowest low, but investments will definitely be countertrend. Losing trades occur in every trading approach, but if investors rely on combinations of geometrical Fibonacci trading tools, they will always know what type of market phase they are in at any particular moment.

Figure 8.7 shows six combinations of PHI-ellipses and Fibonacci time-goal days in the S&P500 Index. All major turning points are double-confirmed by PHI-ellipses and pairs of Fibonacci time-goal days, which point at the trend reversals at time corridors of two days or less.

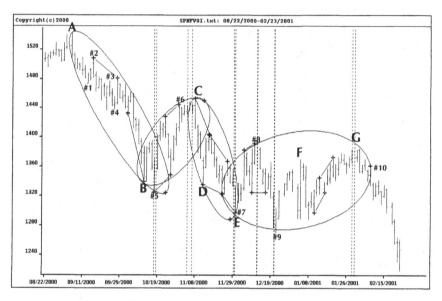

Figure 8.7 Chart of the S&P500 Index from 08–00 to 02–01. PHI-ellipses and Fibonacci time-goal days. *Source: FAM Research,* 2000.

We can integrate a sample PHI-channel with the four basic PHI-ellipses in the same way that Fibonacci time-goal days have been added to the chart of the S&P500 Index.

PHI-channel baselines are established by connecting a high and a low as the starting point and the ending point, respectively, of a trend move. In our example, the baseline connects the peak at point A and the valley at point E. In a PHI-channel analysis, the imaginary line between the two points, B and C, typically intersects.

To receive the width of the PHI-channel, the parallel outside line of the PHI-channel is drawn to the right of the baseline of the

PHI-channel, through the significant peak at point C. The width of the PHI-channel is multiplied by different ratios of the PHI series. The most relevant parallel lines that we use in our analysis are drawn at ratios 0.618 and 1.618 (Figure 8.8).

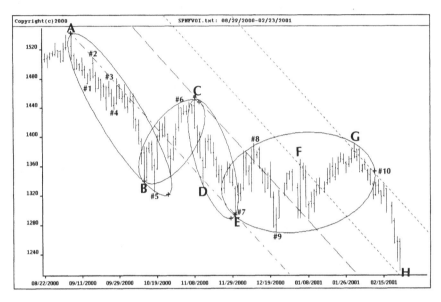

Figure 8.8   Chart of the S&P500 Index from 08–00 to 02–01. PHI-ellipses and PHI-channel. *Source: FAM Research,* 2000.

As expected, the first PHI-channel line is penetrated at point F. The market price retraces back to the original PHI-channel and then advances to the next PHI-channel line at point G. At point G, the PHI-channel line also touches the fourth PHI-ellipse. The following price move retraces back to the previous PHI-channel line at point H.

Instead of combining Fibonacci time-goal days and PHI-channels with our set of core PHI-ellipses in the S&P500 Index, we can draw PHI-spirals on the chart and check the result for multiple confirmations of the major trend reversals.

We are primarily interested in finding the final points of PHI-ellipses confirmed by crossovers of two PHI-spirals. The peak at point #3 is chosen as the center of one PHI-spiral. The valley at point #4 is chosen as the starting point of the PHI-spiral. The PHI-spiral is rotated clockwise and penetrates exactly the end of the price move and the final point of the first PHI-ellipse at point #5 on the third PHI-spiral ring. Even more interesting: the PHI-spiral touches the final point of the third PHI-ellipse at point E on the fourth PHI-spiral ring, as well as the final point of the fourth PHI-ellipse at point #10 on the fifth PHI-spiral ring (Figure 8.9).

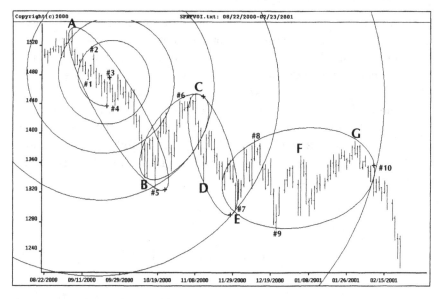

Figure 8.9 Chart of the S&P500 Index from 08–00 to 02–01. PHI-ellipses and PHI-spiral. *Source: FAM Research,* **2000.**

Seldom will one and the same PHI-spiral confirm three trend reversals in a row, on the final points of three consecutive PHI-ellipses. Normally, we need one PHI-spiral (or, to be precise, one separate crossover of two PHI-spirals) per turning point.

The price move in the S&P500 Index is astonishingly symmetrical. We do not show the second PHI-spiral with the crossover points at #5, E, and #10 on the chart. Readers can create the second PHI-spiral themselves by choosing the peak at point #2 as the starting point, and the valley at point #1 as the center of the PHI-spiral. The PHI-spiral should be turned clockwise, to show the expected penetrations at the significant trend reversals.

PHI-ellipses, Fibonacci time-goal days, PHI-channels, and PHI-spirals work together and provide us with an integrated analysis of six months' heavy ups and downs in the S&P500 Index.

Now that we have analyzed two stock index futures, we will discuss the Japanese Yen cash currency.

Japanese Yen Cash Currency Daily

Cash currencies, such as the Japanese Yen and the Euro, are among the most stable and consistent performers for Fibonacci analysis. The reason for the stability of cash currencies in the Fibonacci perspective is: The concentrated worldwide interest in these products goes hand in hand with high volume, marketability, and volatility.

The PHI-ellipse remains our starting geometrical Fibonacci device in the Japanese Yen cash currency. Our analysis covers just over one year, from January 2000 to February 2001, and we have found a total of nine PHI-ellipses that are worth discussing. All nine PHI-ellipses are presented in Figure 8.10.

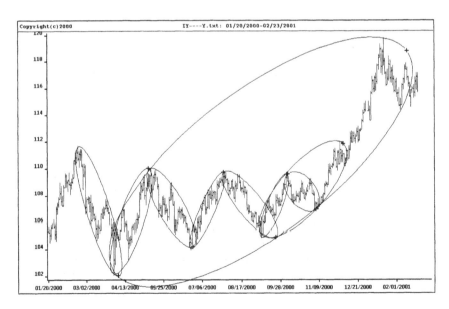

Figure 8.10 Chart of the Japanese Yen cash currency from 01–00 to 02–01. PHI-ellipses. *Source: FAM Research, 2000.*

From the sample PHI-ellipses in Figure 8.10, it becomes clear how PHI-ellipses adjust dynamically to short-term, as well as long-term, market price moves, and how PHI-ellipses are interrelated. The most important thing to observe here is that seven of the eight smaller PHI-ellipses are circumvented by one very-long-term PHI-ellipse.

Most analytic tools work perfectly well on special market moves, but they do not work consistently over longer periods of time. Fibonacci tools are different in this respect. With few exceptions, they work in a reliable manner in volatile markets short-term and long-term, as well as in changing market environments.

The first combination of geometrical Fibonacci trading tools we describe for the Japanese Yen cash currency consists of PHI-ellipses and Fibonacci time-goal days (Figure 8.11).

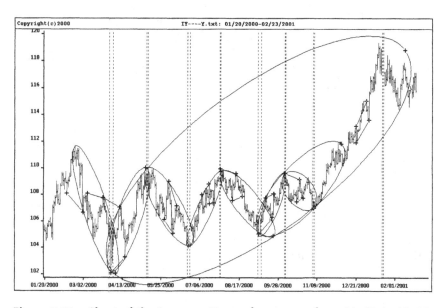

Figure 8.11 Chart of the Japanese Yen cash currency from 01–00 to 02–01. PHI-ellipses and Fibonacci time-goal days. *Source: FAM Research, 2000.*

The final points of PHI-ellipses indicate trend reversals. Almost all of the nine final points of the PHI-ellipses in Figure 8.11 are confirmed by a Fibonacci time-goal day in a corridor of not more than two days. Almost every major turning point in the Japanese Yen cash currency, therefore, has at least a double confirmation by two independent Fibonacci trading tools.

Many readers will be interested in a shorter-term analysis, so we will isolate the third and the fourth of the eight smaller PHI-ellipses that circumvent the price moves in the Japanese Yen cash currency between May 2000 and August 2000.

We first illustrate a combination of the two PHI-ellipses with a PHI-spiral, a time corridor of two Fibonacci time-goal days, and an extension (Figure 8.12).

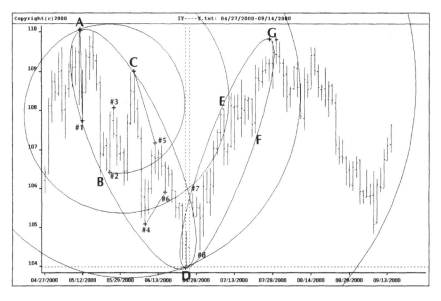

Figure 8.12   Chart of the Japanese Yen cash currency from 04–00 to 09–00. PHI-ellipses, Fibonacci time-goal days, extension and PHI-spiral. *Source: FAM Research,* 2000.

We are especially interested in the significant valley in D, at the end of the strong down move in the Japanese Yen cash currency that starts at the peak in A.

The extension (the dotted horizontal line in Figure 8.12) is calculated by multiplying the size of the initial swing (from the peak at point A to the low at point #1) by the Fibonacci ratio 1.618. The extension confirms the end of the first PHI-ellipse and, thus, the major trend reversal at the valley at point D.

Valley D is also accurately captured by a pair of Fibonacci time-goal days. The two Fibonacci time-goal days are calculated by using the highs at points C and #5, and the lows at points #4 and #6. The resulting Fibonacci time-goal corridor, with a precision of one day, pinpoints the low of the price move at point D and the low at the final point of the PHI-ellipse.

The PHI-spiral has its starting point at the low in #2 and its center at the high in #3. It turns counterclockwise and penetrates the PHI-ellipse at its final point. Readers are asked to draw the second PHI-spiral, which is needed for a crossover confirmation of the valley at point D. The second PHI-spiral will cross over the first one, right at the final point of the PHI-ellipse, by choosing the valley at point #1 as a center and the high at point A as a starting point. The respective PHI-spiral must also be rotated counterclockwise.

The major turning point, at the peak at point G, is also important. We choose the right of the two PHI-ellipses in Figure 8.12 and combine it with a PHI-spiral and a PHI-channel to get to a multiple confirmation of the significant trend reversal (Figure 8.13).

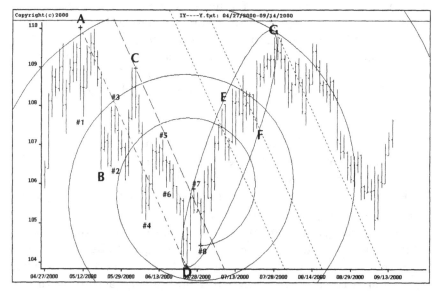

Figure 8.13 Chart of the Japanese Yen cash currency from 04–00 to 09–00. PHI-ellipse, PHI-channel, and PHI-spiral. *Source: FAM Research, 2000.*

294 • COMBINING FIBONACCI TOOLS

The PHI-channel in Figure 8.13 has a baseline that runs from the peak at point A to the valley at point D. The outside parallel to the baseline is drawn through point C. Three PHI-channel parallels are drawn at ratios 1.618, 2.618, and 4.236 times the width of the PHI-channel from the baseline to the outside parallel line. The PHI-channel parallel, calculated at a ratio of 4.236, penetrates the final point G of the PHI-ellipse that starts at the valley at point D.

Point G is also confirmed by the PHI-spiral that turns counter-clockwise with a center at the peak at point #7 and a starting point at the valley at point #8. The PHI-ellipse, PHI-channel, and PHI-spiral all pinpoint the same trend reversal and give multiple confirmation to a major turning point in the Japanese Yen cash currency.

Combinations of Fibonacci trading tools take a lot of the uncertainty out of investing. We hope it is now clear that when we start with the PHI-ellipse as the standard investment tool and add the other Fibonacci trading tools to the charts, we can confirm precalculated trend changes at the final points of the PHI-ellipses.

At times, especially during erratic market moves, we cannot apply the PHI-ellipse to a chart as the standard Fibonacci trading tool. In erratic price moves, we do not find two side points to establish a valid PHI-ellipse. In such cases, investors must choose to either base their investment decision on stand-alone Fibonacci trading devices, or not to invest and, instead, to wait for an alternative trading opportunity where PHI-ellipses again can be established.

Combinations of Fibonacci trading tools work best in volatile sideward markets, and because markets run about 70% of the time in sideward conditions (in almost any product traded), the trading opportunities are plentiful.

Buy or sell signals are not included on the charts for reasons of clarity. As a standard rule, it is safe to invest whenever a starting PHI-ellipse is confirmed by at least two additional geometrical Fibonacci trading tools by the time the market price has moved out of the PHI-ellipse. The stop-loss level should be below the lowest point inside the PHI-ellipse.

This strategy is recommended as long as it is applied to daily data. On weekly data, we expect stop-loss margins to be increased, a factor that is usually not fancied too much by investors. Profit targets, trailing stop rules, or re-entry rules can be used according to our guidelines on corrections and extensions (see Chapter 3). However, we still recommend applying geometrical Fibonacci trading devices to weekly data and comparing the signals on daily and weekly data. Turning points that are confirmed weekly and daily provide us with the best Fibonacci trading signals available.

Before readers use our set of six geometrical Fibonacci trading tools to invest, we highly recommend that they refer to the historical database included with the WINPHI CD-ROM and first try to rebuild the charts that are presented in this book. Only when traders are confident that they have mastered the sample charts should paper trading and real-time trading begin.

Multiple confirmations of trend reversals by different geometrical Fibonacci trading tools make trading decisions easy. Confirmations of four Fibonacci tools that identify one and the same trend change can be better trusted than potential reversals pinpointed by a single Fibonacci trading device.

We must point out, however, that even when several trading tools identify a potential trend change, the market price might still not reach the target price. Fibonacci trading tools help investors recognize patterns that are repeated over time and therefore continually offer numerous trading opportunities.

Geometrical Fibonacci trading devices are best suited for investors who are long-term-oriented. Nevertheless, PHI-ellipses, PHI-channels, PHI-spirals, Fibonacci time-goal days, corrections, and extensions can be successfully applied to very short-term intraday data as well.

STOCK INDEX FUTURES INTRADAY

The analysis of stock index futures intraday will be conducted on two sample products and at four data compression rates: (1) the S&P500 Index on 60-minute data; (2) the S&P500 Index on 15-minute data; (3) the DAX30 Index on 60-minute data; and (4) the DAX30 Index on 15-minute data.

S&P500 Index Intraday 60-Minute

To distinguish intraday Fibonacci analysis from daily analysis, we first present a daily chart of the price pattern in the S&P500 Index for the nine months from June 2000 to February 2001.

The nine significant swing highs and swing lows we are interested in—at a 60-minute data compression rate—are marked daily from A to J in Figure 8.14.

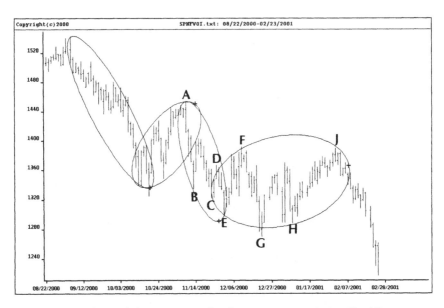

Figure 8.14   Chart of the S&P500 Index from 08–00 to 02–01. Significant turning points daily. *Source: FAM Research,* 2000.

We can mark the significant peaks and valleys accordingly for the segment from the peak at point A to the valley at point H on a 60-minute chart of the S&P500 Index.

By comparing the peaks and valleys daily and hourly, it becomes evident how much more informative 60-minute data are. We can establish three sample PHI-ellipses that circumvent the analyzed market price patterns hourly. This is done in exactly the same way as we described in Chapter 5 for applications of PHI-ellipses to weekly and daily data.

Our first combination of Fibonacci tools hourly is the integration of PHI-channels with the PHI-ellipses as our startup devices.

We can draw the baseline of one PHI-channel as a connective line from the peak at point A to the valley at point E. The outside parallel line runs through point D. A set of PHI-channel parallel trend lines is generated by multiplying the width of the PHI-channel from baseline to outside parallel line by different ratios from the PHI series. A second PHI-channel, providing us with PHI-channel resistance lines, is created by establishing the PHI-channel baseline as a connection of the valley in B and the peak in F, and by laying the outside parallel line through the valley at point C. The PHI-channel resistance lines are drawn as parallels at distances of different ratios from the PHI series.

The chart of the S&P500 Index can be mapped with these trend and resistance lines to show the support and resistance areas for the market price pattern.

Figure 8.15 is an illustration of the combination of PHI-ellipses and PHI-channels in the S&P500 Index on an hourly basis.

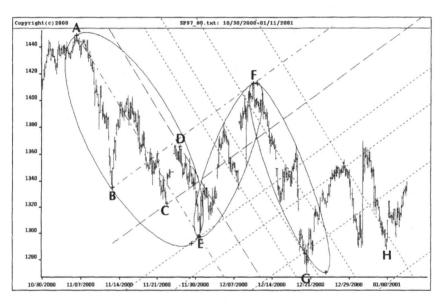

Figure 8.15 Chart of the S&P500 Index from 08–00 to 02–01. PHI-ellipses and PHI-channels. *Source: FAM Research, 2000.*

Crossovers of PHI-spirals can also be used as multiple confirmations of trend reversals on hourly data.

We find crossovers of pairs of PHI-spirals for all significant peaks and valleys in the S&P500 Index. We present two examples of crossovers for the major trend reversals at the valley at point E and at the peak at point F. PHI-spirals were discussed in detail in Chapter 6;

here, we will reduce the demonstration to single charts that show just the pairs of PHI-spirals. Figure 8.16 shows the four PHI-spirals for the crossovers in E and in F.

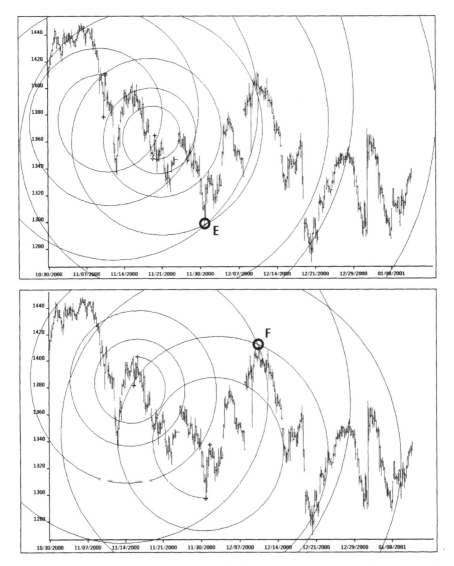

Figure 8.16   Chart of the S&P500 Index from 10–00 to 01–01. Crossovers of PHI-spirals. *Source: FAM Research,* 2000.

To analyze price data, it does not make any difference which data compression rates we choose. The analytical power of crossovers of PHI-spirals remains unchanged, even on intraday data. The major valley at point E and the major peak at point F are identified by crossovers of PHI-spirals.

The price bars in the S&P500 Index can be further broken down from hourly to 15-minute data.

S&P500 Index Intraday 15-Minute

Geometrical Fibonacci trading tools do not depend on types of products or time spans. Working with Fibonacci tools on 15-minute data is, in our opinion, fast enough to stay close to the market action. An analysis on 5-minute data works as well, but the profit potential is reduced because of an increase in the number of trades. Commissions paid and slippage become additional factors that make trading on a 5-minute basis critical.

We start our presentation on 15-minute data with a combination of PHI-ellipses and Fibonacci time-goal days (Figure 8.17).

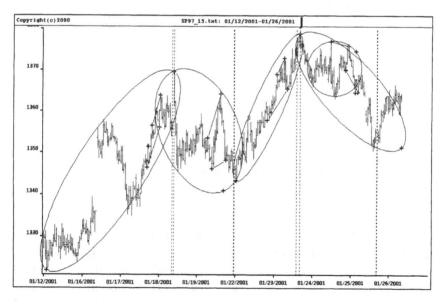

Figure 8.17 Chart of the S&P500 Index from 01–01 to 01–01. PHI-ellipses and Fibonacci time-goal days. *Source: FAM Research, 2000.*

The time span analyzed on 15-minute data is marked from H to J on the daily chart in Figure 8.14. We are most interested in multiple confirmations of the significant peak at point J.

Five PHI-ellipses circumvent the sample 15-minute price moves in the S&P500 Index as of January 2001. The final point of the third of the five PHI-ellipses confirms the trend reversal at point J. The same turning point is confirmed by a pair of Fibonacci time-goal days that meet at peak J in a corridor of only two 15-minute price bars.

Similar to our analysis on an hourly basis, the 15-minute bar chart can be mapped by combining PHI-ellipses and PHI-channels. (See Figure 8.18.)

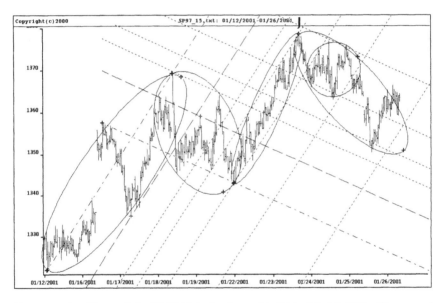

Figure 8.18 **Chart of the S&P500 Index from 01–01 to 01–01. PHI-ellipses and PHI-channels.** *Source: FAM Research, 2000.*

The peak at point J appears at the final point of the third of the five PHI-ellipses. On its way up to the peak at point J, the market move in the S&P500 Index finds strong support and resistance in two PHI-channels. The significant trend reversal finally occurs in the corner of one of the target rectangles formed by the set of PHI-channel trend lines and PHI-channel resistance lines.

In addition, the turning point at peak J can get multiple confirmation via a crossover of two PHI-spirals on a 15-minute basis, too (Figure 8.19).

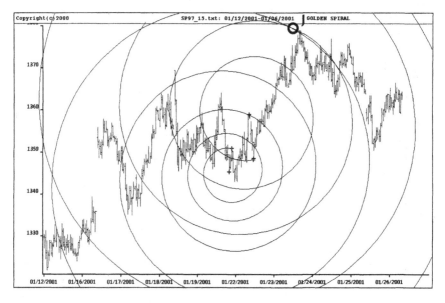

Figure 8.19   Chart of the S&P500 Index from 01–01 to 01–01. Crossover of PHI-spirals. *Source: FAM Research,* 2000.

Crossovers of PHI-spirals that serve to confirm final points of PHI-ellipses are key parts of our Fibonacci analysis. One PHI-spiral is turned clockwise, the other is counterclockwise. The respective PHI-ellipses are familiar from the previous two charts and are not shown here.

Successful intraday analysis based on geometrical Fibonacci trading tools is not limited to the American market for stock index futures. To prove this, we will briefly refer (again, on an hourly and a 15-minute basis) to the DAX30 Index as the leading European benchmark.

DAX30 Index Intraday 60-Minute

We conduct our analysis based on the daily price pattern in the DAX30 Index, from November 2000 to February 2001, and we compare it with a 60-minute chart over the same time span.

Figure 8.20 shows the DAX30 Index on daily data. Two significant trend reversals are marked A and B.

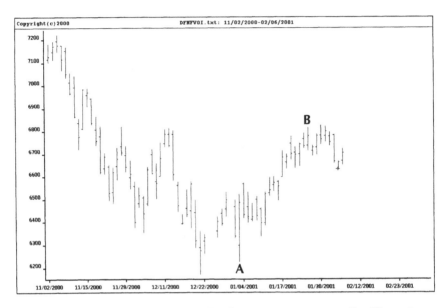

**Figure 8.20   Chart of the DAX30 Index from 11–00 to 02–01. Significant turn-
ing points daily.** *Source: FAM Research,* 2000.

We can draw various PHI-ellipses to an hourly chart of the
DAX30 Index that covers the period between the two turning points
at valley A and at peak B in January 2001.

As soon as PHI-ellipses circumvent a price pattern and two side
points have been established, we need to wait for the final point of
PHI-ellipses to be reached by a price move.

To receive multiple confirmations of the final points of PHI-
ellipses, we integrate Fibonacci time-goal days and PHI-channels into
the analysis. PHI-channels can be applied to any price move, regardless of the data compression rate we choose, as long as there are swing
patterns from which to draw the PHI-channel baseline and the outside parallel line.

Figures 8.21 and 8.22 illustrate the two sample combinations of
PHI-ellipses with Fibonacci time-goal days and with PHI-channels on
hourly data in the DAX30 Index.

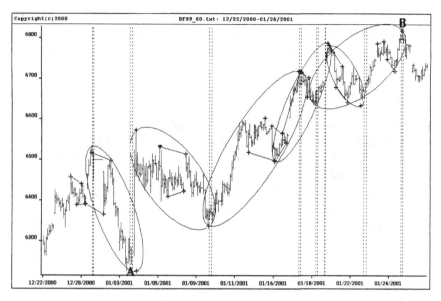

Figure 8.21 Chart of the DAX30 Index from 12–00 to 01–01. PHI-ellipses and Fibonacci time-goal days.

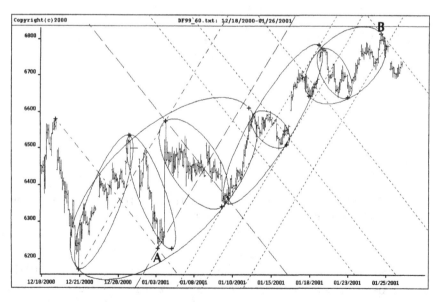

Figure 8.22 Chart of the DAX30 Index from 12–00 to 01–01. PHI-ellipses and PHI-channels. *Source: FAM Research,* 2000.

To conclude our investigation with some promising combinations of Fibonacci trading tools on intraday data, we will present a few examples of turning points in the DAX30 Index on 15-minute bar charts.

DAX30 Index Intraday 15-Minute

We are most interested in the major high in the DAX30 Index at point B, late in January 2001. This high point ended the strong uptrend that had started early in January at the valley at point A (originally on the daily chart in Figure 8.20).

We start with a combination of PHI-ellipses and PHI-channels that effectively captures the trend reversal at point B intraday on a 15-minute bar basis (Figure 8.23).

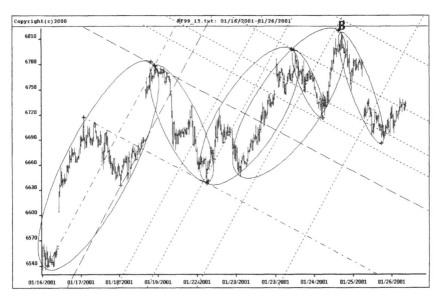

Figure 8.23   Chart of the DAX30 Index from 01–01 to 01–01. PHI-ellipses and PHI-channels. *Source: FAM Research*, 2000.

The significant peak at point B is at the final point of a PHI-ellipse before the market pattern breaks out of it. The trend reversal is confirmed by a target corner, formed by a set of PHI-channel trend lines and PHI-channel resistance lines.

The second sample combination—intraday 15-minute in the DAX30 Index—focuses on another double confirmation by a crossover of two PHI-spirals (Figure 8.24).

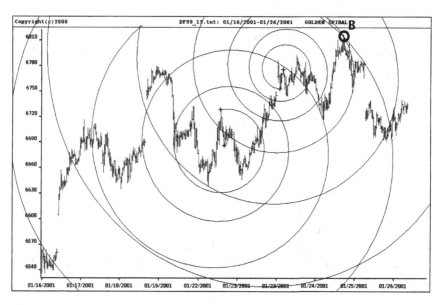

Figure 8.24 Chart of the DAX30 Index from 01–01 to 01–01. Crossover of PHI-spirals. *Source: FAM Research,* 2000.

The generation of the charts in Figures 8.23 and 8.24 is not described in detail because readers now have the expertise to see the relevance of the geometrical Fibonacci trading tools in the charts without further explanations.

This section has been repetitive; it has shown similar charts for different trading vehicles and different data compression rates. We consider this approach necessary, however, because investors who want to put Fibonacci types of investment into trading practice must do the same thing over and over again.

We want to establish confidence in applying geometrical Fibonacci trading tools by explaining how they work on different products and in varied time frames *without* changing their structure. It is not acceptable to have a tool work once, in a special market situation, and then lose its power when price patterns and trading environments change. With very few exceptions, all six geometrical Fibonacci trading devices presented in this book are reliable, regardless of the trading product or time frame used in the analysis. The only requirements for Fibonacci analysis are volatility and marketability.

The general outlook on options for applications of Fibonacci tools is optimistic. Up to now, analysis has been limited to cash currencies and stock index futures. In the final section of this chapter, we will investigate the applicability of geometrical Fibonacci trading devices to stocks.

STOCKS WEEKLY AND DAILY

Futures or cash currencies are only a small portion of all the money that is invested. By far, most money is invested in equities.

It makes no difference what sort of product we apply our Fibonacci tools to, as long as volatility is sufficient and marketability is high. Investor behavior expresses itself in price swings. As long as the swing sizes are not too small, all Fibonacci tools work in a profitable manner. The investor must also have the skill, patience, and discipline to use them correctly.

Among the thousands of stocks that are available for investments, we recommend that investors rely on stocks of the blue-chip segment, which trend strongly at a high volatility.

To demonstrate the use of geometrical Fibonacci trading tools for investment in stocks, we have chosen three examples: Deutsche Bank, Microsoft, and Intel. Deutsche Bank and Microsoft will be presented weekly and daily, and the presentation of Intel will be on daily data only.

Deutsche Bank Stock Weekly

Deutsche Bank is the leading German banking institute. A strong uptrend of the Deutsche Bank stock started in 1996. We find three major trend changes, two upswings, and one strong correction. We begin our presentation with a combination of PHI-ellipses and PHI-channels to map the market moves in the Deutsche Bank stock weekly.

The two uptrends can clearly be identified by two PHI-ellipses. The sharp correction in 1998 cannot be analyzed with PHI-ellipses because of a lack of swing highs and lows on the weekly chart. However, the integration of PHI-channels leads us to a set of PHI-channel trend and resistance lines that captures the significant valley in 1998 at the end of the correction and the highest high in the Deutsche Bank stock in August 2000.

Figure 8.25 illustrates the combination of PHI-ellipses and PHI-channels on the Deutsche Bank stock for five years, from December 1995 to January 2001, weekly.

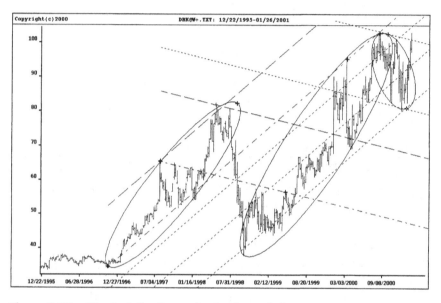

Figure 8.25   Chart of the Deutsche Bank stock from 12–95 to 01–01. PHI-ellipses and PHI-channels. *Source: FAM Research,* 2000.

The most critical turning point on the weekly chart is the major low in September 1998.

We have demonstrated in great detail (see the charts in Chapter 6 on PHI-spirals for a recap) that there is hardly any significant trend reversal in the markets that cannot be identified by a crossover of two PHI-spirals. The significant low in the Deutsche Bank stock in September 1998 is not captured by the final point of a PHI-ellipse. Therefore, we must see whether we can pinpoint the trend reversal by a crossover of two PHI-spirals.

Figure 8.26 provides us with clear evidence of the strength of PHI-spirals as Fibonacci trading tools.

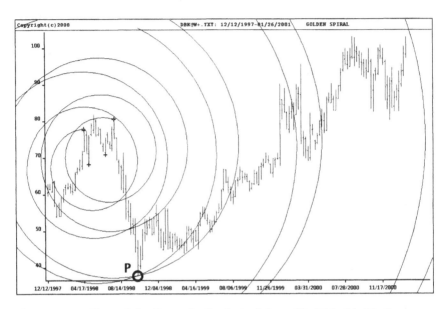

Figure 8.26 Chart of the Deutsche Bank stock from 12–97 to 01–01. Crossover of PHI-spirals. *Source: FAM Research,* 2000.

Both PHI-spirals are turned counterclockwise. Centers and starting points are in April and July, 1998. Both PHI-spirals are penetrated by the market move in the Deutsche Bank stock on their third PHI-spiral rings. The significant valley at the end of the sharp correction in the Deutsche Bank stock is perfectly pinpointed by the crossover of the pair of PHI-spirals at point P.

Deutsche Bank Stock Daily

The analysis for the Deutsche Bank stock daily is conducted on a slightly reduced database over one year, for the period from December 1999 to January 2001.

In this time frame, we find one strong uptrend and one strong down-trend in the Deutsche Bank stock. We are looking for multiple confirmations of the major turning point at the end of the uptrend move, and we start with a combination of a PHI-ellipse, PHI-channels, an extension, and two Fibonacci time goal days.

The combination of the four Fibonacci trading tools is presented in Figure 8.27.

The baseline of the first PHI-channel is drawn from the valley at point A to the peak at point B. The outside parallel to this baseline goes through the valley at point C. A set of PHI-channel trend lines runs in PHI series distances to the right of the PHI-channel.

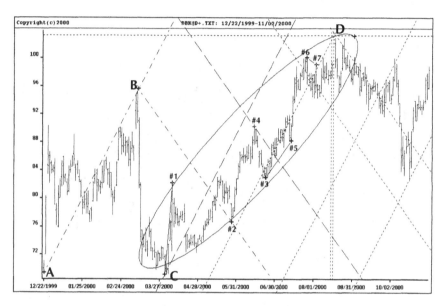

Figure 8.27   Chart of the Deutsche Bank stock from 12–99 to 11–00. PHI-ellipse, PHI-channels, extension, and Fibonacci time-goal days. *Source: FAM Research,* 2000.

The baseline of the second PHI-channel is established between the peak at point B and the low at point #2. The outside parallel line in this case runs through the high at point #4. A set of PHI-channel resistance lines runs in PHI series distances to the right of the PHI-channel. The highest high in the Deutsche Bank stock at the peak at point D is at the corner of the first PHI-channel trend line and the second PHI-channel resistance line.

The extension is calculated (according to the general rules explained in Chapter 3) by multiplying the distance from the valley at point C to the high at point #1 by the Fibonacci ratio 1.618. The price target derived from the extension meets the highest high inside the PHI-ellipse.

The two Fibonacci time-goal days are calculated based on peaks #6 and #7, and valleys #3 and #5. The width of the time corridor is one day. The two Fibonacci time-goal days also point to the highest high inside the PHI-ellipse.

The all-time high in the Deutsche Bank stock (at the peak at point D) is also confirmed by a crossover of two PHI-spirals (Figure 8.28).

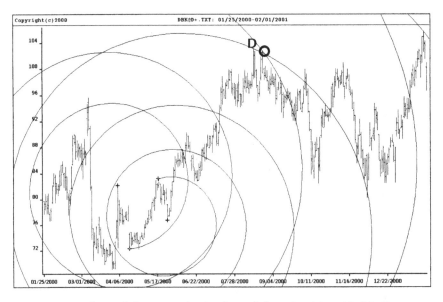

Figure 8.28   Chart of the Deutsche Bank stock from 01–00 to 02–01. Crossover of PHI-spirals. *Source: FAM Research,* **2000.**

One PHI-spiral is rotated counterclockwise; the other one is turned clockwise. Centers and starting points are in April and May 2000. The two PHI-spirals are penetrated by the market move in the Deutsche Bank stock on their third and fourth PHI-spiral rings. The all-time high at the end of the long and strong uptrend in the Deutsche Bank stock is pinpointed by the crossover of the two PHI-spirals at point D.

This crossover is also almost at the end of the PHI-ellipse presented in Figure 8.27, in combination with three other Fibonacci tools. Whenever final points of PHI-ellipses give multiple confirmation by

Fibonacci devices, speculative investors may invest right away, counter to the main trend direction. More conservative investors should wait until the market price moves out of the PHI-ellipse and then act accordingly. The stop-loss protection should be at the lowest low or the highest inside the PHI-ellipse.

The Microsoft stock can be analyzed in the same way as the Deutsche Bank stock. We once more start weekly and then present daily charts.

Microsoft Stock Weekly

Readers now know how to use combinations of Fibonacci tools. One sample chart presentation for the Microsoft stock weekly will therefore be sufficient.

Our focus is on the 30-months' low at 43 USD, late in December 2000. This low is captured by a combination of a PHI-ellipse, a crossover of two PHI-spirals, an extension, and two Fibonacci time-goal days (Figure 8.29).

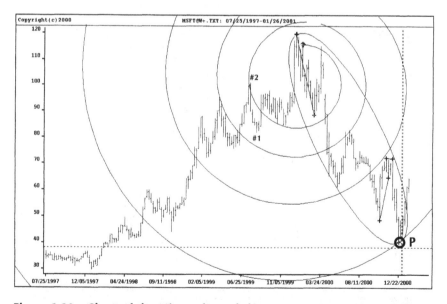

Figure 8.29 Chart of the Microsoft stock from 07–97 to 01–01. PHI-ellipse, extension, Fibonacci time-goal days, and PHI-spiral. *Source: FAM Research, 2000.*

Figure 8.29 also demonstrates that Fibonacci tools can be applied to any product or price pattern. As long as volatility remains high, geometrical Fibonacci trading devices perform in a consistent and profitable manner.

The final point of the PHI-ellipse in Figure 8.29 (as our standard Fibonacci tool) is confirmed by the PHI-spiral, the extension, and the time corridor of the two Fibonacci time-goal days.

The second PHI-spiral, which crosses over the first one, is missing on the chart. Readers can draw the second PHI-spiral with the center at point #1 and the starting point at peak #2. The second PHI-spiral is turned counterclockwise and crosses over the first PHI-spiral at the final point of the PHI-ellipse at point P.

Microsoft Stock Daily

The low in the Microsoft stock (down at 43 USD) that we found on a weekly basis, has multiple confirmation from the combination of a PHI-ellipse, a crossover of PHI-spirals, and two PHI-channels daily (Figure 8.30).

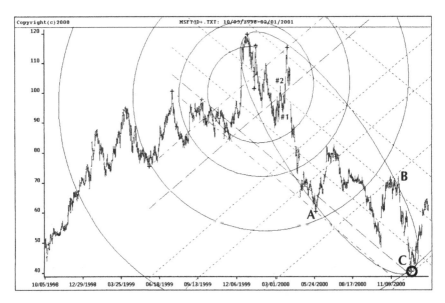

Figure 8.30 Chart of the Microsoft stock from 10–98 to 02–01. PHI-ellipse, PHI-spiral, and PHI-channel. *Source: FAM Research, 2000.*

The main difference between the analysis on weekly and daily data is in the number of peaks and valleys and in the amplitude of swings. Market patterns become more visible on daily price data. However, the advantage of this visibility is contrasted by an increased number of trades when Fibonacci signals are traded more aggressively on a daily basis.

The PHI-ellipse in Figure 8.30 circumvents the price move in the Microsoft stock with side points in A and B. The final point of the PHI-ellipse at the lowest low in C is confirmed by a crossover of two PHI-spirals. One PHI-spiral is shown on the chart. Readers can create the second one by using the center at the valley at point #1 and the starting point at peak #2. The PHI-spiral turns counterclockwise.

Intel Stock Daily

Intel is third on our list of sample stocks. So as not to be repetitive, we present the Intel stock only on a daily basis.

PHI-ellipses, Fibonacci time-goal days, PHI-spirals, and extensions also work in combination on the Intel stock (Figure 8.31).

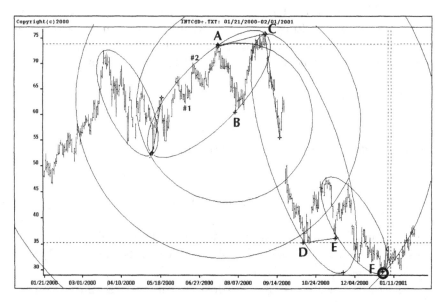

Figure 8.31 Chart of the Intel stock from 01–00 to 02–01. PHI-ellipses, PHI-spiral, extension, and Fibonacci time-goal days. *Source: FAM Research,* 2000.

The first step of the analysis is the generation of PHI-ellipses. The final points of four PHI-ellipses mark significant turning points in the Intel stock over the 13 months from January 2000 to February 2001.

The extension is the first Fibonacci trading tool integrated with the PHI-ellipses. It is calculated by using the distance from the significant peak A to the significant valley B as the initial swing, and then multiplying the swing size by the Fibonacci ratio 1.618. The extension in Figure 8.31 confirms the major valley at point D, which is the side point of the third of the four PHI-ellipses.

The time corridor of the two Fibonacci time-goal days is calculated based on the peaks in A and C, and the valleys in D and E.

The PHI-spiral in Figure 8.31 has its center at the valley at point B and its starting point in A. The PHI-spiral is penetrated by the market move in the Intel stock at the major low at point F. The second PHI-spiral that leads to a crossover at point F can be created by defining valley #1 as a center and peak #2 as a starting point, and rotating the PHI-spiral clockwise.

Weekly and daily market price patterns of volatile individual stocks are similar to the price patterns found in futures and cash currencies. Intel, Microsoft, and Deutsche Bank are three sample stocks that fulfill the criteria for perfect applications of Fibonacci trading tools. The highest volume in international trade is in stocks; therefore, it is good for investors to know that our set of Fibonacci trading tools also serves the needs for forecasting turning points in the stock market.

We will summarize the findings of Chapter 8 before concluding the book with a checklist of characteristic features that are constitutive of Fibonacci traders, and the necessary requirements for successful trading according to Fibonacci rules.

SUMMARY

The quality of our Fibonacci analysis is independent of the data compression rate we chose. Geometrical Fibonacci tools work equally well on weekly, daily, or intraday data.

Fifteen minutes is the smallest increment we analyze on an intraday basis, because, at smaller data-compression rates, the total number of trades is too high. Commissions and slippage become impossible to handle properly, and the costs of trading rise to an unmanageable level.

Fibonacci devices work well, independent of the type of product that is selected. Stocks, futures, or cash currencies can be traded, as long as the products move in a volatile manner in strong trend swings to the upside and to the downside.

All six geometrical Fibonacci trading tools can be applied to charts in order to create profitable trading signals. Geometrical Fibonacci tools are powerful as stand-alone trading devices and also in combination with each other.

The PHI-ellipse is the standard tool that starts each Fibonacci analysis. The other five geometrical Fibonacci trading devices are combined with the standard PHI-ellipse analysis and fit together into an overall profitable and reliable trading strategy.

There might be situations, especially in fast trending markets, when we do not find two side points to establish a PHI-ellipse. Such cases are rare, but if they occur, investors should step aside and wait for a new trading opportunity as soon as another PHI-ellipse has developed, based on valid side points. Alternatively, investors may choose a crossover point of two PHI-spirals (confirmed by additional Fibonacci trading tools) as the next reliable indicator of a profitable investment opportunity.

Whenever a significant trend reversal is identified by a Fibonacci trading tool, aggressive investors can begin a countertrend right away. More conservative investors should choose an entry rule or wait for a market move to leave a PHI-ellipse after the final point has been reached. Our research shows that the high of the peak or the low of the valley prior to market entry, or the highest high or lowest low inside a PHI-ellipse, are the most reliable stop-loss levels. The ways that trailing stop rules, profit target rules, or re-entry rules (see Chapter 3) are applied depends a great deal on the investment mentality of an investor.

Before readers use our six geometrical Fibonacci trading devices to invest, we highly recommend they use the historical database included with the WINPHI CD-ROM and first try to rebuild the charts that are presented. Traders must be confident that they have mastered the sample charts, before paper trading and real-time trading can follow.

Some investors might not feel comfortable with converting weekly or daily data from their data vendors into an ASCII D–O–H–L–C format, in order to be able to chart their data on the WINPHI program. Therefore, we have set up an online version of the WINPHI computer program at www.fibotrader.com for registered members. The Internet platform has the great advantage of supplying a larger universe of trading vehicles from various liquid international markets, and of allowing intraday trading on 60-minute and 15-minute bases.

Working with our set of Fibonacci devices is not as easy as it may look. It takes skill, patience, discipline, and experience to profitably manage the trading tools. Multiple confirmations of trend reversals by different trading tools make trading decisions easy. Confirmations of four Fibonacci tools that identify one and the same trend change can be much better trusted than potential reversals that are only pinpointed by one Fibonacci device.

Traders must remember, however, that even though several trading tools might identify a potential trend change, the market price may never reach the target price. Fibonacci trading tools point into the future, but that future remains uncertain. Trading opportunities sometimes pass us by; meanwhile, new horizons are opening up for profitable investments.

The main reason we feel so content with our Fibonacci trading tools is that they are all based on nature's law and human behavior. The actual market price never trades at the fair value of a product. The market price is either too high or too low compared with the fair value. Greed, fear, news in the media, financial reports, and government statistics are only some of the social influences that move prices. However, a buyer or seller still is required for a trade at any price. No matter where we look, we are always given advice to follow particular trends. Acting counter to the main trend direction is the secret to success. The six Fibonacci trading devices introduced in this book bring the new Fibonacci traders closer to this secret.

AFTERWORD
THE NEW FIBONACCI
TRADERS: WHO ARE THEY?

The new Fibonacci traders are looking for a change. They are unhappy with their performance. They do not understand why a stock that traded at 120 USD a year ago is at 20 USD today, and they no longer want to rely on the expertise of those so-called "experts" who recommended strong buys last year and still favor the same stocks, even though they have lost 80% of their value.

Fibonacci analysis does not need such things as valuation models, because Fibonacci analysis concentrates exclusively on pattern recognition as a representation of investors' behavior.

Fibonacci analysis works equally (and exceptionally) well in bull and in bear market conditions. The sole requirements are clear swing patterns, volatility, and marketability in the products analyzed. There are, however, a few additional essentials. The new Fibonacci traders will require sophistication, open-mindedness, patience, discipline, consistency, and faith in Fibonacci tools.

SOPHISTICATION

The new Fibonacci traders are sophisticated. They understand the value of a new trading concept and are not afraid of using computers and the Internet to enhance their chances of establishing good performance.

The new Fibonacci traders free themselves from the conventional wisdom that markets are random and, no matter what investors do, they cannot make money in the markets.

OPEN-MINDEDNESS

The new Fibonacci traders are open-minded and understand that market prices are driven by forces that actually have very little to do with the short-term effects of earnings reports, sales figures, or dividend yields.

Human behavior is the driving force behind the markets. The new Fibonacci traders accept that investors, as a group, behave in accordance with nature's law, discovered by Fibonacci in the thirteenth century, and made available to a wider audience of investors by R. N. Elliott.

PATIENCE

The new Fibonacci traders are patient. This requirement sounds simple, but it is probably the best virtue a trader can have while executing trading strategies.

Because all geometrical Fibonacci trading tools conceptually work countertrend, it takes patience to wait for trading signals.

Price patterns develop over time, and it is unclear at the beginning what a market is going to do. However, in the unfolding of a price pattern, it becomes obvious whether a PHI-ellipse—as the standard Fibonacci tool to start with—can circumvent a price move. Once the two side points of a PHI-ellipse are established, market pricing has a high tendency to stay within the PHI-ellipse.

The five other Fibonacci tools are then used to confirm the end of the PHI-ellipse. As soon as they have that confirmation, the new Fibonacci traders must wait for the market price to finally reach the precalculated price targets. The development of each price target in time remains dynamic.

DISCIPLINE

Even if market pricing reaches a precalculated price target, it does not mean that executing the trading signal will be an easy undertaking.

Signals are usually countertrend, meaning "sell" if the price is high, and "buy" if the price is low. Hesitation often leads to missing trading signals completely. Order limits should be in the market before the market price reaches the precalculated target price. As soon as an order is executed, a stop-loss level should be entered right away (especially when trading on intraday data). Profit targets, trailing stops, and other protective means should be used as part of the strategy to generate a stable equity curve.

CONSISTENCY

The key advantage of working with computers is that they are fast and do not make mistakes.

Working with our set of geometrical Fibonacci trading devices would be unthinkable without the WINPHI software package or the online WINPHI application. PHI-spirals, PHI-ellipses, and PHI-channels can no longer be calculated by hand. The new Fibonacci traders gain consistency by taking advantage of the WINPHI computer program's precision.

FAITH IN THE FIBONACCI TOOLS

The new Fibonacci traders can expect a stunning symmetry in market patterns that repeat themselves over and over again. What is more, the same symmetry exists on weekly, daily, and intraday data. Each trading product—whether in futures, stock index futures, commodities, cash currencies, or stocks—follows a clear pattern based on investor behavior. This pattern can only be analyzed by using the Fibonacci tools available on the WINPHI CD-ROM.

It is difficult to believe that such a solid Fibonacci analysis with multiple trading tools (PHI-channels, PHI-spirals, PHI-ellipses) exists in a world where everything seems to have been discovered already. The new Fibonacci traders have a profound understanding that, at certain times and on specific price patterns, all six Fibonacci tools work together as one analytical tool.

PHI-channels, PHI-ellipses, and PHI-spirals are the three geometrical Fibonacci devices that are new to the investment world.

PHI-channels are described in Chapter 4. The main feature of PHI-channels is that their trend lines and their resistance lines can be drawn from a baseline (as a peak-to-valley connection, or as a valley-to-peak connection) and a parallel outside line running through a significant peak or valley to the right of the PHI-channel baseline. The PHI-channel trend lines and resistance lines run in PHI series distances parallel to the PHI-channel baseline and form a cobweb of parallels by which price patterns can be mapped.

PHI-ellipses follow in Chapter 5. What makes PHI-ellipses different from other ellipses with alternative charting packages? A Fischer transformation of the underlying mathematical formula provides us with a perfect combination of maintained elliptical beauty and optimal fit to market patterns.

PHI-spirals, described in Chapter 6, prove that price patterns are not random and that there is a stunning symmetry in every volatile and liquid product traded. Our most important discovery is that there is hardly any major trend reversal in futures, cash currencies, or stocks, that cannot be captured by a crossover of two PHI-spirals.

Which data compression rates work best for the new Fibonacci traders will depend on individual risk preferences. Trading signals generated by Fibonacci devices on weekly data are profitable in principle. PHI-spirals work exceptionally well on weekly data. But there are few trading signals on weekly data due to a shortage of swings from which Fibonacci targets have to be calculated. A combined analysis on weekly and on daily data is appropriate on long-term and midterm perspectives. Daily and intraday data go hand in hand for multiple confirmations in short-term perspective.

A second reason to favor combinations of weekly and daily, or daily and intraday analysis is that when trend changes are correctly identified on weekly data, they might not be followed by another significant trend reversal on weekly data, but rather on daily data. The same holds true for a combined daily and intraday analysis. In other words, combinations of time spans might reduce the overall drawdown risk without giving up profit potential.

Almost all examples in this book show countertrend applications of Fibonacci tools. However, a few exceptions to the rule can be clearly defined.

The Fibonacci tool that works best as an indicator of the main trend direction is the PHI-ellipse. The slope of a PHI-ellipse—upward or downward—points in the direction of the main trend. In cases where the slope is negative, when the market price reaches the final point of a PHI-ellipse, we can buy long. If the slope is positive, we get a sell signal at the final point of a PHI-ellipse. However, whenever a stable PHI-ellipse is established with two side points and an upward slope, we can expect a strong breakout to the upside—either at the very end or shortly before the final point of the PHI-ellipse—as a buying opportunity (vice versa for sell signals following the main trend direction and not counter to it). The best example among those presented was the Japanese Yen cash currency (Figure 5.31). This example is an exception, but it is important to know about it.

The new Fibonacci traders must decide what the time frame of their investments will be: weekly, daily, or intraday. The shorter the time span, the more important are the requirements for accuracy in execution. That is why we do not recommend working with data compression rates shorter than 15 minutes.

The new Fibonacci traders can use the WINPHI software package and the historical databases to recreate every single example presented in this book. This approach might be time-consuming, but it will pay off. We highly recommend that, prior to any real-time trading, paper trading is first conducted to get used to the Fibonacci tools and the ways of applying them to different markets and products.

To support these efforts of the new Fibonacci traders, we now have a Web site and have made the WINPHI software available online at www.fibotrader.com for registered members. The online version allows us to automatically and permanently update weekly, daily, and intraday data and to include a wide range of additional trading vehicles from major international markets.

The new Fibonacci traders have a trading platform that makes them independent of other investment tools. It will not be easy; it will take some time to understand the Fibonacci trading tools and to learn how to use them. What we are offering here is just the beginning of a completely new way of analyzing and looking at products and markets.

We are dealing with nature's law, made visible and predictable through six geometrical Fibonacci trading tools.

TUTORIALS

CONCLUDING REMARKS

Readers who have reached these final pages might ask whether it was necessary to describe the Fibonacci trading tools in so much detail and with so many examples. The detailed explanations and numerous examples are provided to demonstrate the strategy's reliability and consistency.

TUTORIAL A: *THE NEW FIBONACCI TRADER WORKBOOK*

Readers who prefer a step-by-step, condensed explanation of the Fibonacci trading tools can refer to the workbook, which was written alongside *The New Fibonacci Trader* and is now available. The workbook provides succinct, summarized explanations of the key concepts, as well as questions and exercises, to both enhance and test one's comprehension of the complex Fibonacci ideas.

TUTORIAL B: *THE NEW FIBOTRADER WEB SITE*

Traders who wish to work with the Fibonacci trading tools online can go to our new Web site, which is available to registered members:

www.fibotrader.com

Part of this Web site is a 15-minute **slideshow tutorial** that includes:

1. Understanding the Fibonacci principle.

2. Crash course: Learning to use the WINPHI program.

3. How to work real-time with the Fibonacci trading tools: two strategies.

4. Learning about the Web site, www.fibotrader.com.

We hope that the Web site will become the focal point for traders worldwide who are looking for successful trading tools, and who want to update their trading knowledge.

LIST OF ABBREVIATIONS

To keep bar charts easy to read when trading signals are added to them, we use a set of abbreviations for entry rules and exit rules according to the following definitions:

Entry Rules

EL	Entry Long
ES	Entry Short

Re-Entry Rules

R-EL	Re-Entry Long
R-ES	Re-Entry Short

Exit Rules

XL	eXit Long
XLPT	eXit Long Profit Target
XLS-L	eXit Long Stop-Loss
XLTS	eXit Long Trailing Stop
XS	eXit Short
XSPT	eXit Short Profit Target
XSS-L	eXit Short Stop-Loss
XSTS	eXit Short Trailing Stop

DISCLAIMER

Please read the following before opening the software package:

This WINPHI software is protected by copyright. The author and John Wiley & Sons, Inc., and their licensors, reserve all rights. You are licensed to use this software on a single computer. Copying the software to another format for use on a single computer does not violate U.S. copyright law. Copying the software for any other purpose is a violation of U.S. copyright law.

This product is not sold. It is provided with *The New Fibonacci Trader* without warranty of any kind, expressed or implied, including but not limited to the implied warranty of merchantability and fitness for a particular purpose. Neither John Wiley & Sons (including its dealers and distributors) nor Fischer Finance Consulting assumes any liability for any alleged or actual damages arising from the use of this software.

This WINPHI software is tested only for Windows 95, Windows 98, Windows 2000, and Window NT with minimum system requirements of Windows 95, 166 MHz Intel Pentium processor, IBM-PC or compatible with CD-ROM drive, 32 MB RAM.

All charts printed in the book are created with a screen resolution of 1024×768 pixels. Different screen resolutions may lead to charts that differ from those shown in the book.

APPENDIX
USER MANUAL WINPHI (CD-ROM):
GETTING STARTED

INSTALLATION OF THE WINPHI SOFTWARE FROM CD-ROM

Insert the WINPHI CD into your CD-ROM drive. Click the **Start** button and choose **Run** from the menu.

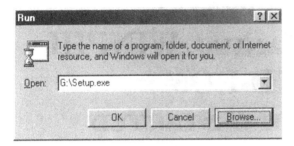

In the **Open** box, enter the path of the WINPHI CD.

Type in the drive letter, followed by a colon (:), a backslash (\), and the word **Setup.exe.**

If you wish to browse the existing directories from which to select, then click the **Browse** button. From a tree of directories, select the CD-ROM drive. Then, from a list of files, select **Setup** and click the **OK** button.

Click **OK.** The WINPHI Installation Wizard starts.

Follow the instructions that appear.

STARTING WINPHI—APPROVAL OF DISCLAIMER

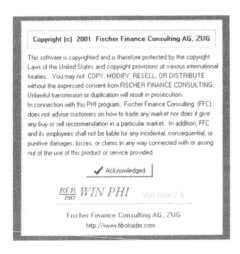

After installation is complete, run the WINPHI program from the Windows Start menu using the sequence **Start** > **Programs** > **WinPhi** > **WinPhi**—or run the executable file **Win-Phi.exe** from the WINPHI directory (the default folder is **\Fibo**).

On startup of the WINPHI program, a disclaimer is brought up. **Acknowledge** the disclaimer by left-clicking the button to get to the WINPHI main screen.

CONFIGURING COMMA DELIMITED ASCII FILES

To **Setup ASCII File Format,** right-click the mouse while the pointer is placed on the **File** speed button.

WINPHI reads the data for processing via ASCII-formatted (text, comma delimited) files. The required data (date, open, high, low, and close), all of which that are present in a file, may not necessarily be in the given order in a delimited file. The following setup screen, then, provides an interface for users to specifically point each parameter (date, open, high, low, or close) to its order in a delimited file.

The default settings are **Date**=1, **Open**=2, **High**=3, **Low**=4, **Close**=5. For example, let us consider a case in which the data fields are arranged as the following in a comma delimited file:
Dummy 1, **Open, Low, High, Close,** Dummy 2, **Date,** Dummy 3.

The correct order in the setup should then be:

Date=7,
Open=2,   **Low**=3,
High=4,   **Close**=5.

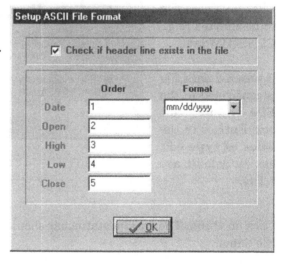

Date format selection is provided since there are many different methods of designating a date. The 'mm' denotes a two digit month; 'dd' for two digit day; 'yy' for two digit year such as 99, 01; and 'yyyy' as four digit year notation such as 1999, 2001.

The **Check if header line exists in the file** checkbox prompts the user to check if the content of the file begins with a header that describes what each data field represents. Some files may outright begin with the data itself without denoting what each data field represents.

CHOOSING DATA FILES

After installing the WINPHI program into the **\Fibo** directory, name of which can be any other name as well, you will note historical data files installed in the designated directory:

CLNBO1W.txt	Crude Oil weekly	INTCD.txt	Intel daily
DBKD.txt	Deutsche Bank daily	INTCW.txt	Intel weekly
DBKW.txt	Deutsche Bank weekly	IY—Y.txt	Japanese Yen daily
DF99-15.txt	DAX intra-day 15 min.	IY—YW.txt	Japanese Yen weekly
DF99-60.txt	DAX intra-day 60 min.	MSFTD.txt	Microsoft daily
DFNBO1W.txt	DAX weekly	MSFTW.txt	Microsoft weekly
DFNVOI.txt	DAX daily	SP97-15.txt	S&P500 intra-day 15 min.
EU—Y.txt	Euro daily	SP97-60.txt	S&P500 intra-day 60 min.
EU—YW.txt	Euro weekly	SPNBO1W.txt	S&P500 weekly
		SPNFVOI.txt	S&P500 daily

To work with the data files, click on the **File** speed button. A window with a list of data files will be opened as displayed.

Click on a data file to be charted (e.g., CLNBO1W.txt).

A selected data file is confirmed in the **File name** edit box. Entries in the **Files of type** edit box by default are ***.Txt.**

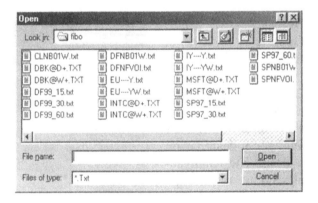

Click on **Open.** The bottom status bar should display the selected data file name.

Click on the **Plot** speed button, and the chart will appear.

Every new or updated data file must be copied into the WINPHI directory to be analyzed, and all files must be in a **comma delimited ASCII** format. **The WINPHI program does not recognize any other ASCII file format.**

SELECTING DATA FROM A DATA FILE

Left-click on the **Dates** speed button. A window captioned **Select Date Range** will open.

Enter the **First record number.**

Enter the **Last record number.**

Press **OK** to continue.

If you wish to leave 'blank' space on the right side of the chart to extra-polate the results of the selected trading tools, you can enter any number of days, from zero day to 50 days into the **# of blank days on right** edit box. Zero day would indicate no extra spacing on the right side of the chart. The **Leave spacing for holidays** check box must be check marked to activate extra spacing in the chart according to the entry in the **# of blank days on right** edit box.

If you wish to chart all historical data in a constant price scale, check mark the **Use one scale throughout all periods** check box. Further explanation of this topic is provided in a separate section, **Working with the Constant Price Scale.**

CHARTING DATA OF A SELECTED DATA FILE

If the correct ASCII field order is set, a data file is selected and loaded, and the records to chart are chosen, then click on the **Plot** speed button. A chart for the selected data file will appear.

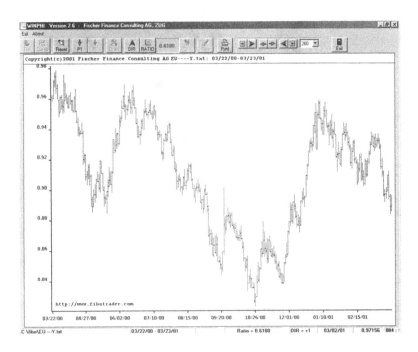

Once the bar chart is plotted successfully, the speed button description toggles from **Plot** to **Reset. File** and **Dates** speed buttons are deactivated as well.

If you click on the **Reset** speed button, the system reverts back to the beginning step, and the original speed buttons (**File, Dates,** and **Plot**) are reactivated.

If you click on the **File** speed button, you can select a new contract as explained under instructions on **Choosing Data Files.**

If you click on the **Dates** speed button, you can modify, for the selected contract, the number of days of price bars to be displayed as explained under instructions on **Selecting Data from a Data File.**

SELECTING FIBONACCI TRADING TOOLS

Click the **P1** speed button.

Move the cursor to any point in the chart where you wish it to be the beginning point of an analysis. Click with the left mouse button on the point of choice to place the first point on the chart.

Click the **P2** speed button.

Move the cursor to any second point in the chart where you wish it to be the second point of an analysis for the selected trading tool. Click with the left mouse button on the second point of choice to place the second point on the chart.

Right-click on the **Draw** speed button to bring forth a list of Fibonacci trading tools.

Move the mouse pointer to a desired Fibonacci trading tool and left-click (a bullet point will appear next to the selected Fibonacci trading tool of the list).

Left-click again on the **Draw** speed button to draw a study.

Six sorts of geometrical Fibonacci trading tools can be applied as studies to the price charts:

Corrections;
Extensions;
PHI-channels;
PHI-ellipses;
PHI-spirals;
Fibonacci time goal analysis.

CHARTING CORRECTIONS

Corrections are a trading tool for analysis in price (see Chapter 3). The WINPHI program draws the retracement lines of 38.2% and 61.8% between highs and lows of choice.

Click the **P1** speed button to mark the **High** (or the **Low**). Move the cursor to the **High** of choice in the chart and click with the left mouse button.

Click the **P2** speed button to mark the **Low** (or the **High**). Move the cursor to the **Low** of choice in the chart and click with the left mouse button.

Click the **Draw** speed button with the right mouse button. Click with the left mouse button on **Corrections** from the list. A bullet point will appear next to the word **Corrections.**

Left-click the **Draw** speed button again. The retracement lines of 38.2% and 61.8% will appear on the chart.

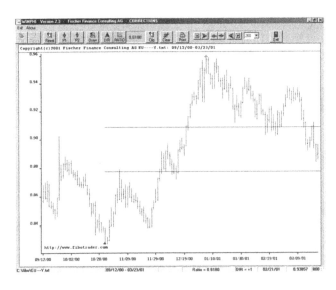

Click the **Clip** speed button, and the retracement lines are saved on the screen. We can overlay the screen with any of the other Fibonacci tools, as well.

CHARTING EXTENSIONS

Extensions are used as Fibonacci trading tools to forecast trend reversals in the markets. The common Fibonacci ratios applied are 0.618, 1.000, 1.618, and 2.618 (see Chapter 3).

Click the **P1** speed button to mark a significant **High** (or a **Low**). Move the cursor to the **High,** and click with the left mouse button.

Click the **P2** speed button to mark a significant **Low** (or a **High**). Move the cursor to the **Low,** and click with the left mouse button.

Click with the right mouse button on the **Draw** speed button. The menu list of the trading tools will appear. Click with the left mouse button **Extensions.** Next to the word **Extensions,** a bullet point will precede the selection.

Left-click the **Draw** speed button again. The WINPHI system calculates the vertical distance between **P1** and **P2** and multiplies this distance by the Fibonacci ratio shown in the box next to the **Ratio** speed button.

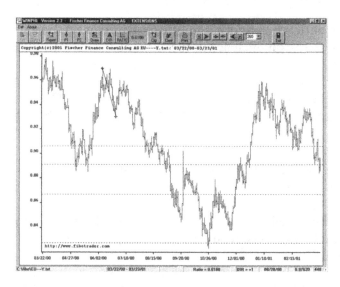

By clicking the **Ratio** button, the Fibonacci ratios change.

When the icon on the **Dir** button points upwards, the Fibonacci ratios will increase when you click the **Ratio** speed button. Conversely, when the icon on the **Dir** button points downwards, the Fibonacci ratios will decrease each time you click the **Ratio** speed button.

As long as the Fibonacci ratios used in the calculation give a price target which is still in the range of the size of the chart, the system will draw a horizontal line on the chart.

Each time you get a price target line, you can save this on the screen by clicking the **Clip** speed button. Once you have the price target lines you want to see, you can add other geometrical Fibonacci trading devices on the same chart.

CHARTING PHI-CHANNELS

Working with PHI-channels generates trend support and resistance lines by multiplying the difference from baseline to parallel outside line of the PHI-channel with different Fibonacci ratios. The baseline of a PHI-channel is created by connecting a significant **High** (or **Low**) with a significant **Low** (or **High**) as described in Chapter 4.

Click the **P1** speed button to mark the significant **High** (or the **Low**). Move the cursor to the **High** of choice in the chart and click with the left mouse button.

Click the **P2** speed button to mark the significant **Low** (or the **High**). Move the cursor to the **Low** of choice in the chart and click with the left mouse button.

Move the cursor to the outside point of the PHI-channel in the chart and click with the left mouse button.

Right-click the **Draw** speed button. Left-click on **PHI-channel** from the list of available trading tools. A bullet point will appear next to the word **PHI-channel.**

Click the **Draw** speed button with the left mouse button again. A chart containing the PHI-channel should be seen at this point. Depending on the choice of a Fibonacci ratio displayed in the ratio box, the system now draws parallel lines to the PHI-channel, by multiplying the width of the PHI-channel with the Fibonacci ratios.

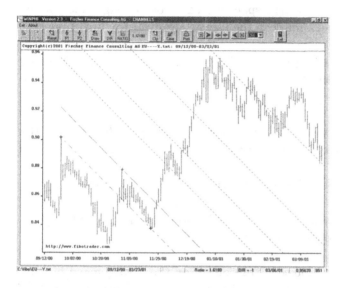

The Fibonacci ratios can be changed using the **Dir** and the **Ratio** buttons.

Left-click the **Clip** speed button each time you want to save a parallel line created with a different Fibonacci ratio.

PHI-channel support and resistance lines can be generated from different PHI-channels, thereby creating a cob-web of parallel lines on the chart (see Chapter 4). On top of the parallel line series representing support and resistance lines, other Fibonacci trading tools can still be overlaid.

CHARTING PHI-ELLIPSES

PHI-ellipses can have many different shapes (see Chapter 5). They can be thinner or thicker, longer or shorter. But they will always have a basic structure founded on the Fibonacci ratios. To get started with a PHI-ellipse, you should look to select a significant high or low, and let the PHI-ellipse envelope the left and right side of a price move.

If you want to draw a PHI-ellipse, and you need additional free space on the right side of the PHI-ellipse in order to reserve enough room to show the full PHI-ellipse, you must go to the **Select Date Range** window as introduced in the **Selecting Data from a Data File** section. Under the **# of blank days on right** option, enter the number of days for which you wish free space allocated on the right side of the chart, and put a check mark in the **Leave spacing for holidays** box.

Left-click the **P1** speed button. Move the cursor to the point in the chart where you want the PHI-ellipse to start, then left-click the mouse.

Left-click the **P2** speed button. Move the cursor to the point in the chart where you want the PHI-ellipse to end, then left-click the mouse.

Click the **Draw** speed button with the right mouse button.

Left-click on the trading tool **PHI-ellipse** of the list. A bullet point will appear next to the word **PHI-ellipse.**

Click with the left mouse button again on the **Draw** speed button. The PHI-ellipse will appear on the chart with a starting point you marked with the **P1** speed button and an end point you marked with the **P2** speed button.

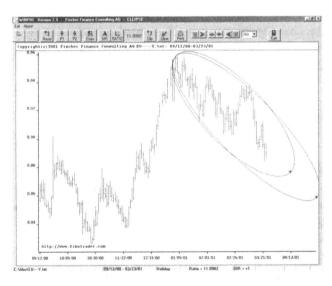

Most likely the first PHI-ellipse you draw will **not surround** the price move you want to analyze. To refine your draw, consider the following options.

To make the PHI-ellipse thicker or thinner, click the **Dir** speed button. The icon will point either upwards or downwards. Let us assume the icon on the **Dir** button points upwards, and you left-click the **Ratio** button. Then, the Fibonacci ratio in the Fibonacci box next to the **Ratio** speed button will increase with each click. While the Fibonacci ratio increases, the shape of the PHI-ellipse becomes thinner. If you click the **Dir** button so that it points downwards, and then click the **Ratio** speed button, the Fibonacci ratio decreases with each click. Each time the Fibonacci ratio decreases, the PHI-ellipse becomes fatter. If the Fibonacci ratio is 1.000, the PHI-ellipse gets shaped as a full circle.

To make the PHI-ellipse longer or shorter, move the cursor to the end point on the very right side of the PHI-ellipse, click with the right mouse button; and while **holding the right mouse button down,** you can drag the PHI-ellipse either to the right, left, up, or down. By doing so, you can make the PHI-ellipse longer or shorter.

You now possess the operational means to possibly fit the PHI-ellipse around the left and right outside points of any price move if there is a 3-wave price pattern. While you have enclosed the price move by the PHI-ellipse, you still do not know in real-time trading where exactly the end point of the price move will be. To identify the end of a price move, you need to read Chapter 5.

By clicking the **Clip** speed button, you can save the PHI-ellipse on the screen and then overlay it with other geometrical Fibonacci tools of your choice.

CHARTING PHI-SPIRALS

The PHI-spiral is a geometrical device for price and time analysis (see Chapter 6). The PHI-spiral rings can be support or resistance lines. The ultimate goal is to identify the point in price and time, where the cross-over of two PHI-spirals is penetrated by the market price.

Left-click the **P1** speed button to select the **Center** of the first PHI-spiral. Click on any point in the chart to select the location of the **Center** of the PHI-spiral on the chart.

Left-click the **P2** speed button to select the **Starting point** of the first PHI-spiral. Click on any point in the chart to select the location of the **Starting point** of the PHI-spiral.

Click on the **Draw** speed button with the right mouse button.

Left-click on **PHI-spiral** from the list of trading tools. A bullet point will appear next to the word **PHI-spiral.**

Left-click on the **Draw** speed button. The selected PHI-spiral will appear on the screen.

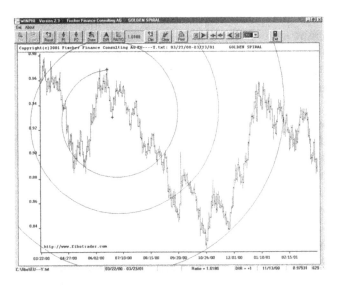

Once the PHI-spiral is drawn on the price bar chart, you can vary the **Center** by clicking on the **P1** button, placing a new point with a left mouse click, and then clicking on the **Draw** button. If you want to change the **Starting point** of the PHI-spiral, click on the **P2** speed button, place a new point with a left mouse click, followed by pressing the **Draw** speed button.

The PHI-spiral must have the Fibonacci ratio of **1.618.** When you start the first PHI-spiral, the default value of the Fibonacci ratio applied may be different than 1.618. To change the ratio, if the **Dir** button points upwards, pressing the **Ratio** button will increase the Fibonacci ratio in the ratio box. If the **Dir** button points downwards, pressing the **Ratio** button will decrease the Fibonacci ratio in the ratio box.

To change the rotation of the PHI-spiral, left-click on the **Dir** button; and the direction of the PHI-spiral will toggle between **counter-clockwise** rotation and **clockwise** rotation.

To save the PHI-spiral on the screen, left-click on the **Clip** speed button, and the PHI-spiral will be saved on the screen. By saving the PHI-spiral on the screen, you can overlay the first PHI-spiral either with another PHI-spiral or with other Fibonacci trading tools from the menu list.

If you have saved the first PHI-spiral by using the **Clip** speed button, you can overlay on the chart another PHI-spiral by clicking the **P1** button, moving the cursor to the new **Center** of the second PHI-spiral, and left-clicking on the chart. For the new **Starting point** of the second PHI-spiral, click the **P2** speed button, move the cursor to the new **Starting point,** and click on the chart with the left mouse button. Left-click the **Draw** speed button, and the second PHI-spiral will appear on the chart.

CHARTING FIBONACCI TIME-GOAL ANALYSIS

The Fibonacci time goal analysis is an analysis for trend reversals in time (see Chapter 7). The WINPHI program can draw the time lines from any high or low in the price chart. The goal is to look for time bands, calculated from highs—highs and lows—lows. It is preferred to work with the ratios 0.618, 1.000, and 1.618, but the more advanced Fibonacci trader will learn how to work also with higher ratios.

Click the **P1** speed button to mark the **Low** (or the **High**). Move the cursor to the **Low** of choice in the chart and left-click.

Click the **P2** speed button to mark the second **Low** (or the second **High**). Move the cursor to the second **Low** of choice in the chart and left-click.

Click the **Draw** speed button with the right mouse button. Click with the left mouse button on **Time Goal Analysis** from the list of trading tools. A bullet point will appear next to the word **Time Goal Analysis.**

Click the **Draw** speed button with the left mouse button again. You will observe on the chart a line which connects the two **Lows** marked by the **P1** and **P2** speed buttons. Depending on the Fibonacci ratio selected in the ratio box, you can draw new time lines which are the distance between the two **Lows** multiplied by the Fibonacci ratio of your choice.

Once you have generated the Fibonacci time goal line with two **Lows,** the same procedure can be used to generate the Fibonacci time goal lines for the **Highs.** By doing so, and using the correct Fibonacci ratios, time bands can be generated as described in Chapter 7.

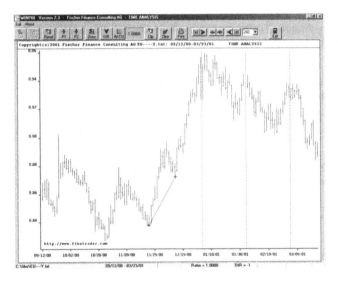

Click the **Clip** speed button, and Fibonacci time goal lines are saved on the screen. You can overlay on the screen any other of the geometrical Fibonacci trading devices, as well.

WORKING WITH THE CONSTANT PRICE SCALE

The constant price scale is important when looking for stable parameters in a product on historical data. Any serious analyst will test his or her findings on historical data first—before moving on to real-time trading.

Select a contract as instructed under **Choosing Data Files** by using the **Files** speed button.

Click the **Dates** button (see **Selecting Data from a Data File** section). Check mark the **Use one scale throughout all periods** check box.

Change the **First record number** to any number of your choice, depending on how much data you want to analyze from the historical data file. Avoid accessing more than 2,000 data records, calculated as the difference between **First record number** and **Last record number.**

Note that there are more records stored in the hourly and 15-minute intra-day DAX and the S&P500 data files. The reason for provision of these long data series is for any serious analyst to compare the signals on significant trend changes on weekly, daily, 60-minute, and 15-minute data over many years backwards in order to test the reliability of the trading tools. Again, **do not load more than 2,000 data** into one file.

Click the **Plot** speed button, and the **entire** data from the data file will appear on the screen.

Next to the **Exit** button located on the upper right side of the screen, you will notice a drop-down box displaying an initial number of **260.** The drop-down list reveals the number of price bars you can select to put on the chart for analysis.

You find also six smaller control buttons left of the drop-down list displaying the number of days to chart. If you place the mouse pointer on any of these buttons, help text should appear to guide you with its function. Starting from the left-most control button, the functions of the six controls are: **Draw beginning period; Lengthen drawing period; Shift to previous period; Shift to next period; Shorten drawing period; Draw whole period.**

If you work with the default value **260** and click on the left-most of the six smaller control buttons, you will have on the screen 260 price bars, starting from the beginning of the selected data file. Use the

Red-arrow control buttons to move the data forwards or backwards the way you wish to analyze it. You can also lengthen or shorten the time periods with the **Blue-arrow** control buttons.

EXITING THE WINPHI SOFTWARE

Left-click the **Exit** speed button from the WINPHI task bar to leave the WINPHI program.

For questions and additional information, visit our website at **www.fi-botrader.com.** Try out the online version of WINPHI with intra-day datafeed, improved charting facilities, and many more international trading vehicles to be analyzed real-time based on geometrical Fibonacci trading tools.

INDEX

For information about the CD-ROM, see the Appendix section of this book.

Printed in the United States
By Bookmasters